To Lin,

The Road Back to Hell

Thanks for joining me on my journey! I hope you enjoy my book.

Diana Lynn

The Road Back to Hell

༄

a Memoir

Diana Lynn

The Road Back to Hell
Copyright © 2015 Diana Lynn
All rights reserved. No part of this book may be reproduced or transmitted in any form or by any means without written permission from the author.
2nd Printing- November, 2015
Printed in USA by 48HrBooks (www.48HrBooks.com).

ISBN-13: 9781541079199
ISBN-10: 1541079191

Please visit me-
www.dianalynnauthor.com
facebook-Diana Lynn

Contents

Author's Notes · vii
Prologue · xi

Chapter 1	The Road Back to Hell ·	·1
Chapter 2	The Beginning ·	·5
Chapter 3	Looking Back at My Roots · · · · · · · · · · · · · · ·	·8
Chapter 4	The Happy Years ·	17
Chapter 5	Laughter in the Rain · · · · · · · · · · · · · · · · · ·	25
Chapter 6	Forever Darling ·	33
Chapter 7	California Here We Come · · · · · · · · · · · · · · ·	43
Chapter 8	California Here We Go · · · · · · · · · · · · · · · · ·	52
Chapter 9	Heading Home ·	60
Chapter 10	Home Again ·	68
Chapter 11	The Ice Cream Man · · · · · · · · · · · · · · · · · ·	73
Chapter 12	Beautiful Dreamer · · · · · · · · · · · · · · · · · · ·	79
Chapter 13	What a Diff'rence a Summer Makes · · · · · · · · · ·	83
Chapter 14	A Fresh Start ·	88
Chapter 15	Finding Peace ·	98
Chapter 16	Flying High ·	104
Chapter 17	Learning the Truth · · · · · · · · · · · · · · · · · · ·	109
Chapter 18	On Top of the World · · · · · · · · · · · · · · · · · ·	118
Chapter 19	Giving In ·	123
Chapter 20	Morning Reality ·	130
Chapter 21	Moving Forward ·	136
Chapter 22	The Hiding Place ·	145

Chapter 23	Survival of the Fittest	156
Chapter 24	A Family United	166
Chapter 25	The Truth	170
Chapter 26	The Wedding	177
Chapter 27	The Canary	185
Chapter 28	Just Over That Hill	191
Chapter 29	Christmas at Our House	197
Chapter 30	The Long Ride Down	205
Chapter 31	1973- The Beginning	217
Chapter 32	1973-The Middle	232
Chapter 33	1973-The End	240
Chapter 34	The Spirit of Christmas	249
Chapter 35	Unraveling	258
Chapter 36	The Separation	267
Chapter 37	The Funeral	278
Chapter 38	Gotta' Get Off of This Ride	285
Chapter 39	My Journey to North Carolina	288
	Epilogue	297
	The Next Road on My Journey	301
	Acknowledgments	305

Author's Notes

THE ROAD BACK to Hell is the true story of my life and the life of my family from 1949-1976. Three of my sisters are still living and have consented to the use of their names in this memoir. However, some names in this book have been changed to protect people's privacy, while others have consented to the use of their names.

While writing this book, I relied on my memory, shared stories with my sisters, Judy, Linda and Lisa, my niece, Amy, and my aunt, Jean Woodard. Many of the stories were passed on to me from relatives who are now deceased. I have related my recollections of the events in my life which took place from 1949 through 1976 to the best of my knowledge. Although the dialogue is not one-hundred percent accurate, it reflects the essence of the conversations. Anything in italics recounts my observations as a child and later as an adult.

Chapter 31 is an exact reprint of my mother's diary. Everything is exactly as she wrote it— complete with spelling and grammatical errors.

*This book is dedicated to Annie Augusta Foote Wilson
My beloved great-grandmother who guided me through life,
And all of the angels on earth and in heaven who helped pave my way.*

Gussie
My Guardian Angel

Prologue

I HAD BEEN traveling on my life's journey a long time before I ever put pen to paper. Many memories of my past were evoked by the music I was exposed to while growing up. The lyrics of a particular song, a certain melody or the sound of a tenor's voice took me back in time. Looking through family photos brought back things I had long forgotten. The stories told to me by members of my family found their way into my head and my heart. Whether the experiences were good or bad, I locked them safely away in the recesses of my mind waiting for the day I would finally write them down.

One of the most vivid memories of my early childhood was my first ballet solo. I picture myself at four, dressed in a black leotard with a pink tutu my mother had made for me; my fine blonde hair was curled around my face, and my blue eyes sparkled. I remember looking back over my shoulder, to acknowledge Mom's encouraging smile as she gently pushed me onto the stage from behind the curtain. With shaking knees, I slowly made my way to the center. When I was ready, I glanced at my father sitting at the piano, signaling him to play. Soon the melancholy notes of "Melody of Love" floated from the piano as his fingers gracefully moved across the keys. After I had finished my performance and the applause began, Mom and Dad joined me on the stage. We stood together holding hands, while we all took a bow.

This moment, etched in my mind, represents a time when we were a close-knit family of three, and my parents were deeply in love. That love would fortify me with the self-confidence, drive and security I would need to get me through some extremely difficult times during my life. My four younger siblings were not as fortunate.

Diana Lynn

Whenever I hear the smoky voice of Dinah Washington singing, "What a Diff'rence a Day Makes," I'm taken back to darker times, when in the wee hours of the morning, I'd see the glowing ash of my father's cigarette as he stood in the darkened hallway waiting for my mother to return home. A ferocious battle ensued when my mother stumbled into the apartment and began slurring her words. My parent's loud shouts could be heard throughout our second-story apartment and probably half-way down the block. On those nights, I'd bring my younger sisters into my bedroom and cuddle with them throughout the night.

The sound of an ambulance passing by my house reminds me of the night of my mother's first suicide attempt. I can still see her coagulating blood slowly dripping down the walls of our bathroom. I vividly remember trying to clean it off before any of my sisters could see it. This was one of many nights I would cradle Judy, Kim, Linda and Lisa into my arms, while trying to shelter them from the chaos of our lives.

This is the bittersweet story of growing up in an extremely dysfunctional home in the 1950's and 1960's. As the oldest child of my biological mother, Bonnie, and my adoptive father, Stew, I was the only daughter who benefited from the strong love my parents shared during the early years of their marriage. Shortly after the birth of my first sibling, Judy, their marriage started to crumble. As it rapidly eroded over the next decade, I assumed the 'mother role' at the age of twelve. I believed it was my responsibility to guide and protect my four sisters through the traumas of alcoholism, the instability of frequent moves, my parents' violent arguments, marital affairs, separations, molestations, and suicide attempts.

While guiding my sisters, I held fast to my dream of escaping the turmoil and drama in my life by attending college. I planned to obtain a career that would financially enable to me reach out to each of them and pull them out of the dark abyss of their lives. To achieve this dream, I had set high goals for myself and worked hard to accomplish them.

The first part of my memoir paints a picture of a happy little girl growing up in a sound environment, surrounded by the love and adoration of her parents. I spent a good deal of time sharing the stories of my early years to illustrate how vitally important a strong, nurturing foundation can be during the first five years of a child's life. Unfortunately, my four younger sisters did not have the same benefits.

As you travel with me on my journey, I will share with you the devastation caused when the family unit is destroyed by alcoholism, marital affairs and incest. While intertwining many stories describing my climb, I also include the story of my fall.

At the age of sixty-three, I decided it was my responsibility to tell the story of our chaotic lives. After reading many memoirs, I realized that our story is not as tragic as some, but nonetheless, it was very painful for everyone growing up in the Smith household.

By writing this book, I hoped to bring some peace and understanding to my three surviving sisters—Judy, Linda and Lisa, and to honor the memory of my sister, Kim, who passed away in 2005. Writing this memoir has been a cathartic experience that has brought me peace.

Looking back at my life helped to convince me that the future can be what you make it. But in order to do that, you have to believe in yourself. I did!

CHAPTER 1

The Road Back to Hell

*I invite you to join me on my journey through
The first twenty-seven years of my life.*

December 3, 2005
I OPENED MY door to the ringing of the phone and reached across the desk to answer it. I picked it up and heard someone sobbing on the other end as I said, "Hello."

"It's bad!" Between the sobs, a weak voice pleaded, "Diana, you've got to help."

It was my youngest sister, Lisa.

"What in the world's wrong?" I asked. "Calm down and catch your breath. I can't understand a word you're saying." My legs started to shake and I dropped into a chair next to the desk.

"It's Kimmie, Diana. Something bad has happened! They took her to a trauma center in Chapel Hill in a 'he…heli…helicopter," she stuttered.

"Oh my God!" *Collect your thoughts*, I told myself. *You need to be strong.* "Was she in an accident?"

After Lisa stopped sobbing, she said, "No. She has an aneurysm and they don't think she's going to make it!"

Hearing my startled voice, my husband, Jim, rushed into the room and approached me. He had a puzzled look in his eyes, so I shook my head to let him know I couldn't explain right then.

I struggled to control my voice before asking Lisa if she was positive of the diagnosis. After assuring me the diagnosis was correct, she explained that Kim had complained of a severe headache earlier that morning. When Kim's daughter, Christine called around noon, she couldn't understand a word her mother was saying. She immediately called Gary, Kim's husband, and told him he needed to get home right away.

Lisa tends to exaggerate, but I knew this was serious. Something very wrong was happening to my sister in North Carolina, and I was in Brookville, Pennsylvania, almost six hundred miles away.

"Calm down, Lisa. Remember when Tom had an aneurysm? The doctors performed surgery to control the bleeding in his brain, and he survived. We have to believe Kim will, too. She's in an excellent hospital being treated by specialists who deal with this type of thing every day. Try to think positively, okay?" I was attempting to instill confidence in Lisa that I didn't feel myself.

"Okay, I'll try, but this is bad. I know it," she said. She told me her daughter, Andrea, and our sister, Linda were on the way to pick her up and drive her to the trauma center in Chapel Hill, North Carolina.

The throbbing in my head made me realize I was in no shape to make decisions. I had to pull myself together. I took a deep breath and calmly told Lisa to call me when she reached the hospital. After we had hung up, I gazed out my window and saw quarter-sized snowflakes falling on the ground and covering my driveway. If I tried to make the journey tonight, a long and risky drive lay ahead.

I collapsed in my chair. God wouldn't let Kim die when so many people needed her, would He? He couldn't let her die when she had finally turned her life around, could He?

Jim stood watching as my tears began to fall. When he wrapped me in his arms, I closed my eyes and prayed, "Dear God, I don't believe I have the strength to deal with all that lies ahead. Please help me."

My first inclination was to pack my bags and head for North Carolina immediately, but Jim convinced me to wait until Lisa called back. "Maybe things aren't as bad as they seem," he said. "If you leave in this snowstorm and have an accident, how can you be of help to anyone?"

Although I decided to take his advice, I felt helpless waiting for the phone to ring. It upset me when I realized Kim's three children, Danny,

Amy and Christine, Kim's husband, Gary and my two sisters, Linda and Lisa, as well as the grandchildren were converging on the hospital while I sat in the comfort of my home. Early that evening, my niece, Amy, called to tell me Kim was in intensive care where the doctors were trying to stop the bleeding around her brain. They had to control that before they could consider operating, which meant the surgery would probably not take place until the next day. She advised me to leave in the morning.

Before I hung up, I promised to pray for Kim and head out early Sunday morning. In the meantime, I reminded her I was only a phone call away. As the evening wore on, I made at least ten calls offering encouragement to my family members while they sat in the hospital waiting room. I tried my best to console them from afar. About eleven o'clock that night, I realized there were at least fifteen adults and children, sitting in the waiting room outside of the ICU.

Where were they going to sleep? What were they going to eat? I knew my family lived from hand-to-mouth with no credit cards and probably very little cash. That's when I realized there was *something* I could do. I called information for the number of the nearest motel and made reservations for a few rooms. Then I phoned Lisa to tell her that anyone who wanted to leave the hospital for a while had a place to sleep that night. It wasn't much, but it made me feel better because I was doing *something*.

After I had gone to bed, all I could see every time I closed my eyes was Kim lying in that bed fighting for her life. Waves of sadness engulfed me. I wondered how her family would manage without her if she died. I also wondered what I would do if she was no longer here. Years before, we'd had a huge argument about the way she was neglecting her three young children.

Consequently, we barely spoke to one another for almost twenty years. In 2001, when Grandma Conklin passed away, we reconciled our differences. Since then, we had enjoyed several wonderful years as sisters and friends. Please don't let it be over so soon, I silently prayed.

As I lay there awake, I recalled the traumas our family had endured over the years. Although I had given them financial support and offered advice on ways to improve their lives, it usually didn't work out. They were still mired down in problems. Drenched in sweat, I finally got out of bed, put on a robe, and went downstairs to start a pot of coffee.

I sat in my easy chair, sipped my steaming cup of coffee and stared at the lights on my Christmas tree. I thought of the beautiful Christmases we'd shared when my sisters and I were younger. I fast-forwarded into the years that followed, a home movie featuring my parents' constant arguments over money, alcohol and affairs. When I remembered the suicide attempts, separations, and the divorce, the movie turned into a horror show.

As the oldest of five girls, I had become a mother figure to my sisters and tried to offer my love and support when they needed it. Eventually, the responsibility became more than I could bear. As a divorced mother raising two sons, I finally had to step away. Although the guilt of my abandonment often overwhelmed me, I understood I had to separate myself from the chaos created by my family if I were to survive.

This time was different. I knew I had to be there for them now, no matter what the cost. I put my cup down, went upstairs, and started packing.

At daybreak, when I pulled out of my driveway and started down Interstate 80, I felt as if I was being pulled into a swamp and feared I would be swallowed up by all of the grief in Kenly, North Carolina. This road was leading me back to bad memories, heartaches and feelings I had buried for many years.

The farther south I drove, the more I felt like I was driving back into my own personal Hell.

CHAPTER 2

The Beginning

"In childhood we press our noses to the pane, looking out; in memories of childhood, we press our noses to the pane, looking in."

- Robert Brault

1951
Pressing my nose to the pane and looking in, I see a happy little girl of three, surrounded by the adoration and support of her parents. She is glowing. You can see it in her bright blue eyes that crinkle at the corners whenever she smiles, which is often. You can see it in her dancing feet as she twirls around the living room entertaining her mother and father. You can hear it in her laughter and her voice. She's a lucky little girl. The love her parents feel for one another at this time in their lives overflows into her, planting the seeds of self-confidence, ambition, and drive. She'll continue to sow these seeds throughout her lifetime. It's unfortunate her parents' love for each other couldn't last forever.

The next scene I see through that pane is the day I was adopted.

Snuggling under my covers early one summer morning, I heard my mother slowly lift the shade, letting the sunshine into my bedroom. She gently shook me. "Diana Lynn, time to get up. We have a big day ahead of us."

Rubbing the sleep from my eyes, I gazed up at her beautiful, smiling face and asked, "Why? Where are we going?" I knew by the sound of her voice something special was about to happen.

"It's a surprise. You have to get up and get ready to go downtown. Stew's taking us to meet an important man."

On the way to the kitchen, I bombarded her with questions. Mom didn't answer any of them. Instead, she teasingly said, "This is going to be a day you'll always remember."

Her words reminded me of another important day— the day Mommy and Stew were married in a lovely little church in Frewsburg, New York.

After the wedding, Stew came to live with us, which made me very happy.

I chattered the entire time my mother dressed me. She softly stroked my cheek with her hand as she pulled my light blonde hair behind my ears. I peered up at her with questioning eyes, *"What's happening today, Mommy?"* My mother knowingly smiled as she secured my hair with blue barrettes and fluffed my silky straight bangs. She lifted my new, yellow-organdy dress over my head, helped me into my black patent leather Mary Janes and turned me towards the mirror.

"See? The ruffled collar on your dress is perfect, just like you." We walked into the living room where Stew was anxiously waiting.

His eyes lit up when he saw the two of us standing there. He smiled and said, "This is my lucky day, I'm taking my two favorite girls to meet someone special."

My heart raced with excitement when I put my small hand into his large one and looked up at him. He gave it a soft squeeze and beamed down at me. I was a little nervous, but as long as he was holding my hand, I knew I'd be safe.

After parking the car, we walked to a large brick building with a big marble lion on each side of the steps. When we approached the top of the stairs, Mom hurried into the building. Stew and I followed the sound of her clicking high-heeled shoes as she rapidly strode down the long marble hallway toward the elevators at the end of the hall. My belly filled with a tickling sensation when the elevator "whooshed" to the sixth floor. I was still clutching Stew's hand when we walked into a big office. A pretty lady looked up from her desk, smiled and said, "Hello, Mr. Smith.

Attorney Johnson is ready to see you." She nodded at Mom, winked at me and led us to a very large room with a couch, some chairs and a stern looking, gray haired man sitting behind a big desk.

Mom sat in one chair, and Stew sat beside her, holding me on his lap.

I fidgeted while the three of them talked about things I didn't understand. After what seemed like forever, Mr. 'Gray-Hair' peered down at me through his wire-rimmed glasses and said, "Diana Lynn, how old are you?"

"Almost three," I pertly replied.

"Do you like Stewart? Is he nice to you?" "Oh, yes!" I replied without hesitation. "Would you like Stewart to be your Daddy?"

I looked over at my mother's smiling face, up into Stew's sparkling eyes, straight back at Mr. 'Gray-Hair' and excitedly replied, "Yes!"

I remember thinking, "He already is my Daddy, isn't he?"

That was the day Stew Smith adopted me, and my name changed from Diana Lynn King to Diana Lynn Smith; the day that changed the course of my life forever.

As we left the building, we joined hands and started to walk to the car. Looking up into the bright blue summer sky, I wished all three of us could climb onto one of those big puffy clouds and float away together forever. But that only happens in fairy tales.

CHAPTER 3

Looking Back at My Roots

1949-1951

THROUGH THE YEARS, I've learned the stories leading up to that beautiful day when Bonnie and Stew married. I was born in Jamestown, New York, on March 31, 1949, to Bonnie Jean Woodard. She was only fifteen when she conceived me out of wedlock. Being an unmarried, pregnant, fifteen-year-old girl was highly unacceptable in those days, so she married before I was born.

Don King was the lucky guy she snared into giving me a name—Diana Lynn King. I don't remember anything about him. Their short-lived marriage ended when Don refused to buy me another new dress. Wouldn't one think after buying me over thirty dresses before my first birthday, he had the right to say no? Apparently it wasn't enough for Bonnie and her beloved baby because she packed everything we owned and moved out while Don was at work. I'm somewhat thankful to him because although he wouldn't buy me my 31st dress, he did give me a name, and I wasn't born a bastard, or is it 'bastardess'?

Mom and I moved into a four-room apartment with my Grandmother Adeline and Grandfather Elmer Woodard who lavished loads of love on their first-born grandchild. I've always been told I was the apple of their eyes.

As the story goes, my mother's mother, Adeline, ran off with Elmer at sixteen to get married, much to the chagrin of my great-grandmother, Annie Augusta Foote. Gussie was extremely distraught when her beautiful, high-spirited daughter ran off with a good-for-nothing guy like Elmer. Adeline was Gussie's daughter from her first marriage to Fred Powell and forever remained Gussie's favorite child. She was a tiny, feisty, strong-willed young woman with a quick Irish temper. She did exactly as she pleased. Gussie assured me Adeline inherited her temperament and spirit from Gussie's father, John Francis Foote, who immigrated from Ireland to Jamaica, New York in 1856.

Elmer was a tall, strapping man with thick, dark eyebrows, a Romanesque nose, and a receding hairline that added to his rugged handsomeness. He was a rough and tumble kind of guy. In his teens, he moved from Arkansas to Jamestown with his twice-widowed mother and six siblings. An easy-go-lucky man, he loved to drink, smoke and raise hell.

Adeline and Elmer had a very tumultuous relationship. They moved from house-to-house and town-to-town while raising three kids in an extremely unstable environment.

Jerry, their oldest son, was born in 1930, followed by Kenny in 1931. Bonnie Jean, my mother, and the only girl, was born in 1933. With three kids to raise and no formal training, Elmer decided collecting junk would be a great way to make a living. He bought a beat up pick-up truck and traveled the countryside collecting scrap metal and junk from local farmers. At the end of each day, he sold whatever he had gathered to the owners of local scrap yards. Sometimes he made a fistful of cash; other days he returned home penniless.

On many days when he'd made a bundle, his first stop would be the nearest bar. The locals were always happy to see him come in the door because they knew he would buy everyone drinks all night long. Although Elmer was a popular guy in the taverns, that wasn't the case when he returned home.

There were many nights Elmer weaved his way up the stairs singing, "Good Night Irene," at the top of his lungs. When Adeline heard him coming, she stood on a chair behind the door with an iron skillet in her hand, ready to pound him over the head the minute he walked into the house. In a rage, Adeline threw anything at him she could find. She jumped up, pounded his chest and pulled his hair, which may explain why he went bald so early in life. Trying to avoid her blows, Elmer ducked down and started cursing a blue streak.

"God damn it, Adeline, what in the hell are you trying to do?"

"Kill you, you fat bastard," she screamed.

Eventually, the name-calling, pot-throwing arguments would stop. She'd fly into his arms, and he would carry her off to bed. Scarlet and Rhett had nothing over Elmer and Adeline.

In the meantime, three young kids stood wide awake, witnessing this bashing and swearing from behind a door or through the rungs of a staircase. It isn't possible to describe the exact scene in the house because they lived in so many. Whenever my grandparents fell behind in the rent, they just packed up in the middle of the night and moved across town or out-of-town to places like Erie or Buffalo. Jerry, Kenny and Mom never had the benefits of being raised in a normal home with three square meals a day, the same bed to sleep in each night, and a group of friends and neighbors to grow up with. My mother continued this gypsy-like lifestyle for the rest of her life.

In telling my family story, I often referred to old pictures from family albums. Unfortunately, all of my relatives who could share stories about the past are deceased. I have to rely on my imagination. One photo, from 1941, paints a very happy picture in the life of the young Woodard children—

It's a sunny, summer day, and Mom, Jerry, and Kenny are each sitting on new two-wheeled bicycles in front of a large maple tree. Mom is in the middle, on the smallest bike. She's wearing a barrette to hold her long, dark brown bangs back from her forehead while making funny faces at the camera. She looks very stylish in her flowered pinafore and saddle shoes. Brother Kenny has the sleeves of his dress shirt rolled up to his elbows, and a broad smile plastered on his face. Jerry is wearing the biggest smile, probably because he's the only one with a basket on his bike. They appear to be very proud of their new bicycles. In the background, a few dirty-faced neighborhood kids are looking on in astonishment. Elmer must have come into some heavy scrap metal that day!

The Road Back to Hell

Another photo was taken in 1942 when Mom was about ten. The Woodard family is enjoying a summer ride on one of the back roads near Jamestown—

Mom's sitting on top of the hood of a 1937 Studebaker, looking very stylish in her plaid jacket and tam. Jerry and Kenny are standing on the front bumper grinning at the camera. If I look closely, I can see Elmer and Adeline peeking up from the back of the car.

Some of Mom's favorite stories were about the family picnics they went on when she was young. She told me Grandma Adeline often woke up on a sunny summer morning and shouted, "Get-up! We're going on a picnic today!" She and Mom scurried around the kitchen making potato salad, baked beans and throwing together whatever else was available. They packed everything into boxes and headed to the nearest park. Whenever she described Adeline like that, I pictured Rosalind Russell in "Gypsy."

There's evidence of one of those summer picnics in a photo from 1944—

Everyone is sitting at a picnic table in Allen Park. Grandpa Elmer looks dapper in his white shirt, vest and tie. It's one of the rare occasions when he isn't wearing a hat. Jenny Goodwill, his mother, has a long unsmiling face and wrinkled skin which reveals the heavy burdens she endured while raising seven hellions with very little income and no husband. Kenny is wearing a baseball cap and smiling at the camera. Mom is sitting across the table from him, craning her neck around Gussie to make sure she gets in the photo. Grandma Adeline is missing from the photo, so I'm assuming she is the one taking the picture. Except for Grandma Goodwill, they all look like they're having a grand time.

Although Mom always painted a lovely picture of her life growing up, I later learned those were extremely difficult years. Whenever Mom talked about Adeline, she made her sound like an angel—she adored her. Even though she never talked badly about her dad or her brothers, I felt she harbored some fear. All three of the Woodard children were wild in their teens. At seventeen, Kenny ended up in Elmira State Prison for attempted robbery. Mom became pregnant at fifteen. Jerry proved to be the wisest of the clan. After getting into a few scrapes, he joined the Army. While stationed in Japan, he met his future wife Jean, whom he later married. That proved to be the best decision he ever made.

When I was about twelve, I questioned my mother about her upbringing. She shared some things with me, but not all. In my teens, I learned more about Mom's life from my great-grandmother, Gussie. Much later, Aunt Lily, Adeline's step-sister, shared even more. It was through their stories I came to understand how completely dysfunctional Mom's family actually was. During my early adolescence, I was desperate for information about my mother's early life because I thought it might explain some of her actions. It has taken me a lifetime to put it all together.

Stew and Bonnie came from very diverse backgrounds. Stew was born in Youngsville, Pennsylvania in 1929 to a very loving mother, Jennette, and a not-so-loving father, Edwin Smith. They lived there until they divorced when Stew was about five. At that time, he and his mother moved in with his grandmother, Gertrude Patch, who helped to raise him.

Stewart Edwin Smith was not my biological father; a fact that never concerned me. He loved me unconditionally from the first moment he met me, at age two, until his death in 1973. His mother, Jennette Conklin, loved me the same way.

There is a photo of Dad and his mother sitting on a table in my hallway. Stew is about eight or nine, and he is standing slightly behind his mother, with his arm gently draped around her shoulders. His curly, blond hair has been carefully combed; his sky-blue eyes are sparkling, and his smile looks like an angel's. They look very similar except for their hair; Grandma's hair was light brown. The strong bond they shared reaches out to me from behind the glass of the frame.

Jennette and Gertrude were hard working women. Gertrude cleaned for several prominent families in the Warren area while Jennette worked in a factory. Their mutual goals were to provide Stew with piano and voice lessons, raise him in a Christian home, and surround him with security and love. The lessons paid off because Stew became an excellent classical pianist who performed throughout the area in his youth. His beautiful tenor voice could be heard in area churches and school choirs until he graduated. When he was only thirteen, he was hired by a local radio station in Warren, WFRA, to perform live on-air. I treasure the old 33's he recorded in the course of those broadcasts.

Often, when I'm missing him, I listen to a very scratchy copy of one of his records. Hearing him sing, "When Irish Eyes Are Smiling" takes me back to those happy nights Mom, Dad and I spent at the Phoenix Grill in Jamestown.

Jennette married Floyd Conklin in 1939, and he became the only father figure Stew ever knew. Even though Dad loved and respected his stepfather, he yearned to reunite with his birth father. When Dad was in his early thirties, my mother contacted Edwin Smith and arranged a meeting. They planned to meet at a quiet bar in downtown Warren. Dad waited for hours, but Edwin never appeared. Nor did he call to explain or apologize. My dad never mentioned his name again.

Grandma Conklin, or Granny C, as I lovingly called her, often shared her wonderful tales of Dad's growing-up years. Her blue eyes shone whenever she described his youthful accomplishments. He was an honor student at Youngsville High School where he participated in band and chorus and lettered in varsity basketball and football.

One day, not long before her death in 2001, Granny C, took me up into her attic. I knelt beside her as she sat in an old rocker looking through some of Dad's memorabilia. The mahogany box she was holding overflowed with newspaper articles, photos, music programs and a host of other things she had saved over the years. Her eyes misted over when she scanned the tattered, yellowed newspaper clippings. One particular article caught her eye. It was printed in the local Youngsville, Pennsylvania newspaper on February, 20, 1947 and read-

"Big Stewie Smith, Youngsville's towering center, broke Merle Welsh's scoring record set last year at 236 points. "Smitty" smashed through the season with 260 markers, to break the Welsh record by 24 points!" He set that record in 1947 at Youngsville High School, and it was unbroken for many years.

While pulling articles and pictures from the box, she found an eight-by-ten black and white photo of Dad with his graduating class. I distinctly remember our conversation-

"Wow, Gram, I love this picture! Look at Dad. He looks so young and happy!"

"He was happy then. You know, he was very popular in school, especially with the girls," she chuckled.

While carefully examining the photo, I noticed Dad's broad smile as he gazed directly down from the top row, into the eyes of a lovely brunette. She was smiling up at him.

"Who is that?" I asked, pointing to the girl in the second row. Granny C closed her eyes as if in a dream, sighed and said,

"That's the girl I hoped he would marry." When she noticed my concerned expression, she put her arms around me and whispered, "But if he'd married her, I wouldn't have you would I?"

She closed the box and handed it to me saying, "Diana, I want you to take this box home with you when you leave today. I know I can trust you to be the keeper of these memories of your Dad. I'll have peace knowing you have them."

I was speechless. I couldn't find the appropriate words to express how deeply touched I was by this kind and loving gesture, so I wrapped my arms around her and whispered into her ear, "I love you, Gram."

Years later, when I was going through that old, wooden box and reading all of the other articles, I realized how accomplished my dad had been. In 1947, his senior year, he was the secretary of his class. That spring, he received a full basketball scholarship to Edinboro State Teacher's College. Other articles described his athletic prowess and musical abilities. I found a yellowed, wax-paper bag with a dried rose in it. The bag contained a program for 'An Evening of Piano and Song', a special concert that featured Stewart E. Smith, singing and playing the piano. The concert took place at the Warren Conservatory of Music on August 4, 1947. According to the program, "Ah, Sweet Mystery of Life", was one of the numbers he sang on that beautiful summer evening.

The following article appeared in the *Warren Times Observer*:

"Stewart Smith, former pupil of Lillian Larsen and now continuing his piano studies with Dr. Leroy B. Campbell, and at the same time a voice pupil of Byron Swanson, was presented in an unusually fine piano and voice recital at the Conservatory of Music at Warren on Monday evening. That Mr. Smith is a young man with much talent and energy, was demonstrated by the fact that he undertook and performed creditably well in both fields. In his first piano group, he played with a splendid tone. His second group was given with a very positive touch.

Mr. Smith has a vibrant voice- rich in resonance and musical feeling. His progress has been almost phenomenal in both voice and piano. Family and friends are watching his musical development with much interest."

At Edinboro State Teacher's College, a freshman away from home for the first time, Stew spent more time drinking and carousing with his friends than he did with his studies. Consequently, his grades were so low he lost his scholarship and dropped out of school at the end the year. My grandparents were devastated. Shortly after returning home, he left for Modesto, California, where he lived with relatives while attending a two-year music program at a local college. Once again, his youthful partying got in the way of his education. He soon returned to Warren.

Despite these youthful failures, and although Dad's mother wasn't wealthy, she made sure he received the love and nurturing he would need to be successful in life.

One blustery, winter Saturday night in 1950, Stew and his best buddy Dick jumped into the car and drove to Jamestown for a night-on-the town.

They were bar-hopping up and down East Second Street when they heard piano music coming from The Phoenix, a local bar and grill. When they walked through the door, a lovely lady sitting behind a piano welcomed them by singing, "Hail, hail the gang's all here!"

When Stew stepped into the crowded room, his sky-blue eyes met the deep-brown eyes of a beautiful brunette sitting at the bar. She had long, dark- brown, curly hair; ruby-red lips and freckles camouflaged by a thin layer of make-up. Her sultry smile drew him like a magnet. He quickly strode across the smoke-filled room, walked up to her and introduced himself and his friend, Dick.

With her seductive voice and coquettish smile, she said, "I'm Bonnie, and this is my cousin, Francis. Would you like to join us?"

After several rounds of drinks and lots of conversation, it was obvious to both Francis and Dick that Stew was smitten with Bonnie. As the evening progressed, Dorothy Brooks invited people from the audience to come to the small stage and sing or play the piano. Stew didn't need a special invitation; he immediately stood up and took his place on the piano stool. When he finished playing several popular songs, he looked across the room, directly at Bonnie, and began to sing one of his favorites, "Because of You." That was all it took for their torrid romance to begin. They wed on May 26, 1951.

I've always understood why Bonnie was attracted to Stew. He was a tall, handsome man with a witty sense of humor and he came from a loving, respectable family. Although he hadn't finished college, his future looked promising. The fact that she needed someone to love and care for both of us made him a good catch.

Bonnie was a very attractive woman who'd had men following her around since she was thirteen, bewitching them with her enchanting eyes and perfectly shaped lips. She was quick-witted and loved to laugh and party. Stew usually dated 'good girls' who were raised with proper etiquette, the type of girls his mother admired. But Bonnie was the attractive young siren he couldn't resist.

CHAPTER 4

The Happy Years

1951-1954

AFTER A FIVE-MONTH whirlwind romance, my mother, Bonnie Jean Woodard married Stewart Edwin Smith on May 26, 1951 in a small Methodist Church in Frewsburg, New York.

The reception was held in the basement of the church, which was a good idea. If they had held it in a hall complete with liquor and beer, I feel confident it would have turned into a "Hatfield and McCoy" reception. Most of the Woodards would have been drunk and brawling before the night ended, which would not have been accepted by the Conklins.

In one of the photographs, Bonnie and Stew are seated at a long table, looking at the photographer who is taking my picture. I'm tip-toeing around the end of the table holding a finger up to my lips as if saying, "Shhh." An older gentleman sitting close-by was chuckling. I appear to be sneaking up on Bonnie and Stew.

They honeymooned for a week in New York City. When they returned, we moved into our first home together on Fairmount Avenue in Jamestown. The next few years would be the happiest of my life with my parents. They were very much in love.

We later moved into an apartment on Crane Street near my grandparents, Adeline and Elmer. My great-grandmother, Gussie, lived in a house just around the corner. We were one big, happy family. My cousins, Carol, Suzie, Sharon, Bobby, and Billy, often came to Gussie's house where we'd play outside while our mothers drank coffee and talked in the kitchen.

Having lived with my grandparents until Mom married Stew, I was very close to them. Adeline adored having a little granddaughter and doted on me. Mom and I spent a lot of time with Grandma Adeline during the day while my grandfather and father worked.

Those visits abruptly ended the day the ambulance arrived and took my grandmother to the hospital. I couldn't understand what was happening; why my mother and Gussie were constantly crying; why Grandpa Elmer was hardly ever home or what all the whispering was about. One night I was awakened by the sound of the ringing phone. The next sound I remember is that of Mom's sobbing. I opened my bedroom door and saw Daddy holding my mother in his arms as she wept. He was crying, too.

Grandpa Elmer had called from the hospital to tell them Grandma Adeline had passed away. She was only forty years old when she died from kidney failure. My mother and great-grandmother's lives were never the same. I was too young to understand why my grandmother wasn't at her house anymore and why she didn't come to see me. Mom told me she went to heaven to live with God. That made me happy.

Of my great-grandmother Gussie's three daughters— Adeline, Dorothy, and Lillian, Adeline had been her favorite. Gussie never missed an opportunity to describe Adeline's beautiful, curly locks of dark-brown hair that cascaded down her back when she was a small child. She could be in the middle of a conversation when she'd suddenly start to giggle as she recalled something spunky Adeline as done as a teen. Although Gussie eventually came to love my grandfather Elmer, I don't believe she ever forgave him for the tough life Adeline endured during their marriage.

I often felt my mother lost part of her heart when she lost her mother. Whenever she talked about my grandmother, she described her as an angel who could do no wrong. Because I was only two when Adeline passed away, I will never know how many of the stories were true and how many were fiction. I do know that neither my mother nor Gussie ever recovered from their loss.

One thing I do remember is walking into the funeral home clutching my mother's hand. I must have been surprised by all of the flowers because my mother told me that Grandma Adeline was loved by many people and they had sent all of the flowers. She also told me she had died *from a disease caused by not urinating often enough. To this day, I rush to the bathroom the minute my bladder feels full!*

Every Easter, all of my relatives gathered at Gussie's for dinner. Everyone was dressed to the nines in new spring coats, Easter hats, gloves and fancy new shoes. When I was older, I began to understand my mother's desire to be well-dressed. Coming from an indigent family, she believed dressing well made you appear prominent and successful, even when you couldn't afford it.

Was this was an indication of her lack of self-esteem? The more I've learned about Mom's upbringing, the more I have come to understand there were other factors that contributed to her incessant need to look pretty.

While looking through an old box of photos and newspaper clippings, I found a picture that appeared on the front-page of the *Jamestown Post-Journal* on April 19, 1953. Mom, Dad and I were decked out in our Easter finery, and gaily strolling down Main Street on Easter Sunday when the newspaper photographer asked us to pose for a photo.

My mother is wearing a beautiful corsage pinned to her light colored full-length coat. Her short, curly hair is topped with a veiled hat. My father is dressed in a dark suit, a white dress shirt, and tie. I'm tucked between the two of them holding my mother's gloved hand. I'm wearing a new spring coat, an Easter bonnet just like Mom's, patent-leather shoes, and a big smile. Mom was the grandest lady in the Easter Parade, Dad was the proudest fellow and I look like the happiest four-year-old on earth.

Some of my happiest childhood memories took place on Crane Street. I remember donning my cowgirl outfit and pretending I was Annie Oakley. I ran around the neighborhood shooting the 'bad guys', usually my cousins Billy and Bobby. When this rough-housing resulted in a cut or bruise, I often ran to my great-grandmother to fix it. After Gussie had applied iodine and a band aid, she kissed the boo-boo, gently patted me on the butt and sent me back outside to play. I loved the kiss but hated the sting of the iodine.

One afternoon, I was in the backyard watching some neighborhood boys doing wheelies on their bikes. I joyously laughed at their comical antics until my knee started to throb. I stood up from my kneeling position and saw the bright red blood flowing down my leg. I screamed. One of the boys hurried to get my mother. Mom ran over, took one look at the deep cut on my knee, picked me up and carried me up the hill to Grandpa Elmer's so he could drive us to the hospital.

When we arrived at the emergency room, a kind nurse calmly explained they were going to give me a shot to numb my knee. After that, the doctor would clean out my wound and stitch it. The word 'shot' terrified me.

"NO!" I screamed. "I want my Daddy! Please Mommy, get Daddy!" Mom left the room and made the call to my father at work. She and my grandfather tried to keep me calm until he arrived. Soon Dad came rushing into the door. He swiftly reached my side, kissed my forehead, held my hand and gently whispered, "Everything is okay. Daddy's here."

I would only allow the doctor to stitch my knee if my father could stay with me and hold my hand. The doctor promptly stitched it up and sent me on my way. The deep gash caused by a piece of glass embedded in my right knee left a big scar, a scar that reminds me of the day when Dad came to my rescue.

At Christmas time, my parents took me to visit Santa. I was a little nervous when I climbed onto his lap for the very first time. My fears vanished the moment I gazed at his twinkling eyes and cheery face. Bolstered by my newly found confidence, I pertly announced, "Santa, all I want for Christmas is a Tiny Tears doll. Please."

I got up very early Christmas morning and ran into my parents' bedroom to wake them up. "Let's see if Santa came!" I exclaimed.

When we walked into the darkened living room, the Christmas lights cast a glow over all of my presents under the tree. I rushed over, lifted my Tiny Tears doll into my arms and kissed her. She became my most treasured possession. I spent hours feeding her, changing her and holding her. As I sat rocking her and singing her to sleep, Mom looked at me with a twinkle in her eye and said, "Maybe next year you'll have a real baby to love."

What in the world did she mean by that?

My mother gave me a birthday party every year, but my fifth birthday is the one I'll always remember. Gussie surprised me with a special party at the Hotel Jamestown. Every Saturday morning, Jim Roselle, a popular local radio announcer, hosted a live broadcast on WJTN called "Breakfast at Bigelow's." The birthday guest was given the seat of honor at a table decorated with balloons and a birthday cake. When my mother and I entered the restaurant we were greeted by Gussie, my aunts, and cousins shouting, "Surprise!" A short time later, Jim Roselle walked over to our table, knelt beside me and announced, "Diana Lynn Smith is here today celebrating her fifth birthday. Diana, are you enjoying your birthday?" When he placed the microphone close to my mouth, I was speechless. However, it didn't take long for me to become comfortable talking on the radio.

After my interview, I began to open my gifts. When I opened the beautifully wrapped tiny box from Gussie and saw a little gold ring with a diamond chip, I was delighted. My eyes were gleaming when I slid it onto my finger. "I love you, Gussie," I said as I wrapped my arms tightly around her.

My parents and I visited Grandma and Grandpa Conklin in Warren almost every Sunday. During the drive, we sang songs together, "You Are My Sunshine" and "Daddy's Little Girl" were among our favorites. The closer we got to my grandmother's house, the louder we sang. When we arrived at her house, I jumped out of the car and ran up the short flight of stairs to the back door where Granny C was standing with her arms open. I nestled in her arms and inhaled the sweet scent of her lilac perfume. The delicious aroma of the baking roast filled the kitchen.

After dinner, Dad sat down at the piano in the living room and patted the space beside him. I quickly climbed up. He entertained us all by playing and singing the songs he had learned as a young man. I loved to watch him close his eyes when he sang; it was as if he was dreaming of something long past. He sang a special song for everyone in the living room. My favorite was "Melody of Love." We didn't have a piano at home, so these musical sessions became a very special time for us.

Diana Lynn

After Christmas, we moved from Crane Street to a second-floor apartment on Stowe Street. Although I missed the nearness of Gussie, I enjoyed spending time alone with my parents. My father got paid on Fridays and almost every Friday night, we rode the bus downtown to Fulton's Fish Market. We sat at a little table and ate our delicious, deep-fried fish right out of the white paper wrapper. After we had eaten, we went across the street to the Toy Shop where they sometimes bought me a new outfit for one of my Ginny dolls. Friday was my favorite night of the week.

Whenever I relive the memories from my past, one of the first to come flooding back are the nights Mom, Dad and I spent at the Phoenix. Writing a letter to my mother describing one of those memorable nights was the best way for me to describe my emotions. Although my mother had been deceased for over thirty years, I wrote this letter anyway. I couldn't put a stamp on it and send it, but in my heart, I believe she got the message—

Dear Mom,
I awoke this morning to another damp pillow. Once again, I'd traveled in my dreams to one of the Friday nights we spent at the Phoenix. Was it '53 or '54? I know I was only three or four years old. Remember, Mom? It was just the three of us--you, Daddy and me.
  After our downtown shopping trip, we took a bus to the Phoenix, the neighborhood bar and grill. This is where we spent many of our Friday nights. The flashing neon lights, the laughter from within and the sounds of the thumping piano keys beckoned us. Once we were inside the smoky bar, Dorothy would look up from the piano, smile at us with her ruby-red lips, and change the music from whatever she was playing to "Hail, hail the gang's all here!" Then she'd announce loud enough for everyone to hear,
  "Look, here comes Stewie, Bonnie, and little Diana."
  Did you get as excited as I did? I felt like every eye in the house was on us and I beamed like a princess or a movie star! Dorothy stood up from the piano stool and gave us all a kiss. I can

still feel her lips on my cheek and smell her strong perfume. Was it Shalimar? Her lipstick imprint probably stayed on my face all evening long. How about those evening gowns she wore? Do you think she ever wore any of them more than once?

Didn't she make you feel special, Mom? I remember tingling with excitement because I knew what a wonderful night lay ahead of us. I was proud that so many people knew us and talked to us as we made our way to our table. Those people were regulars, just like you and Dad, and they too, were probably looking for a few laughs, a few drinks and a few hours away from their lives outside the Phoenix doors.

We'd pick a table close to the piano, and you and Dad would order drinks. I can't remember what you drank. I know it wasn't beer then. Dad would order a beer, and that was fine. It was later when he changed to whiskey that you'd give him a dirty look. You'd order a Shirley Temple for me and whisper in my ear, "You're my Shirley Temple." You were always saying that to me, and I loved it. Looking back, I think I began to believe I was a star like Shirley Temple!

I began to fidget as I waited for Dorothy to call Dad up to sing. She finally walked away from the piano, put her lips up to the microphone and said, "Stewie Smith, are you going to sing and play for us tonight?

Everyone began clapping, and my eyes filled with adoration for Stewie Smith, my dad. I knew you were as proud as I was, Mom because I saw it in your eyes. Dad sat down at the piano and soon we'd hear the beautiful tenor strains of his voice as he sang, "When Irish Eyes are Smiling." Remember how he always closed his eyes whenever he sang? Didn't you think he looked like he was far away in dreamland? Before it was over, everyone in the room was singing along, and when he finished, the room filled with applause. I was bursting with pride!

Then he'd say, "Diana Lynn, come on up here." My knees were shaking as I walked toward the piano. Hoisting me up on top of the table next to him, he'd take the microphone into his hand and look directly into my eyes while he sang, "Daddy's Little Girl." In my head, I can still hear every word and every note of that song. Whenever I've heard that song over the years, I've stopped in my tracks and remembered.

How very special it made me feel, and how lucky I was to have a Dad who loved me so much. I knew then I'd do everything in my power for the rest of my life, to sustain the love and pride he felt for me. After he finished singing to me, he'd look over at you with love in his eyes and say, "This song is for my beautiful wife, Bonnie Jean." Then he'd sing, "Because of You."

The night wasn't over yet. Pretty soon, Dorothy would call you up to sing.

Isn't it sad that I can't remember what you sang? All I remember is being proud of you, too, although I have to admit, I was a little nervous. I worried you might not pull it off. I'd sweat through every note you sang. But with your lovely face, beautiful, dark-brown hair, which was always perfectly coiffed, and your smoky voice, you always carried it off. I clapped and clapped along with everyone else. You were my Mom, and I was proud to be your daughter.

Next it was my turn. Dorothy invited "Darling little Diana" to come up and dance. Dad played the piano, and I began to ballet; the dance you had taught me at home. I felt just like a princess, never wanting the moment to end. Evenings like this that we spent at the Phoenix are the fondest memories I have of my childhood.

So you see, Mom, it wasn't always heartache and pain. It was the best it would ever be— just the three of us when you and Dad were still in love.

Years later when we went to the Phoenix, the magic had faded. Still, whenever I hear the words or the music to any of those songs, my heart and mind travel back to those magical, mystical times. We know though, don't we Mom, that magic doesn't last forever?

Mom, I don't think I ever thanked you while you were alive, so I'm doing it now. Thanks for instilling in me the strength and confidence that helped me become the woman I am today.

I **loved** you Mom,
Your daughter, Diana Lynn

CHAPTER 5

Laughter in the Rain

1954
When I was four, I dreamed of becoming a Prima Ballerina, so Mom enrolled me in formal dance classes. Those dreams were dashed at my first recital. While trying to follow the dancers in my group, I missed the cue when they took a somersault. I anxiously looked out into the audience for my mother, knowing she would give me reassurance, but the bright lights made it impossible to see anyone. I shrugged my shoulders, bent over and proceeded with my somersault—late.

Meanwhile, the other dancers were performing the next part of the routine. The audience erupted into laughter, making me think I had done something wonderful. I smiled brightly and took a bow. This experience led me to consider becoming a comedian.

I'm not sure if I stopped taking formal lessons because I was kicked out or if my parents simply couldn't afford them anymore. I'm sure it was the latter. My mother decided to teach me at home. She put "Melody of Love" on the record player and danced around the room while I watched. Then she gently took my hands and taught me each step. She registered me in several local talent shows where Dad played the piano, I danced, and Mom coached from behind the curtain.

I've often wondered who had taught my mother to dance because I knew her parents couldn't afford lessons. Was it her mother or perhaps Gussie? It really doesn't matter who taught her. What was important were her dainty pirouettes and the gentle smile on her lips as she twirled around the room. It's the most peaceful memory I have of her.

Sometimes during these at-home dance sessions, Mom quit dancing and sat down for a few minutes. After she caught her breath, she explained she had to stop dancing because her tummy hurt. It wasn't long before my parents shared their big secret.

One evening after dinner, Mom walked over to the stove, refilled her coffee cup, lit a cigarette and teasingly said to Dad, "Should we tell her now?"

My immediate response was, "Tell me what?"

Playing along with Mom's little game, Dad replied, "Oh, I don't know, maybe we should wait."

I jumped up from my chair, ran over to him, tugged his hand and pleaded, "What, Daddy? Please tell me now."

My mother knelt beside me and asked, "How would you like a baby brother or sister?'

I squealed with delight and bombarded her with questions. "Will it be a boy or girl? What will we name it? When will the baby get here?"

"Whoa, slow down. The baby will be here this summer, and we won't know what it is until it's born," Dad calmly replied.

Puzzling it out, I asked, "Are you buying the baby at the store?" Mom patted her belly while Dad lifted me high over his head and spun me around. Elated and dizzy, I didn't ask any more questions.

I'd lie in bed at night thinking about my new brother or sister. A myriad of questions passed through my mind—what would the baby look like; how big would it be; what if I don't like the baby; what if the new baby doesn't like me? The most important question to me at that time was, "Will Mom, and Dad still love me as much as they do now? "

My parents apparently felt my concerns because the next week they gave me a big surprise. We didn't own a television set, so I went to a neighbor's house every weekday at four-thirty to watch the Cisco Kid.

One day, my father came to pick me up before the show was over. I was very upset and asked him to wait until it ended. He insisted I leave right then. I pouted the whole way home. My mother was waiting for me at the top of the stairs. As I reached the final step, she put her hands over my eyes and slowly guided me into the living room. When she removed her hands, I saw a brand new black and white television set sitting on top of the table. What a great surprise, now I could watch TV whenever I wanted.

As the weeks passed, it seemed like Mom was always talking on the phone. I heard her tell one of her friends how excited she was about the new baby and how anxious she was to have it all over. A few nights later, Dad came into my bedroom in the middle of the night and told me to put my robe on because I was going to Gussie's. "Why?" I asked. He said he was taking Mom to the hospital to get my new baby brother or sister.

He arrived at Gussie's the next day, lifted me onto his lap and told me I had a brand new sister to love; her name was Judy. A few days later, we went to bring Mom and the new baby home from the hospital. The soft, pink blanket covering my little sister made it nearly impossible to see her tiny face. I carefully lifted the corner and peeked at her. She was beautiful, and I couldn't wait to hold her in my arms. As soon as we arrived home, Mom sat on the couch holding Judy in her arms and invited me to sit beside her. "Diana Lynn, this is your very own little sister, Judy. You'll be her big sister for the rest of your life. Do you want to hold her?"

Reaching for the baby with outstretched arms, I enthusiastically replied, "Oh, yes!"

My mother gently placed this precious, tiny bundle into my arms. It was a very emotional moment for me—I was happy, sad, afraid, nervous and confused. But when I looked at Judy's beautiful little pink face, her tiny, wrinkled fingers and her soft, fuzzy-blonde hair that looked like down feathers, I was overcome with love. Holding her was much better than holding my Tiny Tears doll. Judy was a real live baby I could love and care for as a big sister. My life would never be the same.

Over the next few weeks, our apartment was filled with family and friends coming to see the new baby. One afternoon, Mom sat at the kitchen table sharing her birthing experience with several of her friends when Judy started to cry. She asked me to go into the bedroom and check on her.

Anxious to show off my big sister talents, I hurried into the bedroom. Judy was lying in her bassinette sucking her fist. She had just been fed, so I knew she wasn't hungry. Maybe she has a wet diaper, I thought. I gently removed the pins from her diaper, retrieved a dry one from the shelf and proceeded to change her all by myself. I'll never know what possessed me, but suddenly I had a strong urge to prick her in the butt with the safety pin. I did. She wailed, and my mother rushed into the bedroom to find out was wrong. When I confessed what I had done, Mom was furious. I'm still trying to analyze why I did that. I vowed to myself that day that I would never, ever purposely hurt her again.

At first, it was a difficult transition from being the center of attention to sharing the spotlight with a new sibling. As I began to experience the rewards of being the big sister and accepted the responsibilities that went with it, I overcame most of my jealousy. It didn't take long for me to see how much my little sister needed me to protect her.

On a sunny afternoon at the end of August, we went to visit my grandparents in Warren. The moment we pulled into the driveway, Grandma Conklin, Grandpa Conklin, Great-Grandma Smith, and Uncle Gene, Dad's half-brother, came rushing out to greet us. My grandmothers were anxious to hold this little bundle of joy. Dad's family kept proclaiming how Judy looked just like Stew. She had his sky-blue eyes, light blonde hair, and fair complexion. They were elated. Although Mom smiled while everyone was fussing over the baby, I noticed her mood changed. She seemed sad about something. I vaguely remember Mom and Granny C stepping out on the porch to talk. I'll never know exactly what transpired, but they were very somber when they came back into the house.

A photo from that day that is very telling. Grandma Conklin is sitting on the piano bench holding Judy while Dad, Gene, and Grandpa Conklin are standing behind her. It's the only photo I've ever seen where Grandma Conklin isn't smiling. She's scowling. My mother is seated next to her on the bench looking very unhappy. I'm perched on Mom's knee, pouting. I'll always wonder what had happened that day to put those sad, angry expressions on our faces. Unfortunately, there's no one left to ask, so I've had to come to my own conclusions. I believe this photo represents the first sign that my mother was jealous of all of the attention Judy was getting from Dad's family. It's the first, small crack in our 'family portrait'.

We had outgrown our apartment and moved across town to a lovely, first-floor apartment on Palmer Street. I quickly made friends with a neighbor girl, Vicky Jones. We spent hours playing with our Ginny dolls and squirting each other with the hose on hot days. However, we couldn't do everything together. I didn't own a bike, so I watched Vicky ride hers up and down the block while secretly longing for a bike of my own.

One sunny summer afternoon, a shiny, new red two-wheeler mysteriously appeared on our front porch. A bunch of colorful balloons attached to the handlebars had a tag with my name on it. My dad spent hours trying to teach me to ride it. He hung onto the back fender and ran beside me while I pedaled down the street. I continually shouted over my shoulder, "Dad, are you still there?" He always answered, "Yep." One day, when I asked that question he didn't answer me. I glanced over my shoulder and saw him standing about a block away. I was riding my bike by myself! I proudly rode up and down Palmer Street with Vicky for the remainder of the summer.

The bright sunshine streaking through my window woke me up early one Saturday morning. Through the open bedroom window, I heard the loud voices of my neighbors as they prepared for their weekend outing.

"Did you get the picnic basket?" Mrs. Jones called from the back door "What about my bike? Can I bring it?" Vicky hollered.

I peered out the window just as they were pulling out of their driveway. I wanted to stick my head out and yell, "Hey, can I come along?" But I didn't.

Instead, I got out of bed and went into the kitchen where my Dad sat doing the daily crossword puzzle. He lifted his head and said, "Hey, Snookey, what brings you downstairs so early?" Snookey was his nickname for me.

"I heard Vicky and her family getting ready to go to the lake. Could we go somewhere today, Dad? We could pack a lunch and go to Allen Park for a picnic." Snuggling against him, I gazed up and begged, "Please?"

The color of his eyes swiftly darkened, a sign that he was sad. "Aw, honey, how can we do that? The car isn't running."

That car is NEVER running, I thought to myself, but I didn't say it; the hurt in his voice was enough to stop me. It wasn't his fault we never had any extra money. He worked hard at his factory job, and it saddened him when he couldn't afford to get the car fixed. Most of the time, that old rattletrap of a car didn't provide him with dependable transportation to and from work. When it wasn't running, he walked nearly three miles to get to his job. How could I selfishly expect more of this kind and loving man? Rather than hurt his feelings by reminding him we didn't have a way to go anywhere, I nodded and said, "Okay."

As I walked out of the kitchen, I heard him softly say, "We'll try and find something else to do around here today." Although I had my doubts, there was always hope.

My sadness slipped away as I prepared to work on my summer project— recreating the map of New York State on a large piece of newsprint. I was inspired by the blue and yellow map of New York State on the cover of my new tablet. I swept the front porch, carefully opened my roll of newsprint, spread it the length of the porch, sharpened my number-two pencils and went to work.

As the day wore on, it became sweltering. Late in the afternoon large, gray clouds rolled in; the wind swiftly picked up, and I heard the first rumble of thunder in the distance. I promptly rolled up my map and went inside.

Thunder terrified me. I sat in our living room watching the sheets of rain pelting against the windows. A short while later, the thunder and lightning subsided, and the sun started to peek through the parting clouds.

Dad came up behind me and said, "See, I told you we'd find something to do today."

I curiously asked, "What?"

"Let's run in the rain. We'll put on our bathing suits and go outside and run around in the pouring rain. It's safe now the thunder and lightning have passed. That should cool us off, don't you think?"

What an ingenious idea! Once again, good old Dad came through. I ran to my room and changed into my swimming suit. We stepped off the porch, lifted our faces to the sky and let the fresh, fat raindrops plop down over our heads and bodies. Torrents of rain caused waterways to build up along the curbs. We ran through the swiftly moving puddles. I reached into the rushing water and splashed my dad as he ran past me. While we ran up and down Palmer Street joyously laughing, I realized my father had turned a hot, humid summer day into a memorable event.

The rain plastered Dad's curly blonde hair flat against his head. I looked up and saw his eyes were once again sky-blue; his happy eyes were back. I grabbed his big hand and whispered, "Thank you, Daddy."

When the rain subsided, I knew our little rain game was over for today. This was the first of many days I'd spend running and laughing in the rain with my dad.

Even now, whenever it's hot, humid and pouring rain, I have a notion to get into my suit and run through my big, grassy front yard. Maybe I will someday and when I'm running, I'll look up into the sky and send him a friendly wave and smile. He'd like that.

I barely slept the night before Kindergarten, Throughout the night, I continually checked the school clothes lying on my dresser making sure everything was in order. Next morning, I clung to my mother as we entered Percell School to meet my teacher, Mrs. Archibald. The moment I saw the warm smile on Mrs. Archibald's face, I knew I'd like her.

She reminded me of Granny C – a kind and understanding woman. This thought comforted me and enabled me to let go of my mother's hand. Mom kissed me softly on the cheek and walked out the door. I noticed her wiping her eyes with a tissue.

My mother was chuckling the day she returned from her first teacher-parent conference. She told me Mrs. Archibald enjoyed having me as a student and had said some very nice things about me. I was tickled. A little later, I heard her laughing as she relayed a different story to one of her friends.

"Diana's teacher told me the funniest story today. Last week, Diana stood up during Show & Tell and demonstrated how Stew and I wrestled in bed. She lay down, face-first, and humped the floor! Apparently she remembered what I had told her when she walked into the bedroom while Stew and I were having sex. Her teacher couldn't wait for our conference to share the story."

"Yes, she's quite a girl," Mom commented before she hung up the phone.

CHAPTER 6

Forever Darling

1955-1957

AT THE END of my first school year, my parents became embroiled in a big argument over money. Our landlord, Mr. Carlson, had come to the house to inform my mother we would have to move because we were behind in the rent.

As soon as he left, she went into her bedroom and cried. When Dad walked in the door from work, she came flying out of the bedroom shouting, "Stew, we have to move again because you didn't pay the rent!"

Dad seemed shocked by this verbal assault. He raised his head and retorted, "What a minute, Bonnie. Why is this all my fault? I told you the repairs on the car took most of my last two paychecks, and yet, you insisted on buying a new sofa. When will you understand we have to stick with a budget?"

She defiantly responded, " I guess we'll just have to find another apartment," and stormed out of the room.

Judy toddled over and held her arms out for me to pick her up. I knew she was upset by all of the shouting, so I carried her into my bedroom where I assured her everything would be okay. It was easier consoling a ten-month- old baby than it was convincing myself everything would be all right.

That summer, we moved to a second-story apartment on North Main Street which was located in the S.G Love School District. Although I worried about making friends at a new school, I quickly acclimated to my new surroundings. Every morning, when I passed the office on my way to my classroom, I noticed Mr. Hardenburg, our principal, sitting in a chair, talking to the wall. This mystified me.

After arriving in my class, I immediately walked up to Miss Fuller's desk. "Miss Fuller, is Mr. Hardenburg a little bit crazy?"

Stunned by this bold question, she replied, "Of course not! Why do you ask?"

I explained that I when I passed Mr. Hardenburg's office I noticed him talking to the wall. Miss Fuller's throaty laughter filled the room. She grabbed my hand and led me to the office. While marching down the hall beside her, it occurred to me I might be in trouble. I followed her confident footsteps into the office where she relayed my story to everyone present, including the principal. Relief flooded through me when they all laughed. Apparently I wasn't in trouble; they thought I was funny!

Mr. Hardenburg smiled at me and said, "Follow me into my office, young lady."

When we entered his room, he walked up to the panel attached to the wall. He pointed to the screen and explained it was the intercom system he spoke into when making his daily announcements. Noticing my astonished expression, he asked, "Would you like to try it?" Intrigued but frightened, I slowly nodded my head. I approached the screen and softly said, "Good morning everyone." This was my second public speaking experience.

1956 started out with a bang. Judy and I spent New Year's Eve with my grandparents in Warren while Mom and Dad enjoyed an evening barhopping in Jamestown. At midnight, we donned our winter coats, grabbed some pans from the kitchen and went out on the front porch. As the church bells began to ring, we banged our pots and loudly shouted, "Happy New Year!" Granny C lifted my face, kissed me and whispered, "Happy New Year, Diana. I'm praying it will be a good one for all of you."

The excitement of the New Year continued throughout January and into early February with the announcement that Lucille Ball and Desi Arnaz were coming to Jamestown for the premier of "Forever Darling" in February. My cousin, Suzie and I had good reason to be excited. For years, Gussie and our mothers had shared stories about the great friendship between my grandmother Adeline and Lucy while they were in high-school.

Although these stories were never officially confirmed, they satisfied the imaginations of two young girls. According to my mother, Adeline and Lucy kept in touch after Lucy had moved away and attained stardom. Lucy contacted Adeline to arrange a meeting whenever she came to town. Sometime in the mid-'40's, my grandparents went to the ballroom in Midway Park on Chautauqua Lake to meet her. They brought Bonnie with them. My mother became starry-eyed whenever she described sitting beside Lucille Ball and listening to her fabulous stories about her life in New York City and Hollywood.

Whenever my mother told me this story, I could almost feel the warmth of the summer breeze coming off the lake and hear the soft sounds of the big band music. I could feel her excitement as she described having a face-to-face conversation with Lucille Ball. It was a perfect night in my mother's young life that she always remembered.

On the evening of February 7, 1956, Third Street in downtown Jamestown, overflowed with thousands of fans and well-wishers. They lined both sides of the street for hours waiting for Lucy and Desi to come out of the Hotel Jamestown. From there, they would ride in a sleek, black limousine down the street to the Palace Theater. The colorful lights on the marquee flashed, "Jamestown Welcomes Lucy & Desi for the Premier of Forever Darling."

My cousin Suzie and I stood in the lobby of the hotel with our parents waiting for Lucy and Desi to come downstairs to get into the limo. As more people wedged themselves into the crowded hallway, Suzie and I became separated from our parents. She grabbed my hand and said, "Follow me."

We wriggled through the crowd and found ourselves at the end of a long hallway where we noticed a stairway cordoned off with a red velvet rope. Suzie quickly ducked under the rope and ran up the steps. I followed. We stopped at each landing, peered around for some sign of Lucy and continued up another level. When we reached the last floor, we paused to catch our breath. Suddenly a door opened, and three men dressed in dark suits and top coats emerged. Soon, a beautiful, bejeweled, red-headed Lucy strolled out of the room! We stared at her elegant, gold, glittering evening gown, her white fur stole, and her long, white gloves. Fascinated, we watched as she gracefully lifted her long cigarette holder to her lips. Slowly blowing the wispy, white smoke from her lungs she drawled, "Gentlemen, shall we go?" When the doors to the elevator opened, Lucy turned to us and said, "Girls, why don't you join us?" Speechless, we followed. I'll never forget that magical elevator ride.

We followed Lucy and her entourage out of the elevator and into the arms of our frantic fathers. Dad and Uncle Morrie started to scold us for leaving without telling anyone. Mom rushed up and asked, "Were you in that elevator with Lucy?" In a trancelike state, the only thing I could do was nod.

"Did you tell her you were Adeline Woodard's granddaughter? I slowly found my voice and weakly replied, "No."

"Are you serious? You didn't tell her who you were? Why?" she asked. "You taught me never to interrupt adults when they were talking." My family laughed about this story for years.

One morning, shortly after that magical night, I opened the door to the bathroom and discovered Mom vomiting into the toilet. Concerned, I grabbed a wet wash cloth and handed it to her. While she wiped the spittle from her chin, I asked if she was ill and she replied, "I'm not sick, I'm pregnant again."

This news surprised me. She didn't sound happy about the situation so I didn't ask any more questions.

As Mom's morning sickness continued, I would often come home from school and find her sitting on the couch staring off into space. When I asked her what was wrong she wouldn't answer me. Instead of improving the relationship between my parents, her pregnancy seemed to push them farther apart. They continued to argue about the same old thing—never having enough money. To avoid the chaos, I'd retreat to my room and lie there wondering what I could do to fix things so the fighting would stop.

The constant battles wore Dad down. He solved the problem by finding a part-time job as a playground superintendent for the Jamestown

Department of Recreation. He was assigned to work at the Love School playground, Monday through Friday evenings, from late spring until early fall.

Every day Dad rushed home from work, grabbed a bite to eat, gathered up a big, gray canvas bag filled with balls and bats and went to the playground. I usually tagged along. The smiles on the kids' faces whenever my father appeared to open the gate, made me proud. When the gate swung open, everyone ran onto the playground, heading to the swings, a basketball court or the arts and crafts tables. I'd join in one of the activities and play until closing at nine o'clock.

Love School was one of the only interracial schools in Jamestown in 1956. The color of someone's skin never mattered to Dad; he treated everyone fairly. If someone was hurt, he would tenderly care for their injury. If kids started physically fighting, he would put an end to it, and if someone needed to talk about a personal problem, he would readily listen. As I witnessed my father's fairness and understanding with children, I could see that race wasn't a factor with him like it was with some people.

One night, a young black boy named Jimmy tried to join a basketball game already in progress. When some of the older boys pushed him away, an argument broke out. As the shoving and shouting worsened, Dad blew his whistle to get their attention. They all stopped and stared at him. He walked up to the ring-leader, a tall, cocky, blue-eyed blonde, and asked him what was wrong. All of the basketball players stood silently looking down at their feet. At six-three and two hundred plus pounds, Dad towered over them. In his sternest voice he said, "I guess there aren't any problems, right? Let Jimmy play, and if I see this type of behavior again, you'll all be told to leave the playground for the rest of the summer." Before the night was over, several more black boys had joined the game. They continued to play basketball together throughout that long, hot summer.

Because Mom continued to be ill throughout most of her pregnancy, I tried to help out by caring for Judy. I would read books to her, make her lunch, bathe her at night and often tuck her into bed. Many nights

Judy cried because she wanted Mommy to do it. I would gently rub her eyebrows like my mother used to do to me until she fell asleep. Before leaving the room, I whispered in her ear that things would be better once Mom had the baby.

My mother was only eight months pregnant when she went into labor. My sister, Kim, was born on August 12, 1956. While Mom was in the hospital, Judy and I stayed with Mom's good friend, Ann Hart. At seven, I couldn't understand what was happening but I knew it was dangerous by the worried look on Dad's face when he stopped each evening to check on us. I overheard him and Ann as they whispered about some health problems with the new baby. I prayed to God and asked Him to make Kim better. About a week later, Mom returned home without her. Kim had been born prematurely and had to remain in the hospital until she weighed five pounds. We all continued to pray.

After Mom had come home, concerned friends and relatives called or stopped by our apartment nearly every day. I eavesdropped as they sat at the kitchen table drinking coffee, smoking cigarettes and talking about the difficulties my mother endured during the delivery. I heard my mother say,

"It was horrible! Kim's umbilical cord was wrapped around her neck, choking her. When they first brought her to me, she was black and blue from the lack of oxygen. I didn't think she'd make it. I believe my mother, Adeline, heard my prayers because Kim is getting better every day."

"Bonnie, don't you mean God heard your prayers?" Arlene inquired.
"Arlene, I had the most surreal experience. During delivery, while under the anesthetic, I dreamed I was walking through a long, dark tunnel. I saw a light at the end of the tunnel and followed it, thinking it would lead me out. When I came to the end of the tunnel, I saw my mother's face and reached up to her, begging her to pull me out. I heard her voice telling me it wasn't time for me to join her. She told me to turn around and go back."

Mom bowed her head and softly said, "The next day my doctor came in to see me and told me they'd almost lost me during the delivery. He said he didn't think I'd make it, but suddenly, my vital signs improved and everything was back to normal." She went on to say, "Arlene, I believe that's when my mother told me to go back to be with my family. And yes, I do believe God listened to my prayers, but it was my mother's voice I was hearing. "

I was frightened by what I had overheard. I worried about it until I realized Grandma Adeline must have been watching over my mother from heaven.

A week later, my parents brought Kim home. She was a pretty little baby, considering all she'd been through. She had the smallest fingers and toes I had ever seen. Like Judy, she strongly resembled Dad's side of the family.

Everyone fussed over her. I was old enough to understand why everyone was fussing over the baby but Judy had just turned two and couldn't understand why everyone paid attention to Kim and seemed to ignore her.

She looked at me and cried, "I want Mommy." I picked her up and took her to my room where I entertained her until she forgot about it. Unfortunately, my promise to her that things would get better with Mom after she had the baby was never fulfilled.

This was the onset of the middle-child syndrome that haunted Judy for years. It was at this time I actively assumed my role as Judy's surrogate mother.

As fall turned to winter, the conditions at home settled down. Because of the problems with Kim's birth, Mom devoted most of her time doting on her. She seemed much happier in this role. Dad's part-time, summer job had ended and he was much more relaxed.

The only problems seemed to be between Judy and me. Every time I turned around, she would be in my bedroom playing with my Ginny dolls; completely undressing them and pulling out the rubber bands that held their pony tails or braids in place. My Ginny's looked like wild trolls instead of cute, little five-year- old girls. I'd find a blue, one-inch shoe here, a white sock there, and pieces and parts of all their sweet little outfits scattered all over my room. I tried calmly talking to her about it. I even gave her one of her own so she'd leave mine alone. Nothing worked. Exasperated, I yelled at her one day.

"Judy, this is MY room and these are MY dolls. If I catch you in here again I'm going to spank you!" She'd never seen me so mad. Watching as her blue eyes clouded over, her lips puckered and she started to wail, broke my heart. Then I did what most, older sisters do—I picked her up, held her close and told her I was sorry for getting so angry. After that, whenever she came into my room, she only played with the doll I had given her and left the rest alone.

Things rapidly changed one blustery winter day in March when I stayed home from school because I was sick. Midway through the day, a large, blue and yellow truck pulled up outside of our apartment. My mother peeked out the upstairs window and saw a man stepping out of the truck and walking toward the stairs to our apartment. She hurriedly handed Kim to me, pulled Judy by the hand, and pushed us into the hall closet. She whispered, "Don't make a sound. I'll tell you when to come out."

Huddling together in that dark closet, I thought, *"What if this man is coming to hurt us?"*

Suddenly, I heard a loud knock on the door, followed by several more knocks. Finally, a deep-voiced man announced, "Gasman. Open up." After repeating it a couple of times, he realized no one was going to answer the door. A few seconds later we heard his heavy boots stomping down the steps. When Mom was certain he was gone, she opened the door and let us out of the closet. Then she rushed to the phone to call my dad at work. After she had hung up the phone, she sat down at the kitchen table and began to cry. I didn't know what to say to her.

She finally composed herself, went into the bedroom, opened the dresser drawers and started throwing her clothes into suitcases and bags. She did the same with our things. When Dad arrived home from work, he loaded the car with our belongings and piled us all in. We drove to Ann Hart's where we would spend the next four months. That night, I cuddled with Judy in a soft, cozy double-bed in the back bedroom. She drifted off to sleep while I lay there listening to my parents' whispers from the next room. They weren't fighting, but I knew by their muffled voices they weren't happy.

In July, Mom announced we were going on a long trip; we were moving to Modesto, California. *Why California? What about going to the playground with Dad and our summer picnics with Mom's family?*

I finally gathered the courage to ask, "How can we leave Gussie and everyone else? Why are we moving so far away?"

"We're going to stay with Dad's relatives in Modesto, won't that be exciting?" my mother, the ultimate sales person, replied. Dad broke into the conversation to tell us he had a lot of relatives in Modesto. We would get to meet Grandma Conklin's brother, Bob Patch and his wife, Ruby, who were excited we were moving there. It was the first time I had heard of these relatives; I was a little skeptical. After my father assured me our lives would be happier once we moved to Modesto, I was satisfied.

Very early in the morning of August 12, 1957, Kim's first birthday, Grandpa Woodard and Gussie picked us up at Ann's house and drove us to the train station on Second Street in Jamestown. I stood in front of the massive building and stared at the words, *Erie Railroad*, etched on the stone. The huge clock above it read five o'clock. Upon entering the lobby, I was intrigued with the large blocks of white marble covering the walls. I rushed to the dark, green marble water fountain to taste the cold water. Brass lamps hung on the walls, filling the room with a soft, glowing light as I followed Dad to the Ticket Office window. When he identified himself to the lady behind the desk, she handed him some tickets and gave him instructions about our trip.

After getting the tickets, we walked to a narrow hallway lined with big, wooden benches. We sat there anxiously waiting for our train to arrive. It was impossible to sit still. An older gentleman, dressed in a navy-blue suit trimmed with gold and white stripes and wearing a white brimmed cap on his head, finally arrived. When he called our names, it was our cue to go down the stairs that led to the tracks and board our train. Although I was extremely excited to board that big train, I was also very sad to be leaving Grandpa and Gussie— especially Gussie. She was seventy-two years old, and although she was in very good health, I worried she might die before we ever returned.

Gussie held me tightly in her arms and whispered, "You'll like California, but I'm sure you'll be back. I'll miss you very much while you're gone. Remember to write to me, okay?"

I bravely choked back my tears and gently kissed her on the cheek.

Grandpa Woodard picked me up and gave me one of his famous bear hugs. He told me he loved me and he'd miss me. He promised to visit us in California. With these loving good-byes and assurances, I was ready for *the BIG TRIP*.

As I ran toward the train, I saw Mom and the girls peering out of the windows. My dad was waiting on the platform to hoist me up the steps. The train engines were running, the whistle was blowing, and tears were streaming down my cheeks as I waved good-bye to Grandpa Woodard and Gussie from the train window.

CHAPTER 7

California Here We Come

1957

WHEN THE TRAIN started chugging along the tracks, I watched out the window as we flew past familiar places in Chautauqua County. I waved good-bye to the large maple trees whose green leaves would soon turn the vivid colors of orange, red and gold and the breath-taking, aqua waters of Chautauqua Lake. I said farewell to the cows grazing in the pasture, the grape filled vineyards and everything else I wouldn't see for a long time. Then I closed my eyes and sent a silent good-bye to the family and friends I was leaving behind.

My thoughts were interrupted when a kind gentleman with graying hair poking out from beneath his cap, said in a baritone voice, "Tickets, please."

Dad reached into his coat pocket and withdrew the tickets. The conductor inquired, "Where in California are you headed, sir?"

"Sacramento and from there to Modesto, California," Dad proudly replied.

"My-oh-my," the conductor commented." "That's quite a trip. I'll bet this is your first train trip. Am I correct, young lady?"

I blushed when I realized he was talking to me. "Yes it is. Daddy has family there."

"Well, you enjoy your train ride and if there's anything you need just let us know. Maybe your Daddy can show you around the train so you'll know where everything's located." He winked at me and moved on to welcome the people in the next seat.

I batted my baby-blues at my father. He stood up, took me by the hand and led me to the next car. I waved at Mom while she sat holding Kim in her arms. Judy was snuggled up next to her sound asleep.

Dad and I strode down the aisle to the door at the back of the car. When he opened it, a strong, gusty wind blasted me in the face. He stepped onto the platform leading to the next car and told me to follow him. The swiftly moving train and the surging winds frightened me. When I grabbed onto Dad's hand and cautiously stepped down, my fear was whipped away by the wind. I spent the next three days exploring every inch of that train.

The coach cars had cushioned seats on both sides of the aisle, while a few of the cars had small sleeping rooms on each side. As we entered the sleeping car, I peeked into a door that was slightly ajar. I envisioned myself lying on the bed at night, staring out the window at the stars in the sky and the bright moon. My dreams were dashed when Dad told me we'd be sleeping in the coach car because the sleepers were too expensive.

The next stop was the dining car. The tables were covered with white, linen cloths and set with fine china and crystal. How could the dishes and glasses possibly stay in place on this speeding train? I never did figure it out. The last car we explored was the lounge where men and women sat smoking and drinking, while others played cards, read books or stared out the window, admiring the passing scenery.

As we traveled through Utah, I spotted the Great Salt Lake just ahead. My eyes widened with fear when I realized we'd be going on the large bridge that spanned the lake.

Remembering my fear of water and heights, my dad promised we'd be safe. I gulped and said, "Really?"

"Yup. You know why?" I shook my head no. He explained, "There's so much natural salt in this lake even if the train fell into the water, it would float!" Once again, I believed him.

After three days on the train, we finally arrived at the station in Sacramento where two strangers were waiting to meet us. I knew immediately it was Uncle Bob because he looked just like my Grandmother Conklin with the same soft, blue eyes that sparkled when he smiled and the same light brown curly hair. His wife, Ruby, was a large woman, with long, black hair twisted into a bun, a ruddy complexion and kind, dark eyes. As soon as she smiled I knew I'd love her.

Uncle Bob and Aunt Ruby welcomed us into their hearts and into their lovely home. Shortly after our arrival, they invited Dad's relatives for a picnic. Although everyone seemed kind and loving, my mother appeared to be intimidated by them. Noticing Mom's discomfort, Ruby took Mom 'under her wing.' She spent days driving us from place to place to look for rentals.

Mom and Dad finally found a white-stucco, two-story house across the street from a park. It was in a lovely neighborhood on a tree-lined street.

When we walked up the path toward the house, the neighbor lady lifted her head from the flower bed she was weeding, smiled and said, "Hello."

Meanwhile, Uncle Bob helped Dad find a job. He was hired as a manager at a local service station close to our house. Uncle Bob and Aunt Ruby helped furnish our new home and assisted with the move. After living with other people for over six months, we were finally in our own place again I spent my days taking Judy to the park to swing, slide and play in the sandbox. After returning her safely home, I would go back to the park by myself. I stood there watching the kids around me playing on the monkey bars, swinging and sitting in small groups talking. For the first time in my life, I felt utterly alone. I couldn't find the courage to walk up to anyone and introduce myself. It's the only time I can remember feeling paralyzed with shyness. I silently prayed someone would seek me out.

One hot summer afternoon I jumped into the pool to cool off. Suddenly, a girl swam up beside me and introduced herself. She said her name was Mary, she was ten years old and lived on the other side of the park. I was delighted to finally meet someone. After swimming for a while, we decided to get out of the pool. When Mary stood up in the shallow water, I noticed for the first time that she had no left-arm below her elbow. I had never seen anyone with a deformity like this before, and the shock terrified me. I screamed and quickly emerged from the pool. Grabbing my towel, I ran home crying. I never went back.

Many times over the years, I've admonished myself for reacting that way. How could I have hurt someone like that and not gone back to apologize? I'm sure I told my mother about it, and I've never understood why she didn't make me go over to the park to apologize to Mary for the way I had acted. I've often wished I could remember Mary's full name because with today's technology I may have been able to find her and send her a letter of apology. This probably was just one of many times Mary experienced this reaction to her deformity. I regret being the person responsible for one of those times.

One night, something terrifying happened while Dad was working. We were sitting at the kitchen table eating dinner when we heard a knock on the back door. Mom got up from the table to answer it. I followed her.

"Hello," she greeted the strange man.

Peeking over her shoulder, I could see a tall, scruffy looking man with gray hair and a scraggly gray beard, standing there. He was dressed in dirty overalls and a tattered plaid shirt. He frightened me.

"Ma'am," he said as he took his cap off and bent his head, "I'm out of work and was wonderin' if you have any odd jobs I can do to earn a few bucks."

Mom's voice was shaky when she answered. "I'm sorry, we don't need any work done. My husband does it all." Before closing the door, she hesitated and went on to say, "Wait, just a minute."

She grabbed an old plate from the cupboard, filled it with a piece of fried chicken, some mashed potatoes with a dab of gravy and green beans. She covered it with a piece of waxed paper, walked back to the door and handed it to the man.

"I can't hire you to work, but I can share part of our meal. I hope this helps you."

When she returned to the table, her hands were still shaking. She was visibly frightened. Mom explained that while she was afraid of the stranger at our door, she didn't want to anger him. She had given him the food in hopes he would not bother us again. Then she called Dad at work to tell him about the incident. He advised her to keep the doors locked, and the curtains closed until he came home from work at midnight. We followed his instructions and closed all of the curtains, except for two small windows on each side of the fireplace. Although there were no curtains on these windows, Mom wasn't concerned. She thought they were too high for anyone to peer into.

That evening, we huddled together on the sofa watching TV until it was time for bed. While crawling into bed, I realized I was still frightened by the strange man who'd come to our door. Noticing the fear in Judy's eyes, I pulled her close and reassured her we were safe. A few minutes later, Mom tucked us in and told us the same thing—the man would not return. She kissed us goodnight and went downstairs. She sat on the sofa watching television, occasionally checking the slowly moving hands on the clock while anxiously waiting for Dad to come home from work. A short time later, Judy and I heard a blood-curdling scream. I jumped out of bed and ran downstairs to find out what had happened.

Mom stood there trembling. Her eyes were filled with fear as she shouted, "Oh my God! That man was just staring at me through the window!" She ran to the phone and called Dad. I heard Kim wailing from her crib in my parents' bedroom. She was clutching the rails of the crib and sobbing when Judy and I rushed in. Judy clung to me while I carried Kim into the living room. After Mom hung up the phone, she told us Dad was calling the police. We huddled together on the couch waiting for the sound of a siren.

A police car soon pulled up in front of our house. Mom let the police officer inside and recounted the incident with the stranger. The officer wrote down the description of the man who had come to our door at dinner time.

Then he walked around the house with a big flashlight to check things out. When he came back into the house, he announced he had found a large, wooden box just under the window beside the chimney. He believed the big footprints on the soft ground beside the box, belonged to a man. He indicated it could have been the same man who had stopped earlier. The officer remained at our house until Dad came home.

Next day, we were still pretty shaken. My mother decided it was time to look for another place to live. Dad agreed and once again Aunt Ruby drove Mom around town hunting for a new rental. Mom was bursting with enthusiasm when she described the beautiful house she'd found on the other side of Modesto. She couldn't wait for my dad to see it.

The following day, we went to look at the lovely house my mother could not stop talking about. From the outside, it was as beautiful as Mom had described. It was a fairly new, ranch styled home on a quiet street on the outskirts of Modesto. There was a large, red brick chimney separating the house from the garage. Just below the large picture window the pink azaleas and red roses were in full bloom. We followed Mom through the welcoming front door. She was ecstatic as she walked us through the house pointing out all of the features. "Don't you love the living room?" she asked. She pointed to the brick fireplace along one wall and said, "Imagine how beautiful this house will be at Christmas!" I remember, thinking at the time, maybe she should try selling houses.

I was awestruck as Mom continued the house tour. The kitchen was filled with bright sunlight coming in through the windows facing the big, backyard. The built-in appliances were something we'd never had. Open shelving separated the dining room from the kitchen. Mom described all the fancy knick-knacks she planned to buy to fill these empty spaces. Next, we traveled down a carpeted hallway. There was a bathroom on the right and two, small bedrooms on each side. The master bedroom was at the end of the hall. "Will I have my own room?" I excitedly asked. "Can I have that bathroom? Can we toast marshmallows in the fireplace?"

"Whoa! Slow down," Dad commented. "We have a lot to think about before we actually decide to move in."

My mother noticed the disappointment on my face and seized the moment. "It's the loveliest house we've ever considered renting. How can you say no, Stew?"

His brow furrowed as he shrugged his shoulders and walked into the backyard. Mom and I continued to admire the great features throughout the house as the girls ran from room-to-room. A week later, we packed up and moved into our new home at 1401 Lotus Lane.

In addition to his full-time job at the service station, Dad had to get a part-time job to help cover the high cost of the rent. We had only lived there a month, when my parents began arguing again. Hearing them fight made my stomach ache and caused me to worry so I silently retreated to my room or took Judy and Kim outside to play.

It always made me happy whenever our relatives or Dad's old friends came to visit because I knew my parents would not argue in front of them. Dad's best friend from college, Joe and his wife, Anne, were my favorites. Joe was extremely handsome with dark, curly hair, pearly-white teeth and brown eyes that could melt anyone's heart. Mom thought he resembled Julius La Rosa.

Anne was a very attractive, soft-spoken woman with short blonde hair, radiant green eyes and a gentle, comforting smile. She was quick to offer compliments to everyone and paid close attention to anything anyone had to say. Joe and Anne had two daughters about the same ages as Judy and Kim. Whenever they came to visit, our house was alive with commotion and laughter, a much needed respite from the everyday arguments.

As Halloween approached, Anne invited my parents to a Halloween party they were hosting. Mom spent hours talking to Anne on the phone about the plans for the party and what type of costumes to wear. Dad didn't appear to be as enthusiastic about the upcoming event as Mom. A few days before the party, I overheard their conversation.

"Anne is looking forward to their Halloween party. I'm still not sure what we're wearing. Do you have any ideas?" she coyly asked Dad. Hidden behind the sports section of the newspaper, Dad lifted his head and asked, "What party?"

Exasperated by his comment, Mom curtly replied, "Stew, I've mentioned this to you for weeks. I think it's the most exciting thing that's happened since we moved to California. What's the problem?"

"I'm dealing with more important things than what to wear to a damn party!" Dad retorted.

"Oh brother, here we go again. If it's the money, you're worried about—don't! I'm not spending a damn dime. I'll find things around here to make our costumes," Mom shot back. She stormed into the living room and turned on the TV set.

Over the next few days, she put up the recently purchased Halloween decorations and worked on costumes for her and Dad. She had decided to dress as a Pixie. Finding an old, dark-green tablecloth, she cut holes for her head and arms. Then she slashed points around the bottom. She sewed the seams by hand, which amazed me because I had never seen her use a needle and thread. When she was finished, she slipped it on, put a piece of rope around her waist to serve as a belt and started dancing around the living room. Judy, Kim and I were mesmerized.

"What do you think, girls? Do I look like a Pixie?" Kim nodded and offered her standard response, "Yes, yes, yes." My mother smiled when I told her she was the most beautiful Pixie in the world.

"What are you wearing underneath it?" I inquired. "It's a little short." "I'm buying a pair of black tights and some new slippers," she replied. "I heard you tell Daddy you wouldn't spend any money."

"Diana, were you listening in again? I get furious when you listen to your father and me talking about things that don't concern you. Besides, those things won't cost much." Like a reprimanded child, she turned on her heels and fled the room. Apparently I'd said the wrong thing.

Mom was in a terrific mood the day of the party. She strolled around singing something about being wild again, a whimpering child again who couldn't sleep and wouldn't sleep. Although I didn't know what song she was singing, I was glad to see her so happy and full of life. She went into her closet and pulled out a large, flowered dress and a pair of shoes Aunt

The Road Back to Hell

Ruby had given her. I had no idea what she was planning to do with these things, and she wouldn't reveal her secret.

When Dad came home from work on Saturday afternoon, Mom announced he was going to the party dressed as a woman. I started giggling when I tried to picture my tall dad dressed as a female. My laughter was contagious; even Dad began to laugh. While they were getting ready for the party, I served my sisters' supper. Pretty soon, Mom and Dad came into the kitchen dressed in the cutest costumes I had ever seen.

Dad made quite 'the lady' in Ruby's flowered dress and black heels. He was wearing a black-dyed string mop on his head with a big, floppy red hat perched on top of the wig. Mom had done an excellent job applying foundation to his freshly shaven face. Thick black mascara covered his light eyelashes and made them 'pop'. The crimson lipstick and red rouge added just the right touch, turning him into a ravishing beauty. My mother made him wear one of Ruby's old bras which she stuffed with rags to make him look like he had boobs. We doubled over laughing when he strutted around the room in heels. Mom beamed with pride as we fussed over the way she'd dressed Dad.

"I can't believe you made these costumes, Mom! Daddy looks funny as a woman, and you look adorable as a Pixie." I exclaimed. "He's even wearing your perfume; he smells like Shalimar instead of Old Spice."

Mom was adorable in her dark-green Pixie outfit. The little Pixie hat on top of her new, short haircut completed her outfit. Dad jokingly commented Mom's skirt was a bit too short as he pulled her into his arms and danced around the kitchen with her.

"You'll be the most beautiful Pixie at the party," I heard him whisper in her ear.

CHAPTER 8

California Here We Go

1957-1958

THE NEXT MORNING, I was awakened by the sounds of a barking dog. I arose from bed and followed the barking noise to the garage. Upon opening the door, I spotted a darling little black 'wiener dog' running around the garage. (I later learned the proper name was Dachshund). I picked her up, carried her into Mom and Dad's bedroom, shook Dad and said, "Daddy, wake up. Look what I found in the garage!"

The dog slipped out of my arms onto the bed and began licking Dad's face as he slept. My father slowly opened his eyes and started to chuckle.

Apparently, he had taken first place in the dress-up contest at Joe and Anne's party, and this little dog was the prize. Squealing with delight, I rushed into the bedroom to show Judy and Kim our new puppy. We named her Suzie.

Later that morning, while the three of us were playing with Suzie, I noticed Mom and Dad seemed at odds with one another again. I wondered if they were tired from the party or if they had a fight; they often fought when they were drinking. I let go of these thoughts because I had to take care of my spunky little pup.

As Thanksgiving approached, Mom invited Dad's cousin, George and his family for Thanksgiving dinner. When George, his wife Sally and their two daughters entered the house, Judy and Kim led the girls to their bedroom.

The four of them dragged the toy box into the living room and dumped it on the floor—so much for our cleaning efforts.

"The Road Back to Hell"

Please visit my website dianalynnauthor.com to learn more about my memoir and subscribe to my blog

Visit my facebook page at
https://www.facebook.com/dianalynnauthorpage/

Buy a copy or review my book at
http://www.amazonbooks.com/

Dad and George poured themselves a drink and went into the living room to try to watch television amidst all of the chaos. Mom and Sally sat at the kitchen table and gossiped while I played with Suzie in the garage.

When it was time for dinner, my mother called everyone into the dining room. After we had been seated, George filled the adults' glasses with liquor and the kids' glasses with tomato juice. Then he made a toast that went something like this; "It's a great pleasure to be spending this Thanksgiving Day with my cousin, Stew, and his family. Here's to many more holiday celebrations together!" With that, he promptly downed his drink and went for a refill. Let the party begin!

After we had finished dinner and cleaned the kitchen, the adults sat at the dining room table enjoying their cocktails and cigarettes. The kids lay on the floor in the living room watching TV. There was no one my age to spend time with so I drifted from room-to-room. Mom and Sally were talking about the upcoming holiday and what their children wanted from Santa. I heard my mother say, "Diana Lynn wants a Madame Alexander ballerina doll, but it's pretty expensive."

I thought to myself, " *How can it be expensive if it's from Santa?*"

I soon had my answer when George retorted, "For God's sake, Bonnie, why would you spend a lot of money on a doll for a kid?"

"Because she wants it, and she believes Santa will bring it!" Mom shot back.

"Are you kidding? Diana still believes in Santa? Maybe it's time you told her the truth—there is no Santa!"

I wished I hadn't been listening. My mother was surprised when she saw me standing in the doorway with a bewildered, hurt look on my face. I fled to my bedroom, flopped down on the bed and thought about what George had said. I could not believe he said there was no Santa. Some kids on the school bus were whispering about this possibility the other day; I just ignored them. At eight, I had begun to have serious doubts about Santa's existence, but hearing these words coming from an adult devastated me.

A little while later, Mom came into my room and knelt down beside me. She gently patted my head and told me she was sorry I had overheard what George had said. She assured me it wasn't true, there really was a Santa. Then she asked, "Do *you* believe there is a Santa?"

"I guess so," I said through my tears.

"That's all that matters." She kissed me on the forehead and wished me sweet dreams. I lay awake for hours wondering what the truth was. I decided I would learn the truth about Santa on Christmas morning. If there wasn't a beautiful ballerina doll beneath the tree that would mean there is no Santa because my parents couldn't afford to buy me one.

We spent Christmas Eve with Uncle Bob and Aunt Ruby, enjoying the thoughtful gifts Aunt Ruby had purchased for us. When we finished, I sat there remembering the Christmas Eves we always spent at Gussie's. I missed her a lot. When I glanced over at Mom, I knew she was thinking the same thing.

When we returned home, Mom and Dad told us to get ready for bed so Santa Claus could come. I must have fallen asleep quickly because the next thing I knew, it was Christmas morning. It was still dark outside when I tiptoed into my parent's bedroom to wake them. Mom's eyes popped open and she told me it was okay to wake up Judy and Kim. I walked into their room, gently shook them and whispered, "Santa's been here. It's time to get up."

With our eyes closed and our hands joined together, we slowly found our way into the living room. Santa never wrapped our gifts. Instead, he displayed them under the tree in individual sections for each of us. The beauty of the colored lights and tinsel shining over our presents made it look like a toy store. We opened our eyes as soon as Mom said it was okay. It took me longer to open my eyes this year because I was afraid my ballerina wouldn't be there.

I gasped when I saw my Madame Alexander ballerina standing beneath the tree! She was stunning. Her dainty face, long black eyelashes, and rosy cheeks made her the most beautiful doll I had ever seen. The dark hair pulled tightly into a chignon on top of her head was surrounded by a ring of tiny pink and white flowers. Her light pink tulle tutu over her white satin leotard was covered in the same small flowers. White tights covered her long, slender legs. Supported by a doll stand, her slipper clad feet were in the *en pointe* position.

I rushed to the tree and gently cradled her in my arms. "I knew Santa would bring you," I whispered into her tiny ear. Christmas morning in Modesto will live in my memory forever.

As New Year's Eve approached, Mom grew increasingly excited about the celebration. My parents always went somewhere special to celebrate New Year's Eve. This year, Mom seemed more excited than usual. They were going out with their good friends, Joe and Anne, to the local country club for a night of dinner, dancing and drinking. She and Anne talked nearly every day about what they were wearing. One evening while Dad was watching TV, I heard my mother whisper into the phone, "Stew is going to have a fit when he finds out how much I spent on my dress."

I remember thinking, *"Oh brother, now there's going to be trouble."*

My father was generally an easy-going guy who only complained about my mother's spending habits when our budget was very tight. He had recently asked Mom not to frivolously spend money because our living expenses were more than his income and he was struggling to make ends meet. To avoid another argument, Mom had hidden her new dress in a closet, making us promise not to tell Dad because it was a surprise.

New Year's Eve arrived and while Dad was picking up the babysitter, Mom finished dressing for their big evening. When he returned, she strolled into the living room. He stopped in his tracks, took a long look at her and whistled.

In a picture from that evening, my mother was a knock-out in her full-length, strapless gown. Her floor-length pink, satin dress had a black lace overlay. Her makeup was perfectly applied. With her crimson lipstick and her dark-brown hair pulled into a French twist, she looked like a movie star. Standing next to her, my dad is wearing a navy blue suit, white dress shirt, and a snazzy tie. They made an extremely handsome couple.

Joe whistled at Mom when he and Anne walked into the house, which seemed to annoy Anne. I did not understand why she was upset because I thought she looked just as beautiful in her full-length silver gown and her sparkling diamond necklace and earrings. After a quick cocktail, they all got into Joe's car and left for their night-on-the-town.

About two o'clock in the morning, I was awakened by loud shouting and banging in our kitchen. I lay still in my bed listening to one of the worst battles my parents ever had. It sounded like they were throwing things at each other. I was frightened. Dad shouted obscenities at Mom, and she screamed back. I crept from my bed, opened my door a crack and peeked out to see what was happening.

I remember their heated argument going something like this—"God damn it Bonnie! This is the worst thing you've ever done to me during our marriage!

How could you do it?"

My mother yelled back, "I didn't do anything! Everyone was kissing everyone else at midnight. What's wrong with that?"

"You're right. Everyone was kissing at midnight, but it was one o'clock in the morning when Audrey and I finally found you! Joe was clutching you so tightly I'm surprised you could breathe. What in the hell were you two doing?"

Mom sobbed uncontrollably. "We were just talking. Joe knew I was upset, so we walked outside to talk about it."

"Talk about what? It looked like you two were doing more than talking for God's sake."

"I was telling him how homesick I am. I didn't want to say anything to you because I knew it would make you angry. It was easier to share my feelings with him than it is with you," she meekly replied.

The room became silent. Dad finally spoke up. "I'm your husband for chrissakes. I'm the one you should be talking to about these things, not my best friend. Anne is so upset I doubt if she'll be talking to us for a long time."

Mom gently touched his arm, smiled up at him and said, "I'm sorry Stew. I'll call her tomorrow and get it all straightened out, okay?"

He paused for a few moments, let out a deep sigh and said, "I guess it will have to be okay. I don't want to discuss it anymore tonight because we've both had too much to drink. Let's go to bed and talk it over in the morning. This is no way to start the New Year."

With that, they both went into their bedroom. I climbed back into my bed, thankful my sisters hadn't been awakened by all of the shouting. I lay there for a long time trying to figure out what I had just heard. What had Mom and Joe done that angered Dad and Anne so much? I closed my eyes and prayed to God asking Him to help Mom fix things with Anne so my dad wouldn't stay mad.

Over the next few days, things settled down a bit. My mother's spirits had been lifted by a call from her brother. At Christmas time, she had called Uncle Jerry and tried to convince him to move with his family to Modesto. On New Year's Day, he called back and said they had decided to come and would be heading west by the end of the month. Grandpa Woodard was coming, too. Although he was only staying in California for a few weeks, it would give us a chance to spend time together.

The heaviness of the air surrounding our family seemed to lift when we heard this news. I hadn't seen my cousins, Bobby and Billy for a long time, and I missed them. Billy and I were the same ages and I hoped we would be attending the same school. Bobby and Judy were close in age, and I knew she'd enjoy him as a playmate. It would be great to have my funny Uncle Jerry around and I couldn't wait to hug my sweet Aunt Jean. Most of all, I was looking forward to seeing my grandfather.

The anticipation of their arrival made all of the other problems vanish. At least that's what I thought until the day Anne came to the house to talk to Mom. That's when everything changed.

When I got off the school bus, I noticed Anne's car parked in our driveway. The sight of her car made me happy; maybe she and Mom were making up. I ran into the kitchen and hugged her. The twinkle in her eyes had died and the expression on her face told me something was terribly wrong.

Mom's eyes were puffy and swollen as if she'd been crying.

Dumbfounded, I mumbled, "I have homework. I'd better go to my room and get it done." I shut the door to my bedroom because I did not want to know what they were talking about; it obviously wasn't good. I changed my clothes, picked up my book and started to read. Suddenly I heard the back door slam shut and the sound of Mom's feet as she ran into her bedroom. I softly knocked on her door and asked, "Is everything okay, Mom?"

Her voice sounded weak when she replied, "I don't feel very well. Will you keep an eye on the girls and start supper?" she meekly replied.

"Sure," I answered.

The Woodards arrived a little earlier than planned. I was happy they were staying with us because their presence seemed to distract my parents from their current problems. Our house was filled with laughter rather than shouting. I was so busy playing with my cousins that I didn't pay any attention to the solemn conversations the adults were having.

Three weeks after the Woodard's arrived, Mom and Dad called Judy, Kim and me into the living room for a family discussion. Uncle Jerry, Aunt Jean and the boys had gone out for the day so we could talk privately Both of my parents looked better than they had in weeks. Mom had some color back in her cheeks and my father seemed much calmer. Judy, Kim and I were sitting on the couch when Mom asked, "How would you girls feel about going home?"

"Home?" I questioned. "We are home."

Mom broke into a big grin. "I'm talking about our real home—Jamestown."

I think she expected me to shout with joy at this suggestion, but I couldn't. Modesto had grown on me. I had new friends; I enjoyed school and I was thrilled Bobby and Billy had moved here. I was shocked by this news.

"What about Uncle Jerry, Aunt Jean, and the boys?" I questioned.

When Judy heard this, she started to cry. Kim was too young to understand what was happening. Seeing our reaction, Mom jumped into sales woman mode. "Everything will work out great. Uncle Jerry and Aunt Jean haven't been able to find the right house, so they'll stay here until they do."

"What about our things? What about Suzie?" I asked as I sat holding my puppy close to my chest.

"You can take your dolls and games. Aunt Jean or Aunt Ruby will mail us the rest after we get settled in Jamestown. Okay?" Mom always had a quick answer.

When she hadn't responded to part of my question, I repeated, "What about Suzie?" She never gave me an answer.

Later that night, Dad was sitting at the kitchen table doing a crossword puzzle when I walked over and sat on his lap. I nuzzled myself into his chest, lifted my head and whispered, "Daddy, do you want to go back to Jamestown?"

He sighed, took a big sip of his dark, black coffee and a long drag off of his unfiltered Old Gold. When he exhaled, I watched as a puff of smoke slowly drifted into the air. It took him some time to respond. "I'm not sure, Snookey. Time will tell. We'll just have to hope for the best."

That's what we did. We hoped for the best.

CHAPTER 9

Heading Home

1958

WE SPENT ABOUT a week sorting through our clothes, toys, and personal possessions as we prepared for our big move back east. Judy and I shed a lot of tears setting aside things that would not fit into Grandpa's station wagon. Mom promised that once we became settled in Jamestown, Aunt Jean or Aunt Ruby would mail some of the things we were leaving behind. That never happened.

Just before daybreak, Mom woke us and said it was time to leave. The brightly shining moon provided the only light in the pitch black sky. With tears streaming down my face, I bid goodbye to my aunt, uncle, and cousins. Then I picked Suzie up and held her in my arms, promising her Aunt Jean and my cousins would take good care of her. I was heartbroken to be leaving her behind.

Grandpa's beat-up gray station wagon was filled to the brim with pillows, blankets, a rusty, old cooler, a few boxes and just enough space for Judy and me to sleep. The rest of our belongings were tied onto the roof of the car, covered with a big plastic tarp.

My grandfather slowly drove out of the driveway. Once again, I found myself waving goodbye to the things I would miss most—the Woodards; Uncle Bob and Aunt Ruby; our beautiful house and my neighborhood friends. Passing under the big, arched sign spanning the I Street entrance to Modesto, I read the words, 'Modesto— Water, Wealth, Contentment and Health', for the last time.

Thus began our three-thousand-mile journey across the country.

The Road Back to Hell

From the back of the car, I watched as the night's darkness was slowly replaced by pink and yellow streaks of light peeking over the horizon. When the sun rose in the east, so did my spirits. I finally became enthusiastic about returning to Jamestown. My mother's mood became much lighter the further south we traveled. I knew she was happy again when she started singing, "You Are My Sunshine." When she glanced back at us, I noticed the worry lines covering her brow for the past few weeks had disappeared. Her facial expression was softer, and her eyes gleamed when everyone joined in the song. I remembered Dad's words, 'hope for the best.' Maybe his words were beginning to come true.

It was well over one-hundred degrees when we passed through Needles, California. Sweltering and cranky, we were happy when Grandpa pulled into a gas station to fill the gas tank and get us some cold drinks.

Crossing the desert was quite an adventure. All, I could see for miles, were the low-lying mountains; the dry, sandy soil; cacti of all shapes and sizes; short shrubs and an occasional Joshua tree. The barren landscape became pretty boring until Grandpa brought the car to a sudden stop.

"Why are we stopping here?" I asked.

Dad whispered, "Be quiet and climb over the seat so you can see."

A huge rattlesnake was curled up in the middle of the road. Never having seen one before, my eyes were riveted on it while my heart raced with fear. Dark, diamond shapes covered its tan, scaly body. As it lifted its triangular-shaped head, I saw its small, slanted, black eyes. Transfixed, I watched this coiled up creature for what seemed like hours, until it slowly started to slither across the road towards a big rock. Dad turned toward us and said, "That's a Mojave Desert Rattlesnake, the most poisonous snake in North America."

I sighed with relief as we started down the highway once more.

As the sun began to hide behind the mountains, large streaks of pink, yellow and orange filtered through the clouds and spread across the sky. My grandfather parked the car along the side of the road so we could enjoy the breathtaking sunset. When the sun completely descended the mountain slopes, thousands of twinkling stars shone in the dark sky, lighting it up like fireworks. Judy and I stared at the stars as we continued down the highway. I pointed to the biggest, brightest star in the sky and told Judy to make a wish. She squinted her eyes tightly shut and whispered, "I wish Mommy loved me as much as she does Kim." I had forgotten to tell her to make her wish silently.

We were very weary by the time Mom spotted a neon 'VACANCY' sign flashing in the distance. Grandpa pulled into the driveway while Dad went to the office of the roadside motel to register for the night. Judy and I scrambled out of the car and ran around the parking lot. Kim was fast asleep in Mom's arms as she carried her into a little white cottage. Upon opening the door, we spotted a double bed along one wall and a single bed against the other.

"I know it's small, but it has a nice, clean shower," Mom announced as she peered into the bathroom. I figured my parents would sleep in the double bed while Judy, Kim and I shared the single. "Where's Grandpa going to sleep?" I asked with concern.

"He'll sleep in the car. It has a big back seat so he can stretch out."

The Cape Cod curtains and a small table beneath the window made the room cozy. The faded bedspreads were a little tattered, but they smelled clean and felt soft. When I stuck my head inside the bathroom, the fresh aroma of Dove soap filled the air. This smell reminded me of Granny C's house. I closed my eyes and envisioned her smiling face. Thinking about her made me homesick.

"Please God, help us get home soon," I prayed.

Dad bought some lunch meat, bread and milk in a little store attached to the office. We ate our sandwiches, took our showers, and crashed as soon as we hit the bed. Fourteen hours in the car made for a long, long day.

During the middle of the night, I was awakened by the squeaking of bedsprings and my parents' whispers. These sounds comforted me; I knew they weren't fighting. I quickly drifted back to sleep.

We arose early the next morning to start the second day of our journey. Today, it was Dad's turn to drive. As we pulled away from the motel, he announced we were leaving Flagstaff, Arizona and heading to Amarillo, Texas. As usual, I bombarded him with questions —how long it will it take, what will we see and where will we eat breakfast? "Pipe down," he commented. "It's gonna' be another long day."

Midway through the day, the thrill of the trip and sight-seeing lost its appeal. I closed my eyes and daydreamed about returning to Jamestown. The second wave of homesickness hit when I thought about Gussie and how much I missed her. I envisioned her big, gray and white Victorian-styled house across from the park on Seventh Street. I loved everything about that house— the wrap-around front porch; the sheer Priscilla curtains crisscrossing the windows; the huge maple trees in the front yard and the thick, double oak door. Whenever I opened that door, I would rush through the oak-paneled foyer shouting, "Gussie, I'm here!" She would come scurrying out of the kitchen, wiping her hands on her apron and give me a big hug. In my daydream, I could almost feel her tiny body and soft skin. I imagined looking up into her pretty, smiling face and seeing those mischievous, blue eyes that crinkled at the corners whenever she smiled. Her soft, white hair was usually pulled into a knot on the top of her head. My mother had once told me the reason I loved Gussie so much was because I was a lot like her. I had her mischievous eyes, her same sense of humor and her endless energy.

"What does mischievous mean?" I asked.

"It means playfully funny," she elucidated. It thrilled me to think I was like my great-grandmother Gussie; I admired her more than anyone in the world. I wished my dad would drive faster so we would get home sooner.

Later that morning, when Dad noticed a big sign that read 'EAT', he pulled in and parked in front of a restaurant that looked like a log cabin.

"Looks like a great place to stop, Stew. Hope they have plenty of coffee brewing," Grandpa commented as he stepped out of the car. We followed the aromas of bacon frying and coffee brewing. When we entered the restaurant, a perky waitress welcomed us at the door and led us to our table. Men in cowboy hats sat at the counter talking, laughing and shoveling scrumptious looking home-cooked food into their mouths. A soft, blue haze from cigarette and cigar smoke clung to the ceiling. Most of the men tipped their hats and greeted us with a hearty "Howdy" as we passed on the way to our table. After everyone was seated, the waitress inquired, "Where ya'll from?"

"Jamestown, New York," I proudly replied.

"Wow, that's whare Luceeelle Ball is from, ain't it?" I started to giggle because of the funny way she pronounced Lucy's name.

"My Grandmother Adeline was good friends with Lucy," I enthusiastically replied. The waitress winked at my grandfather as if she thought I was making up a story. After she took our orders and started toward the kitchen, I nudged Grandpa with my foot. "Why didn't let her know I was telling the truth about Grandma Adeline?"

"Aw, honey, it's hard for people to believe. We know it's true; that's all that matters."

It wasn't long before the waitress reappeared, carrying a big tray piled high with plates of pancakes, eggs, bacon, sausage, and home fries. The delicious smells emanating from the plate made me forget all about it. Our bellies were full, and our spirits were high when we left the restaurant.

The rest of the days were more of the same, arising before dawn and driving towards home. As we drove through Missouri, Illinois, and Indiana we became wearier and wearier. Mom was very frustrated by the commotion caused by Judy and Kim; Dad and Grandpa were exhausted from hours of driving, and I was terribly whiny. We couldn't wait to reach our destination. The songs we had sung as we started our journey lost their luster; our feelings of excitement had worn thin and the hope we had in our hearts began to sag. We had become a bedraggled group of travelers very eager to reach our destination.

When the sun came up on the fifth day of our trip, Grandpa shouted, "If everyone gets a move-on we could make it home tonight." We hustled!

I fell asleep dreaming about home. A couple of hours later, I was abruptly awakened by the 'chug-chug-clang-clang' of the car engine. The car sputtered to a sudden stop, and Grandpa yelled, "Damn it. What in the hell is wrong with this car?" After several unsuccessful attempts to restart the car, Grandpa, and Dad got out. Grandpa opened the hood and declared, "We're in serious trouble. I'm not sure what the hell is going on with this damn car, but we're going to have to get a tow truck or some help."

My heart sank. We were in the middle of nowhere with smoke pouring out of the engine, and I had no idea how we would get home. Chaos broke out. The adults began shouting at each other while the three of us huddled together in the back of the station wagon, burying our heads in our pillows. Finally, Dad directed us to get out of the car because we had to walk to the nearest restaurant or motel. Mom grabbed whatever she could carry. My father carried Kim and told me and Judy to follow. We walked for a long time until we came to a bar with a 'WELCOME' sign out front. The man behind the bar looked surprised when all six of us stumbled through the door. He smiled and said, "Can I help you?"

Grandpa spoke first. "I sure as hell hope so. We're on our way to Jamestown, New York, and my fucking car just broke down!" Grandpa always used awful words whenever he became angry.

The friendly bartender grinned and replied, "Sit your tired ass down buddy. You've come to the right place."

The waitress seated us at a table in the back of the bar. She cheerfully asked what we'd like to order. We were all exhausted and speechless. Dad finally spoke-up, telling her about our problems. He explained we had traveled from Modesto, California and we were on our way home to Jamestown, New York; our car had broken down, and we were short on cash. He offered to do odd jobs to help pay for our meals.

When the waitress saw the desperation on my father's face and heard the sincerity in his voice, she said, "Mister, you've come to the right place because we'll do whatever we can to help ya'll."

Hearing those words lifted the heavy weights surrounding my heart. I loved her!

Over the years, whenever I've thought about this time in my life, I have asked myself why I worried about these problems. At almost nine, they shouldn't have been my concern. I have come to realize I was driven by the memories of the happier times in my early childhood. I felt if I could find a way to fix things, maybe that happiness would return and everyone in our family would have peace. Consequently, I could not turn away from the problems. They became my cross to bear.

What began as a very dire experience turned joyful. We gorged ourselves on the bountiful food our wonderful waitress set down at our table. Mom seemed to be relaxing a little while Grandpa regaled the guys at the bar with his tales of woe. My dad returned to the table and announced that he had called Uncle Kenny, Mom's brother, and he was on his way from Jamestown to get us. He would be there in about three hours. Hallelujah!

When a friendly, older man put quarters in the jukebox, Judy and I ran onto the dance floor. Kim soon toddled over and joined us. We danced for hours to the loud music coming from the jukebox. The bar patrons apparently enjoyed watching us dance because they fed the jukebox with money all afternoon. By the end of that day I knew every word to the "Yellow Rose of Texas"! When I noticed my grandfather slipping out the side door, I raced from the dance floor to follow him. I asked where he was going. He said he wanted to check the car one more time to see if it would start. I grabbed his big hand. He smiled down at me and said, "Okay, baby. Let's go."

While strolling down the highway, I stared up at his six-foot-four, imposing frame, into his deep-set dark, brown eyes and asked, "Grandpa, why is Mommy always mad at Dad?"

He stopped in his tracks, looked directly at me and said, "Your Momma is often very confused. It's not her fault. Sometimes I think she'll never be happy." As we walked on, I heard him mutter something about 'the grass always looking greener on the other side of the fence'.

I wondered what that meant. It would take me many years to figure out what he was trying to tell me.

After checking the car and determining it wasn't going anywhere, Grandpa and I returned to the bar. The sun had set, the sky had darkened and it had started snowing. Upon entering the bar, I heard a man with a deep, gravelly voice telling jokes to everyone sitting at the bar. Although his back was to me, I knew it was Uncle Kenny. He had come to get us! I squealed with delight, ran up to the bar and jumped into his waiting arms. I hugged him tightly and start to bawl into the crook of his neck. He gently patted my head and told me everything would be okay. He would get us all safely back to Jamestown.

We spent over six hours in that cozy, little bar in eastern Ohio. On our way out, we said goodbye to all the kind strangers who befriended us by paying for our food and feeding the jukebox. We continued to thank them as we walked out the door to Uncle Kenny's awaiting car.

Once outside of the tavern, we were greeted by beautiful, huge snowflakes drifting from the overcast sky. I turned my face to the heavens, letting the snow cover my hair and eyelashes and said, "Thank you, God."

After traveling almost 3,000 miles and spending five, long days in the car, we cheerfully climbed into Uncle Kenny's car and FINALLY headed home to Jamestown.

CHAPTER 10

Home Again

1958

THE BLINDING SNOW-STORM slowed our travel time on our drive to Jamestown. We arrived at Gussie's house a little after midnight. When I noticed the lights shining through the parlor windows, I knew she was still up, waiting to welcome us.

I scurried out of the car and into her welcoming foyer. She had opened the door before I reached it. I wrapped my arms around her and cried as she gently patted my head. My bedraggled family followed me into the house where we spent the next hour sitting in the dining room, eating sandwiches and describing our long trip. It was almost two o'clock in the morning before we finally went upstairs and fell into bed.

My parents shared a big bedroom at the top of the stairs. They slept in the double bed while Judy and Kim shared the single bed. I slept in the room next to theirs, a cozy little space not much larger than a closet. Gussie's boarders also lived on that floor and although they seemed like very nice men, I was uncomfortable and afraid to sleep alone in this room. *What if one of them tries to come into my room in the middle of the night?*

Mom allayed my fears by locking the door to the hallway. "I'll leave the door to our room open a little. If you get scared, just come into our bed or call me. I'll hear you."

After she had left, I covered my face and hands with the almond-cherry scented Jergen's lotion Gussie left for me on the bed stand. I crawled under the warm covers, inhaled the soothing smell of that lotion and fell fast asleep.

One of the things I loved most about staying with Gussie was helping her with the daily chores. I spent my weekends and days off from school following her around. I did whatever she needed me to do.

Although Gussie was only five-foot-two and weighed about one hundred pounds, she was a powerhouse of energy. She woke up every day at five o'clock in the morning and had a hot breakfast on the table for the boarders by six o'clock. She filled their lunch boxes and had them ready when they left for work. After they left, I often got up and went downstairs to drink tea with Gussie while we discussed the plans for that day.

When the kitchen was cleaned, we went upstairs to make the boarders' beds and tidy their rooms. Gussie planned specific chores on specific days – Monday was wash day; Tuesday was ironing day; on Wednesday she changed the sheets, and so on. She was able to complete all of her daily tasks because she was extremely organized.

If I wanted to spend time with her, I realized I needed to assist her with the daily chores. I followed her like a little puppy, listening to her stories as we worked. She shared stories about her early life in Jamaica, New York, her beloved daughter, Adeline, and the story of her first husband's death by suicide in New York City during the depression. She gossiped a little about her boarders or her card club friends. She told me things about my family I would never have known if I hadn't worked beside her on my days off from school and on the weekends.

After the daily chores were finished, we took a little break. Gussie usually spent this time calling one of her many friends. While sitting at the mahogany telephone table in her bay window chatting away, I'd watch as she parted the curtains to look out the window at the passing traffic. I often heard her laugh and reply to her friends, "Isn't that ducky?" This was one of her favorite expressions and it pretty much expressed her optimistic feelings about life. Whenever she hosted Canasta Club or Bingo parties, I was often her assistant. I loved eavesdropping on the lively conversations. While observing the interaction of Gussie with her friends, I came to understand that it was her warm, loving personality that made her the leader of these women. I longed to be just like her.

When her break was over, she began preparing dinner, which she served promptly at five o'clock each evening. After we had eaten and cleaned up the kitchen, we would watch television in the living room. Even then she couldn't sit still. Her hands deftly moved as she embroidered a pillow case or mended a sock while watching Lawrence Welk or the Ed Sullivan Show. After the eleven o'clock news, she would kiss me goodnight and watch as I climbed the stairs to my little bedroom.

Years later, I realized how much my experiences with my great-grandmother taught me about life. The examples Gussie set instilled in me a strong work-ethic, the ability to set long-term goals and the drive to succeed. When I needed her sunny smile and understanding, she was always there. She gave me hope during some of the darkest times in my life. I often wonder what my life would have been like without her.

My parents appeared to be much happier since we had returned from California. Dad found a job delivering milk for a local dairy while Mom spent most of her days trying to keep my young sisters occupied. Kim, who was almost two and very active, was intrigued by the dozens of salt and pepper shakers lining the shelves in Gussie's parlor. While Judy was dusting the knick- knacks, Kim would reach over and try to help. One afternoon, during a tussle, they knocked over the knick-knack shelf, and several items were broken. Gussie remained surprisingly calm, but my mother blew up. She screamed at them, paddled their butts and took them upstairs to the bedroom.

That night, I heard her explaining to my father that we needed to get a place of our own because it was difficult keeping Judy and Kim from destroying her grandmother's belongings. Dad let out a long sigh before acknowledging that he understood we needed our own place to live, but we weren't in a financial position to do it just yet. He reminded her we had to completely furnish an apartment because we had sold our furniture when we'd moved back to Jamestown.

When their conversation ended, I heard Mom crying. I worried.

Earlier that week I had noticed an ad in my Weekly Reader about some kind of salve you could sell to make money. Next day, I filled out the order form, asked Gussie for an envelope and a stamp and put it in the mailbox. About two weeks later, the mailman delivered a hefty box addressed to me. I was ecstatic! I marveled at the cans of salve inside and promptly carried the box to my room to make a list of people who might buy it. Mom entered my room and asked what I was doing.

I smiled confidently and declared, "I have a job. I'm going to sell these cans of Watkins Salve and make a lot of money so we can move."

After reading the instructions, my mother became concerned. "Diana, you can't do this. This agreement states your father and I are responsible for paying for all of this stuff, whether you sell it or not. Why didn't you talk to me before you ordered it?"

Instead of being happy about what I was attempting to do, my mother was upset. I fought back the tears as I explained, "I was just trying to help."

When Mom noticed the tear that had escaped down my cheek, she sat beside me on the bed and in a much softer voice said, "Honey, the money we need is not your problem. Dad and I will figure something out. It was a great idea, but the company should never have sent this to you without a parent's signature. I'm going to send it back with a letter explaining why I won't permit you to sell it."

She hugged me, dried the tears from my eyes and sent me downstairs to help Gussie with dinner. That was the last I heard about the salve.

I returned to Love School when we came home from California, and a few of the kids in my fourth-grade class remembered me. One of them was a girl named Linda who lived around the corner from Gussie's. We spent hours at her house making doll houses out of egg crates for our Ginny dolls.

One day while Linda was practicing the piano, I asked her the name of the song she was playing. She told me it was "Beautiful Dreamer" by Stephen Foster. I recognized his name because I had recently seen it while perusing an encyclopedia at the James Prendergast Library. His life story impressed me.

While Linda continued to practice, I grabbed a pencil and a pad from the desk, sat in a chair in the corner and began to write a play about his life. When I arrived back at Gussie's, I went straight upstairs to the apartment of Ray and Joan Black.

Gussie had converted three upstairs bedrooms into a small apartment for Ray and Joan, a married couple who had moved from the eastern part of the state to Jamestown. One of the first things I did when we moved into Gussie's was make friends with this friendly young couple. I spent most of my spare time in their apartment where Joan graciously allowed me to use her manual typewriter. That typewriter opened up a whole new world for me.

I knocked on the door and when Joan opened it, I burst inside gushing with excitement. I held up my newly written pages and explained I was writing a play. She encouraged me to use her typewriter. I pecked away for days, typing a sentence or two, making mistakes, pulling out the paper and starting over. When Joan noticed my frustration and the pile of wasted paper, she volunteered to type the play for me. I let her.

As the close of the school year approached, my parents announced they had found the perfect apartment and we'd be moving to 114 Stowe Street in June. I made sure I took my recently written play with me.

CHAPTER 11

The Ice Cream Man

1959-Summer

IT WAS WONDERFUL having our own place again. Our second-floor apartment had three bedrooms, a nice sized living room, a small porch off the kitchen and a big yard out back. We had plenty of neighborhood kids to play with every day. At five, Judy was able to play out back unattended, which freed me from constantly watching over her.

After returning to Jamestown, my mother had reunited with her two best friends, Arlene and Shirley. Although my father was very friendly and outgoing in social situations, he didn't encourage close personal friendships so I was quite surprised when he started talking about this guy named Frank he'd met at work.

Frank ran a small business selling hot coffee, sandwiches, pastries, and ice cream to the workers at local factories. He stopped at Dairylea, where my father worked, early every morning and again at lunch time. Through these daily encounters, he and Dad struck up a friendship.

Almost every day when my father came home from work, he shared a funny story about Frank. I loved the sound of my mother's laughter when Dad talked about some of Frank's escapades. Mom was a very social person, while Dad was more of a loner, and I was pleased when she encouraged him to invite Frank over some evening to meet the family.

About a week later, I was playing in the backyard with my sisters when Mom called us inside. She told us to wash-up and change our clothes because Dad's friend, Frank, was coming to meet us. Judy and Kim squealed with delight when I mentioned Frank would probably cause quite a buzz in the neighborhood when he parked his ice cream truck in front of our house.

In anticipation of his visit, Mom had scrubbed our apartment from top-to-bottom. She had also spent a considerable amount of time on her appearance. Dad even remarked, "Bonnie, don't make such a fuss, he's just a regular guy, not the King of England." I chuckled as I envisioned a man stepping out of his ice cream truck clad in a red velvet robe with a big, gold crown on his head.

When we had finished washing-up and changing into clean clothes, the three of us sat on the front porch, anxiously awaiting the arrival of this 'mystery man'. It wasn't long until we heard the faint tinkling of bells. The sound got louder as the truck came closer. The tinkling stopped when Frank parked his truck in front of our house. As predicted, most of the neighborhood kids came running to see what was happening at 114 Stowe Street.

A fairly good-looking, dark-complexioned, Italian man stepped out of the truck and started to walk toward us. He was about five-foot-ten, with curly black hair, dark brown eyes and a winning smile. His smiled broadened as he approached. With a deep, smoky voice, he greeted us, "Hi, girls, I'm Frank." That's all it took to steal the hearts of three young, starry-eyed girls. It was the first of many evenings Frank came to visit during that long, hot summer.

In the beginning, Frank stopped to visit about once a week. These evening visits soon increased to two or three times a week. We looked forward to seeing him because he usually brought us small toys or gave us money to put in our piggybanks. A lot of times, he treated the neighborhood kids to free ice cream. That may explain why we were the most popular kids in the neighborhood that summer.

One visit I'll never forget is the night he brought us a soft, furry bunny rabbit; a live rabbit, not the stuffed kind. When he carried the rabbit into the house, Mom was dead set against it. Then Frank winked at her and said, "Bonnie, how can you say no to these beautiful little girls?" Frank and my mother exchanged a meaningful look. When she finally relented, Judy and Kim shouted, "Yippee!"

During this encounter, my father stayed in the background. I realized by his facial expression he was unhappy about the situation. Did my dad object to the new bunny or to all of the attention Frank was getting? I detected some jealousy emanating from him. When Dad realized I was watching him, he quickly smiled and asked, "Where will you keep this silly rabbit at night?"

Judy piped-in and said the bunny could sleep with her. Kim wasn't quite sure how to respond, and I just shrugged my shoulders. After a little discussion, we decided since it was summer, the rabbit could sleep on the side porch.

Next we needed to come up with a name for this furry creature. Because he had black and white spots, someone shouted, "Let's name him Spot." Everyone made suggestions, as we watched the little rabbit sniff and jump around the kitchen. I finally spoke up and said, "What about Jumper?" That became his name for the remainder of his short life on Stowe Street.

The rest of the evening, the girls chased Jumper all around the apartment, pulling him out from his hiding places under the beds and behind the dressers. My job was to carry the paper towels and clean up the little pellets he left everywhere. It was also my job to keep the peace between Judy and Kim while Mom, Dad, and Frank went into the living room to sit around and talk.

Judy was much bigger than Kim and constantly picked Jumper up so Kim couldn't get a hold of him. Kim started bawling until I took Jumper away from Judy and handed him to Kim. I finally had had enough of this game and announced it was time for Jumper to go to bed. That's when we realized we didn't have a bed for Jumper to sleep in. We marched into the living room to discuss it with my parents.

After listening to our dilemma, Mom looked at Dad and in her sweetest voice said, "Stew, do you mind going to the store to get a box for Jumper to sleep in?"

Dad was accustomed to doing her bidding, so he immediately stood up and headed for the bedroom to get his wallet. As an afterthought, she added, "While you're there, will you get a six-pack of Blatz and two packs of Tareytons? Please?" By the sounds of things, Frank wouldn't be leaving anytime soon.

While Dad was gone, I scurried around looking for something warm and soft to use as Jumper's blanket. I walked towards the bathroom to get a towel but when I tried to open the door, I was surprised to find it locked.

We seldom locked that door. Assuming it had been accidentally locked by one of the kids, I went in pursuit of my mother. When I couldn't find her in the living room or any other room in our apartment, I figured Frank must have gone home, and she was the one in the bathroom. I approached the bathroom again. This time I heard the sound of voices quietly whispering. I knocked on the door and said, "Mom, I need a towel for Jumper's bed."

When she slowly opened the door, I saw Frank looking into the medicine cabinet. My mother seemed flustered as she explained, "Frank has a headache, and I'm helping him find some aspirin."

It was a very awkward moment for all of us. I wanted to ask why the door had been locked, but the words would not come out of my mouth. Frank excused himself as he brushed past me. I stared at Mom and icily said, "I need a towel for Jumper's bed." She handed me a towel and shot me a questioning look.

Why was she looking at me that way? I'm the one who should be looking *at her that way.* At ten, I was surprisingly mature, and realized it was very odd for her and Frank to be in the bathroom together with the door locked. Why hadn't she just gone into the bathroom herself and taken him some aspirin?

And why was she so flustered when she opened the door? I pondered these questions for the rest of the night.

Dad was coming up the stairs just as Frank was leaving. "What? You're leaving already?" he asked Frank. "I brought home a six-pack so we could enjoy a couple beers."

"Thanks, but not tonight. I just remembered I need to order some extra supplies for tomorrow. Catch ya' next time."

Mom rushed to the door. "Not so fast. You're not leaving before the girls get a chance to thank you for the rabbit."

With that comment, she motioned for us to come and say good-night to Frank. The girls ran giggling into his arms while I stood back. It took everything I had to walk over and give him a short hug. What I wanted to do was slap him across the face.

For a night that started out so happily, it ended with me feeling inexplicably sad. My thoughts were muddled. I couldn't grasp what was going on with Mom and Frank. What were they doing in the bathroom together? Is this all going to turn out like the time with Joe in California? At the time, I had no idea what an 'affair' was.

As the summer flew by, we continued to play with our friends and to take Jumper into the backyard for his daily exercise. The first thing I did each morning was feed Jumper and clean out his bed. One morning, when I went to the porch, Jumper's bed was empty. There was virtually no place for him to hide on the small porch. We had covered the opening between the porch floor and the bottom rung of the railing with cardboard to prevent him from escaping. After looking around a second time, I realized he was gone. It was then I noticed a piece of the cardboard had fallen down.

The thought of Jumper falling off the porch sickened me. My dad was working, and Mom and the girls were still asleep. I had to find Jumper before they woke up. Frantic, I walked to the railing and peered over. Directly below on the sidewalk lay the body of little Jumper. I prayed as I ran down the stairs, "Please let him be hurt and not dead."

As I approached him, I noticed a spray of blood on the sidewalk and dried blood on his face, and realized Jumper was dead. Hot tears streamed down my face as I tried to think of what to do. Should I wake Mom up?

Should I call Dad at work? I knew Dad couldn't come home, but the thought of talking to him eased the pain in my heart a little. I tip-toed back upstairs and quietly picked up the phone to call him. I explained to the secretary I was Stew's daughter, and something awful had happened at home, stressing my need to talk to him right away. After a few minutes, he came to the phone.

He was out of breath when he answered. He must have run all the way to the office. "Honey, what's wrong?"

Through my tears, I mumbled, "Daddy, Jumpers dead!"

A short silence followed. Then I explained what had happened. Dad asked me if anyone else was up yet.

"N..N..No..." I stuttered.

"I know this will be difficult for you, but you need to wrap a towel around him and push him under the porch. Leave him there until I get home. Can you do that?"

"I think I can," I whispered.

"Once you've taken care of Jumper, wake-up Mom and tell her what happened. Have her tell the girls Jumper ran away. I'll take care of everything as soon as I get home."

"Okay, Daddy, I will."

It seemed like forever before Dad came home that night. I met him at the bottom of the steps and showed him where I had hidden Jumper. He squatted down and looked under the porch. When he stood up, he took me into his arms and let me cry my heart out.

When my tears had subsided, Dad smiled at me and said, "Snookey, you're a very strong young girl to be able to do what you did today. I'm very proud of you."

Hugging him tightly, I softly replied, "Thanks, Daddy."

Those words of comfort have stayed with me forever, and I remember them whenever I face a crisis. His words assured me of how deeply he loved me and that he would protect me as long as he lived.

It took some time to get over the death of Jumper. Fortunately, school was about to start, giving Judy and me something to look forward to. Kim turned three in August and kept busy playing with Thumper, the name she had chosen for the stuffed bunny Frank had given her on her birthday.

One afternoon in late August, my friend Terry and I were lying on a blanket in the backyard, making up names for the puffy, popcorn-like clouds floating high in the bright, blue sky above us. As the afternoon wore on, the clouds moved closer together until the sky was covered with a dark, gray blanket. At the first sounds of a loud clap of thunder in the distance, we quickly ran for cover and watched as a large flash of lightening hit the earth. That night, I closed my eyes and tried to fall asleep, but the memory of those dark clouds gathering in the sky, filled my head and made me shudder. I remembered how the bright sunny sky quickly dissipated when the storm began.

CHAPTER 12

Beautiful Dreamer

1959-1960

I LOOKED FORWARD to starting fifth-grade at CC Ring Elementary School. On the first day of school, Mom went with us because Judy was starting kindergarten. After that, Judy and I walked to school together every day. She fussed and cried every morning while getting ready for school because she did not want to go. Mom explained she had no choice in the matter; the law required all five-year-old children to attend school. That didn't seem to make any difference. I still had to drag her out the door every morning. She sobbed most of the way to school.

One morning, Judy stopped dead in her tracks and defiantly screamed, **"** I AM NOT GOING TO SCHOOL!" She let go of my hand and bolted for home.

Exasperated with the whole ordeal, I yelled, "Go ahead! I'm sick of fighting with you every morning!" I watched as she ran back to the house. When I knew she was safely inside, I continued on my way.

I arrived home from school that day and found my parents sitting at the kitchen table discussing Judy's problems with school.

"What happened with Judy today?" I asked.

My mother replied, "I talked to Judy's teacher today, and we've decided to keep her home in her room for the next few days. Don't play with her or baby her because she'll think everything's okay. We hope this little punishment will make her want to go back to school. Understand?"

"Sure. I hate dragging her by the hand and forcing her to go every day because it makes me late. That works for me."

Diana Lynn

I was always anxious to get to school to see Miss Funk. She was the gentlest, most caring teacher I'd ever had. She made her students feel as if they were the only person in the classroom whenever she spoke to them. One day, during the music portion of our class, Miss Funk introduced the songs of Stephen Foster. My heart raced with excitement as I thought about the play I had written. I couldn't wait to tell Miss Funk about it. At the end of the day, I walked up to her desk and said, "Miss Funk, I became interested in Stephen Foster last summer when I read about him at the Prendergast Library and I wrote a play about his life."

Miss Funk was very interested in my project and asked me to bring my play into school so she could read it. My heart soared as I raced home to tell my parents.

Next morning, when I turned my play into Miss Funk, she promised. to read it and discuss it with me when she finished. My play was fairly short and I hoped she would get back to me quickly. When she didn't mention it over the next few days, I began to worry that she didn't like it. About a week later, she winked at me when I entered the classroom and asked me to stay after school so we could discuss my play. When the dismissal bell finally rang at three o'clock, I silently waited at my desk. As the last student walked out the door, Miss Funk invited me to come and sit beside her. My legs shook as I made my way to the front of the room.

Her eyes sparkled like diamonds as she said, "Diana, this is one of the best pieces of writing by a student I've ever read."

I couldn't believe what she had just said. "Honestly?"

"I'm sorry it took so long to get back to you. I spent time sharing your play with the principal and some of the other teachers and we think it would be wonderful to have our class perform "The Life of Stephen Foster" for the school. How do you feel about that idea?"

I swallowed the lump in my throat, jumped up from my chair, put my arms around her shoulders and exclaimed, "Thank you so much. I can't believe you liked it!"

While discussing the production of the play, Miss Funk asked me to be the director. After a few weeks of practice, my class performed "The Life of Stephen Foster" in the school auditorium. All of the elementary students attended. My parents, my sisters and Gussie sat in the front row. It was one of the proudest moments of my life.

As my fifth-grade year at CC Ring progressed, Miss Funk and I bonded more and more. She spent time with me after school suggesting good books to read and discussing ideas for writing. I will never forget the excitement I felt on Valentine's Day when she accompanied me to my house for a special luncheon my mother was serving as a special thanks for all Miss Funk had done for me. During that school year, I continued to write several poems and short-stories. Through her encouragement, I developed a life-long love of writing.

Miss Funk was one of the most influential people in my life. She turned my fifth-grade experience into my best year as an elementary student. She spent an enormous amount of time encouraging me to write and create a vision for my future. Through her, I came to understand if I worked hard and set goals for myself, I might be able to go to college. I can still picture her face. She had small wrinkles around her eyes, long, gray hair and a beautiful smile that made me feel special. The beauty of her soul shone through her eyes. I believed she was a saint.

She never married and had no children. Perhaps Miss Funk thought of me as one of her surrogate daughters while she tenderly nurtured my emotional and intellectual needs. For these reasons, I feel fortunate to have known her.

At the end of that summer in 1959, we moved once again. I attended sixth-grade at SG Love School. During American Education Week, Mrs. Patti, my teacher, instructed our class to write a play. I raised my hand and told her I had written a play the year before about the life of Stephen Foster. She recalled hearing about it from other teachers and suggested we perform it again at S.G. Love School. I was delighted!

This time, I requested to play the part of Stephen Foster rather than direct it. Once again, my family attended. In the final scene, while portraying Stephen Foster as he lay dying, I heard the sounds of "Beautiful Dreamer" in the background. Maybe my beautiful dreams were coming true?

In November, a photo of me dressed as Stephen Foster appeared on the front page of the Jamestown Post Journal. The caption under the picture read— "Diana Smith- Maybe Another Edna Ferber in the Making. Eleven-year-old Love School Student Wears Top Hat in Stephen Foster Role for Play She Wrote About America's Bard of the South."

The article stated I'd written a play during summer vacation while at a friend's house. It went on to say, "Mrs. Patti has always requested her class to write plays during American Education Week. She thinks Diana's is about the best she's ever received. Diana sent the play to a publisher, but they returned it stating that it was the 'not the right material for just now.'

I'm quoted as saying, 'I'm writing a novel. I've finished three chapters. I don't have much time, or I'd be further along. Boys and that stuff, you know?'

Although it was a silly remark for me to make, the article further explains it.

'She also has a frank sense of humor. When she was asked if she wanted to write just for fun or for money, she gave her head a piquant jerk and uttered a one-word reply. Both.'

CHAPTER 13

What a Diff'rence a Summer Makes

1960

W<small>E WERE STILL</small> living on Stowe Street in the summer of 1960. I had made a lot of new friends in fifth-grade and spent most of my days playing with them at their homes.

Returning home on a hot, summer afternoon, I could hear the familiar strains of "What a Diff'rence a Day Makes," floating through an open window of our apartment. That song disturbed me. It usually meant I'd find my mother standing over the ironing board with a cigarette burning in an ashtray and a can of Blatz beer sitting beside it. Whatever happened to the coffee she used to drink all day?

When I opened the door to our apartment, Mom was standing there, just as I had pictured. Her hair was covered in bobby pins, and she was staring out the window with that 'dreamy look' in her eyes. The woman standing there wasn't the mother I loved and admired—the mother who taught me to do ballet when I was three; the mother who made the most perfect coconut cream pies in the world; the mother who comforted me when I had bad dreams. She was another lady inhabiting her body. I wanted to scream and tell this new 'mother' to leave right now! Of course, I couldn't. Talking to an adult that way at eleven years old was not appropriate behavior.

Instead, I walked up to her, put my arms around her waist and asked, "Going bowling again tonight, Mom?"

She smiled at me with that far-away look in her eyes, a look I had just begun to notice. "Uh-huh. I have to leave a little early to meet Shirley and the girls so I thought you could make supper, okay?"

"Sure," I sullenly answered. "I noticed you laid burger on the counter. Should I make goulash or hamburgers?" When she didn't respond, I realized her opinion didn't matter. Dad and the girls would be happy with whatever I served them.

As I headed into my bedroom, I heard Dinah's deep, gravelly voice singing about her yesterdays being blue now, her lonely nights being through now and something about someone making her *his*.

I lay down on my bed and watched the pink, polka dot curtains swaying in the breeze from the open window. I wondered what this song my mother kept playing had to do with *her*. Why were Mom's nights lonely? Are they through now? Who was making *her* 'his'? How could she be lonely when Dad stayed home every night and watched television with us?

Who could answer these questions? I couldn't ask my father because he became upset whenever I broached the subject of Mom's new interest in bowling. The last time I mentioned it, I watched as the ghost of sadness slowly shadowed his eyes. I thought about this for quite a while. Unable to come up with any answers, I set these thoughts aside and went into the kitchen to start cooking supper.

Walking past Mom's room on the way to the kitchen, I could hear her humming as she dressed to go bowling. The familiar scent of Shalimar drew me to her open door. She took my breath away as she stood before the mirror. Her short, dark hairstyle reminded me of Mitzi Gaynor's. The bobby-pins had turned the straight ends of her hair into tiny curls. Her make-up was perfectly applied. Fire-engine red lipstick covered her sensuous lips. She was wearing the brown and white checked dress she had been ironing when I came home. It was difficult to envision her throwing a bowling ball down the lane while wearing a full-skirted dress and high heeled shoes. Oh well, what did I know about bowling?

I was ready to comment on how beautiful she looked when I heard Dad whistling as he walked up the steps to our apartment. My heart began to beat rapidly. I knew what was about to happen and wished I could stop it.

Encountering Mom in the kitchen, Dad asked, "Hey, honey, why are you all dressed up?"

"Shirley and I are meeting some of our friends for dinner before we go bowling. Diana's making supper so I didn't think you'd mind if I'm not here," Mom replied in her sweetest voice.

With an edge to his voice, he said, "You just went bowling Monday night, didn't you?"

"This is a different team. They invited Shirley and me to sub. Are you upset?"

"Since when have my feelings mattered? I don't mind you leaving early; it's getting home late that makes me angry."

Mom ignored his comments, walked past him and bent over to kiss Judy and Kim good-bye. She reminded them to behave for Daddy and me while she was gone. Then she brushed her lips lightly against my cheek.

Without a backward glance, she exited through the door.

Dad stormed into the bathroom, slamming the door behind him. I was left holding the pan of goulash and wondering what-in-the-hell was going on. Hell was a strong word for an eleven-year-old to consider.

My father became very upset when my mother started bowling two nights a week. She usually returned by midnight, but on a few occasions, she came home much later. Whenever she was extremely late, Dad stood at the top of the stairs, with his cigarette glowing in the dark, waiting for her to return. The moment she walked in the door, the fighting began.

Their loud shouts could be heard throughout our apartment and probably half-way down the street. Several times she came home in the wee hours of the morning teetering and slurring her words. That's when Dad called her a drunk and accused her of doing things I didn't understand. The tone of his voice told me these things weren't very nice. She screamed back, saying he had no right to accuse her because she'd done nothing wrong and shouting that he was jealous of all of her friends. It would go on like this for a while.

Quite often, Judy and Kim were awakened by the commotion and tiptoed into my bedroom. Judy's eyes were often filled with tears and Kim looked frightened when they climbed into bed with me. If the fights quickly ended, we fell asleep together. If my parents' arguments lasted for a while, I lulled the girls to sleep by softly rubbing their eyelids. I would lie there praying the noise would stop. In fact, I prayed that the whole sordid affair would end, and our lives would get back to normal. At the time, I didn't realize how ominous the word 'affair' actually was.

One afternoon, later that summer, I was outside playing with my friends when Judy came running up the street with Kim in tow. She ran past me excitedly shouting, "I'm going upstairs to tell Mom that Uncle Frank is coming. His ice cream truck is parked down the street!"

I was mystified. Frank visited in the evenings when Dad was home. Why would he be coming during the day? Just then, Mom and Judy came rushing out the door and headed to the corner. When I arrived at the scene, Judy was pointing down the street saying, "See Mom! I told you Uncle Frank was coming to see us. He was talking to the lady on the porch and then they went inside. His truck has been in her driveway a long time. I'll bet he's in the house giving her kids some ice cream!"

Mom's face rapidly turned red, matching the fire in her eyes as she spun on her heels and ran home. We tried to follow her up the stairs but she firmly instructed us to stay outside because she needed to make an important phone call. Her sudden mood change frightened my sisters. At that moment, I thought I knew what was going on. I recalled reading about affairs in one of the *True Story* magazines Mom often left on the living room table. It felt as if someone had slapped me across the face. My stomach churned as I ran into the bushes and puked.

A short while later, Mom sternly called Judy upstairs. I followed behind, but my mother shut the door in my face, telling me this was between her and Judy. I listened through the door and heard Mom's raised voice as she berated Judy for making up stories about Frank following the lady into her house. Mom claimed Frank never went into that house with a woman.

Judy protested. "Mommy, I'm not lying. Uncle Frank did go into her house."

By this time, Mom was seething mad and wouldn't listen to anything Judy had to say. Judy's protests turned into wails as Mom continued to yell and call her a liar.

I couldn't stand there while my six-year-old sister was being accused of lying. It was then I realized who the real liar was, and I thought I knew what the lies were about. When Judy ran sobbing into her bedroom, I decided it was time to confront my mother with what I believed was happening. I'd never before questioned Mom's decisions or commands or deliberately disrespected her. I could no longer stay silent.

My legs trembled as I crossed the room. I looked directly in her eyes and said, "Mom, I know what you and Frank are doing, and it makes me sick! I won't tell Daddy because it'll kill him, but I will say this–*you disgust me!*"

I will never forget the look on her face. Shocked by my outburst, it took her a few minutes to respond. She glared at me and said, "I can't believe what you're implying, Diana Lynn! Exactly what is it Frank and I are supposedly doing?"

"I can't say!" I shouted as I ran from the room.

Catching up with me, she grabbed me by the shoulders. "Frank and I are just friends. If you mention any of this to your dad, he'll get very upset and possibly lose a good friend."

The long, hot summer of 1960 was a turning point in my life. I went from being an innocent girl to a confused adolescent as my world collapsed around me. The first ten years of my life had been relatively normal. During those years, Mom was still loving and attentive; Dad was my role model and my younger sisters were a source of joy.

When Frank entered our lives, it all changed. At first, it was exciting to be around this charismatic, entrancing man who made us laugh. We all looked forward to his next visit. By the end of that summer, I began to believe my mother was in love with Frank, although she vehemently denied it. At times, she seemed to love Frank more than she loved her husband and her daughters. That's when I started to dread the sound of his truck pulling up outside of our house.

As the fights between my parents escalated, I wanted to run away from it all. But where would I go?

CHAPTER 14

A Fresh Start

1960-1961

My mother answered my silent question of 'where I could run to' when she announced we were moving to a duplex on Seventh Street. Usually, I dreaded moving because it meant leaving my friends and starting over at a new school. This time was different. I wanted to move, thinking it might be a fresh start for all of us. Maybe we would leave the bad memories behind.

Maybe Frank wouldn't visit anymore. Maybe Mom and Dad would stop fighting. That's a lot of 'maybes.'

We moved just before school started in the fall of 1960. Although I hated to leave Miss Funk, it was comforting to go back to S.G. Love School where I'd hopefully know some of the kids in my sixth grade class. The best part of the move was that we were only two blocks away from Gussie's house. I could easily escape to her house whenever I needed to get away from the chaos at home.

After we moved, the chaos seemed to settle and our lives slowly improved. Occasionally, I would Mom and Dad embracing or catch them whispering in the corner of the room. Once I caught Dad patting Mom on the butt. She giggled. Unfortunately, Frank began to visit again which made me very uncomfortable. My feelings towards him had drastically changed and it was difficult for me to understand why my parents allowed him back into our lives. I put it out of my mind by convincing myself it was none of my business.

We spent Thanksgiving Day at Grandma Conklin's. After greeting us with the usual hugs and kisses, Granny C handed Mom an apron, and they went to work putting the finishes touches on dinner.

When the freshly carved turkey had been placed on the table, everyone sat down. We bowed our heads while Grandpa Conklin offered the Thanksgiving prayer. When Grandpa Conklin said "Amen," we raised our rooster glasses filled with tomato juice for a toast. Each year, making the toast was Dad's job. This Thanksgiving, he stood up, lifted his glass into the air, smiled at Mom and said, "Bonnie and I have a special announcement. We're having another baby in July."

A few seconds of stunned silence followed. Granny C broke the silence by saying, "That's wonderful news. Here's to another grandchild and a new sister or brother for the girls!"

Now I understood what my parents had been whispering about. Maybe God was answering my prayers. Sharing our love with a new baby might be just what our family needed.

Christmas Eve was the next holiday and we always celebrated it at Gussie's house with all of the aunts, uncles and cousins. After everyone arrived, we went into the dining room and filled our plates with the various dishes my great-grandmother had prepared. I tried to be one of the first in line so I could secure my favorite seat beside the Christmas tree in the front parlor. I had kept Gussie's secret about the new aluminum tree, and was anxious to see everyone's reaction to the rotating wheel as it showered vivid shades of red, green, yellow and blue on the silver tree. I hoped they would be as mesmerized as I had been when I first saw it.

My cousin, Suzie, leaned over and whispered into my ear, "When did Gussie get this tree? What happened to the real ones she used to get?"

"Oh, you know Gussie. She likes to be different," I perkily replied.

As I listened to the laughter and watched the smiling faces, I was reminded why my mother and I had become so homesick on Christmas Eve in Modesto. Spending Christmas Eve at my great-grandmother's with all of Mom's relatives was a family tradition; one that I'd hoped would last forever.

Unfortunately, this was one of the last times we spent together on Christmas Eve. That winter, I spent a lot of time with Gussie on the weekends. One cold, snowy night in January, I returned from a visit at her house to find Frank sitting in the living room laughing and smoking with Mom and Dad. It always annoyed me when I came home and he was there. He made my skin crawl. My mother quickly spoke up when she noticed my expression, "Look who came to visit, Diana. Frank brought you girls some Christmas gifts. Wasn't that nice?"

I glared at Frank and mumbled something about spending the night with my great-grandmother. I ran to my room, threw some clothes in a bag and hastily made my exit. As I wiped my tears away while trudging through the blinding snow, I kept asking myself how my parents could welcome Frank back into our lives. What were they thinking?

Gussie was startled when I burst into her living room, threw myself in her lap and sobbed. She kept asking what was wrong, but I couldn't tell her. The only thing I could think to say was, "Mom and Dad are having another fight."

She immediately got up from her chair and went into the kitchen to make me a cup of hot tea. By the time she brought me the tea, I had stopped crying. I cuddled up to her on the couch and watched television. I must have fallen asleep because the next thing I knew she was her telling me to go into her room and get in bed.

I crawled into her side of the bed, pulled the covers up to my chin and dozed off. I had only been sleeping a little while when I felt a warm body nestling close to me. The sound of the heavy breathing in my ear made me uneasy. When a hand touched my leg and fingers slowly moved toward my crotch, I froze. It took me a moment to realize it was my great-grandfather, Daddy Wilson, who was caressing me. I jumped out of bed and ran back into the living room.

Startled by my presence, Gussie looked up from her embroidery and said, "What's the matter honey, can't you sleep?"

"No," I answered. "I woke up from a bad dream and decided to sleep out here tonight." She went into the closet and came back with a blanket and pillow. After making me comfortable, she kissed my cheek and told me to have sweet dreams, that everything would be better tomorrow.

The Road Back to Hell

I never told anyone about what had happened that night. I couldn't tell my mother because I knew she would confront Daddy Wilson about it and it would cause major problems. Gussie was the only person I could turn to when I was hurt and I certainly couldn't tell her about it. I finally convinced myself Daddy Wilson thought I was Gussie sleeping next to him that night when he touched me. However, I never slept at my great-grandmother's house again.

The long, snowy winter finally ended. Large patches of ugly, brown snow were replaced by blooming yellow daffodils, purple and white hyacinths and bright red and pink tulips. The sweet scent of lilacs filled the air as their bushes sprang to life in May. In June, we looked forward to the school year ending. Our thoughts turned to picnics in Allen Park, riding our bicycles down the street; playing flash- light tag with our friends and spending a week or two with Granny C.

We were also excited about the arrival of the new baby as we watched Mom's belly get bigger. Sometimes, she'd invite us to sit beside her on the couch and feel the baby kicking inside her stomach.

In beginning of July, Mom's best friend Shirley held a baby shower for her at our house. Dad took Judy and Kim out for the afternoon, and I stayed home to help. I was cleaning up the kitchen when I noticed Mom and Shirley whispering in the corner like a couple of schoolgirls. Shirley suddenly burst into laughter.

Puzzled, I asked, "What's so funny?"

"It's nothing, honey, just a little joke between us girls," Mom answered. If this response was intended to satisfy my curiosity, it didn't.

The house soon filled with Mom's friends and relatives bearing gifts for the new baby. After everyone had settled into the living room, I sat down beside my mother and handed her the packages. As she opened them, she read each card so everyone would know who the gift was from. When my mother opened one of the cards, she hesitated before announcing, "This gift is from Angela and Frank."

A silent hush fell over the room. Several women seemed surprised by the names on the card. They paid close attention as Mom slowly pulled a sterling silver baby cup and a child-size set of sterling silverware out of the box. "What a thoughtful gift. I'll send them a nice thank you note," Mom graciously said as she hastily set the package on the floor.

After my mother finished opening the gifts, Shirley invited everyone into the dining room for refreshments. I stayed behind to clean up the discarded wrapping paper. Aunt Dorothy obviously didn't realize I was still in the room when she sarcastically remarked to Arlene, "Hmph! I wonder what Stew will think of that gift."

Just before the baby was born, I asked my dad if he wanted a boy or a girl. He said it didn't matter as long as the baby was healthy. Linda Sue Smith was born on July 20, 1961. She had dark brown eyes, curly brown hair, and a lovely, soft, olive complexion. She weighed a little over six pounds. Linda was a perfectly happy, beautiful little baby. The first time I held her, I spoke softly in her ear, "I'll always be your big sister, and I will protect you forever."

When we had spent Thanksgiving Day at Grandma Conklin's and my father had announced Mom was pregnant again, I was hopeful it would help restore some peace in our family. That dream was short-lived because instead of improving things, they seemed to worsen. Once again, my mother appeared to be jealous of her newborn baby, Linda. At the time, I could not understand why she felt that way. In my late teens, I finally realized my mother had been jealous of Judy because my father had paid so much attention to her. It took me years to figure out why she resented Linda.

The remainder of that summer, I spent a lot of time thinking about starting seventh-grade in the fall at Lincoln Junior High. I tried to imagine what it would be like changing classes every hour. Although I was eager to participate in the extra-curricular activities, I was extremely nervous about making new friends. All of my friends from Love School were attending Washington Junior High, which meant I wouldn't know a soul at Lincoln. This thought terrified me.

The morning of my first day at Lincoln, Dad drove me to school. I sat beside him clutching my blue three-ring notebook close to my chest. He reached over, patted my hand and said, "You'll do just fine, Snookey. You have what it takes." I nodded and prayed he was right.

He sat in his truck and watched as I slowly made my way up the long side walk leading to the school. My knees shook; my hands were clammy and beads of perspiration formed underneath my bangs. Because I didn't know anyone, it was difficult to decide which door to enter. I wished there was a familiar face in the crowd, someone who would yell, "Hey, Diana, come over here!"

I understood that selecting the right door to enter the school was critical because entering a wrong door could brand me. There was a large crowd of kids gathered outside the first door, smoking. I shied away. While walking towards the second door, I spotted a group of girls dressed like me in white, starched blouses with Peter Pan collars, plaid pleated skirts, and knee socks. I quietly stood in the background, listening as they cheerfully greeted one another. I felt very alone and frightened. Suddenly, someone tapped me on my shoulder. When I turned around, I was face-to-face with a cute, chubby-cheeked girl with dimples, soft brown hair, bright blue eyes, and a sweet smile.

"Hi, I'm JoAnne Ottoson. Are you new here?"

Relief flooded through me. Someone had sought me out! I finally found my voice and replied, "Yes, and I don't know a soul. I'm Diana Smith."

The bell rang, and everyone rushed into the school. JoAnne grabbed my hand and said, "Follow me, I'll show you the way." That was the beginning of a friendship that would span over fifty years.

JoAnne led me to the auditorium where orientation was being held. After it was over, she pointed me in the direction of my homeroom. When I entered the classroom, Mrs. Swanson was sitting behind the desk looking over some papers. She was a heavy-set woman with short curly gray hair on her head and her chin. I had to control a giggle because she reminded me of a Bassett Hound with big, droopy eyes and droopy jowls. As the students entered her room, she never looked up from the papers she was perusing. I assumed she was a bitch. It didn't take long for her to prove me wrong.

Diana Lynn

Upon receiving my class schedule, I was amazed to find I had been placed in all advanced classes. When Mrs. Swanson passed out a list of extra- curricular activities and clubs, I was instantly drawn to the school's journalism program, of which, she was the advisor. I decided to speak to her about it as soon as possible.

Entering my first class of the day, I spotted JoAnne sitting by the window. I rushed over and took a seat beside her. As we compared our schedules, I was delighted to learn we'd be together in most of our classes. When the dismissal bell rang at the end of the day, I lingered outside of the school, thinking about all that I'd experienced during my first, full day at Lincoln Junior High. I couldn't wait to return.

The next morning while crossing the Sixth Street Bridge, I looked up at the beautiful sunny sky and was reminded that in a few weeks, colorful leaves would be floating to the ground. I could almost hear the sounds of the dry leaves crunching under my feet as I briskly walked to meet JoAnne. She had invited me to walk to school with her and her friends Barb, Mary, Sue, Lorrie, and Cherrie; I was eager to meet them. They all lived on the west side of town, had been friends all through elementary school and met every morning for the trek to Lincoln. I hoped they would welcome me into their group.

As soon as I entered my homeroom, I approached Mrs. Swanson about the journalism position I had seen posted. Every Thursday, the *Jamestown Post-Journal* published a feature called "Junior High Notes", a weekly article highlighting school events and honoring the outstanding students and teachers at each junior high school. These columns included recaps of the weekly sporting events and announcements of upcoming activities. The photos and bylines of each columnist were posted above the article. I didn't know if I qualified for the position, but I had decided to apply.

Mrs. Swanson was correcting papers when I approached her desk, so I cleared my throat to get her attention. She slowly lifted her big, sleepy eyes, looked up at me and said, "Yes?"

"I would like to apply for the journalism position."

Those nine words quickly got her attention. Her smile softened, her eyes came alive, and she said, "That's wonderful, Diana. Tell me why you're interested."

I explained that I enjoyed writing and had written a play, several short stories, a few poems and three chapters of a book. When I finished, she nodded and invited me to come back after classes to discuss what the position entailed.

She was waiting for me when I returned at the end of seventh period. She handed me a piece of paper listing the requirements. During the first year, the upcoming journalist would be trained by the current reporter and would have to stay after school each day gathering current school news and interviewing staff members and students. The school journalist was responsible for completing the column by Friday and delivering it to the newspaper each Tuesday by 4:00 p.m. When we finished discussing the duties, Mrs. Swanson added, "I almost forgot to mention you will not be permitted to participate in any other extra-curricular activities. This position has to be your number-one priority. There is a lot to consider before you apply. I suggest you go home and talk it over with your parents."

Although this information was overwhelming, I didn't hesitate to respond. "That's not necessary, Mrs. Swanson. It's up to me. I know my parents will support whatever I choose to do. I'd like to apply for it."

Her broad smile revealed that my strong response had elevated me to a new level. I walked out of that room elated.

A few days later, I heard my name announced over the PA system, instructing me to report to Mrs. Swanson's Latin class directly after school. As I entered the room, another classmate, Kathy Brown, was sitting there. I became concerned, assuming we were competing for the position. Mrs. Swanson allayed my fears when she announced she had decided we would share the duties of Junior High Reporter.

"Each of you has excellent writing skills. I believe it would be best if Diana reports the social news and Kathy covers sports." Thus began my writing career and an excellent relationship with Kathy and Mrs. Swanson.

Diana Lynn

During the first month of school, I made a number of new friends. One girl in particular, Sharon, was easy to talk to and very friendly. During our daily chats, we discovered our mutual interests—football games, dancing, music and flirting with cute boys. She invited me to her house to talk about an idea she had. I readily accepted her invitation.

When I arrived on Saturday, Sharon immediately ushered me into her room. I sat on the bed as she bounced around the room like a pixie, animatedly describing her plans for us to co-host a hayride later that fall. She ended her presentation by saying, "Doesn't that sound like a blast?" What could be more fun than riding on a hay wagon for two hours with dreamy boys? Afterward, we could sit around a big bonfire and roast hot dogs. Don't you love it?"

Admittedly, I was intrigued by the idea because I'd been thinking of hosting some type of party for my new friends but I became apprehensive when she started discussing the guest list. I didn't know a lot of the kids she mentioned; most of them were ninth graders with pretty wild reputations.

I finally spoke up. "I'm not sure about those ninth-grade boys. Aren't they a little old for us?'"

"Are you kidding? That's the reason for the hayride," she replied sassily. "A few of them are on the football team. Isn't that exciting?"

"Exciting in what way?" I naively inquired. "Have you ever been on a hayride?"

When I shook my head no, Sharon breathlessly went on to say, "Hayrides are cool. Everyone huddles together under blankets, and before the night is over, you never know what boy you'll be making out with. I'm hoping I'll get lucky, and Ron will pick me. I've heard he's the best kisser in ninth grade!"

Just before leaving, I promised to call Sharon after I talked to my mom. I needed time to sort out my feelings about this whole party idea. Walking home gave me the opportunity to think about my trepidations. I was uncomfortable making friends with these older kids. In my opinion, some of them were hoods, and I didn't want to associate with them.

Would it be a mistake to become involved in this hayride? How could I make out with a boy I didn't know? Would I risk losing my new friends?

I had grown to really like JoAnne and the girls I walked to school with each morning and felt they were beginning to accept me. I envied them because they had something I didn't—long-lasting friendships. If I took part in this hayride, what would they think of me? I knew I was facing a crucial decision in my life, and needed my mother to help me sort it out.

She was in the kitchen fixing supper when I arrived home. When she asked if I had a good time at Sharon's house, I shrugged my shoulders and replied, "Kind of."

Noticing my despondency, she inquired, "What's wrong, honey?" "I have a big decision to make and I need your advice."

We sat at the table while I told her my concerns about the hayride. "I'm proud of you. That's a pretty mature way to look at things. Why don't you just have your own Halloween party right here and invite the kids you want?" Despite my recent feelings of disappointment with my mother, I was grateful she was there when I needed her.

The next morning, I called Sharon to tell her I couldn't participate because my mother didn't think the hayride was a good idea. I asked her if she'd like to help me with my Halloween party. She declined. That pretty much ended our friendship.

The Halloween Party was another significant turning point in my life.

Everyone I invited seemed to really enjoy themselves. We started out the evening as acquaintances and ended it as good friends. Some of the girls became my best friends and we still get together whenever I go to Jamestown.

CHAPTER 15

Finding Peace

1961-1962

Although my home life appeared to be stable, a current of unrest bubbled just below the surface like an undertow. My mother had joined a second bowling team which meant she went out two nights a week. On those nights, it was my responsibility to prepare supper, clean the kitchen and help Dad with the girls. I usually enjoyed holding and feeding Linda and helping Judy and Kim with their school work, but sometimes I resented it, especially if I had homework. I found myself mumbling, "This is Mom's job. Why isn't she home doing it?"

One night Dad overheard me and replied, "Good question. I've been thinking the same thing." I shot him a questioning look implying, *Why don't you do something about it, Dad?*

I found myself handling more and more of my mother's responsibilities while she was out with her friends, and I was beginning to resent it. I had friends of my own that I longed to spend more time with but often couldn't because I had to watch the girls. I'd ask myself why she had four children if she didn't want to spend time with them. Had her friends become more important than her family? I also resented the fact that I stayed up later than usual doing the homework I couldn't get done earlier in the evening while I was babysitting. It didn't seem fair!

Late that night, when Mom returned home, the familiar sounds of their arguing carried up to my bedroom. They were fighting about Mom bowling another night a week and something about Frank. I was glad my father was finally confronting the situation. I closed my bedroom door to drown out the noise and fell asleep thinking about school.

It was about this time that I started to become moody and experienced stomach cramps. When Mom noticed, she explained the facts-of-life to me. I didn't tell her my friend, Ann, and I had already figured it out by reading passages in the Bible. We read some verses in the Old Testament referring to a woman begetting the seed from some man. I could barely suppress my giggles when she told me how a man inserted his sperm into a woman's egg. I envisioned a tall, bearded man in a long robe, humping a woman clad in a cumbersome skirt with a big scarf covering her face. Stifling my laughter, I paid closer attention as she explained menstrual bleeding. Yuk!

One morning, not long after our mother-daughter talk, I woke up and discovered blood on my panties. Frightened, I ran to get my mother. We went into the bathroom where she handed me a large sanitary napkin and showed me how to put it on. When she noticed me struggling when I walked, she suggested I stay home from school. Then she sent me to the corner grocer's to purchase a smaller, teen-sized box of Kotex. Donning my winter coat and boots, I slowly trudged through the snow to the store.

Thankfully, the female owner was working that day. When she asked what I was looking for, I whispered into her ear. She pointed and loudly said, "They're down that aisle on the right. It's a blue box marked Junior Size." Three men were standing behind me in the check-out line. I was mortified.

I was still struggling with the large, uncomfortable pad between my legs when I arrived back home. As I walked into the living room, I discovered Frank and Mom sitting on the sofa. My first thought was, "What's he doing here?" When I realized they were snickering about the way I was walking, I shouted, "This isn't funny! And it's none of your business, Frank!" I stormed off to my room.

I heard the front door closing as Frank left and the sounds of Mom's footsteps coming up the steps. She opened the door and found me lying on my bed still dressed in my coat and boots. She tried to apologize, but I turned my head and commanded, "Just go away." Hearing the anger in my voice, she quickly left me alone. I remained in my room for a long time sorting out my feelings. Had I reacted that way because I was moody from starting my period or was I upset because Frank was at the house? What was he doing here during the day? He usually visited in the evenings when Dad was home. That's when I remembered I should have been in school that day and wondered how often he visited my mother when we were in school, and Dad was at work. After stewing about this for awhile, I got up and went downstairs to get something to eat. I was fixing myself a sandwich when Mom approached me.

"I remember how tough it was when I started my periods. Your whole body changes and you get really moody. I understand why you're upset today. It's okay."

My body stiffened. She thought my moodiness caused my outburst.

Didn't she know I was upset because Frank was here? My anger erupted. "You just don't get it, do you Mom? I'm not a baby anymore—the lady at the store told me I'm a young woman now and that means some of the things I couldn't understand before are much clearer to me now. What you're doing hurts me very much."

She ignored my insinuations and placated me by giving me some Midol. Then she suggested I take a nap; it would make me feel better. I slammed my peanut butter slathered knife on the counter and fled the room.

As soon as Dad came home from work, he knocked on my bedroom door, walked in and sat beside me on the bed.

"Hey, Snookey, Mom told me you became a 'young lady' today. That may be true, but you'll always be my little girl." He went on to explain why Frank was at the house today. According to him, Frank dropped in to lend my mother some money because she had given me the last of her cash to go to the store. I couldn't believe what I was hearing! Mom apparently called my father about Frank coming to the house because she was afraid I would tell my dad. She was very sly and offered Dad a believable excuse for Frank's daytime visit. Although my father appeared to believe her, I knew it was just another lie.

As the winter quickly turned to spring, I looked forward to my summer plans as a form of escape. I was especially eager to attend church camp for the first time.

The Road Back to Hell

On a beautiful Sunday afternoon in August, JoAnne, Martha, Cheryl, and I loaded our suitcases into the trunk of Ottosons' car. We talked non-stop on the thirty-minute drive to the Methodist Church camp in Findley Lake, New York. After we arrived and got settled, we went to the Central Hall for orientation where we were given our schedules for the week and a review of the rules. The strictest rule stated boys must remain on their side of their hill and the girls on the other. No fraternization of the opposite sex was permitted in the cabins. "Like we'd invite boys to our room," I whispered to JoAnne.

Our days were filled with activities—craft making, Bible studies, hiking, and swimming. At the end of each day, we went to our room to change into dress clothes for dinner and the evening church service. After the evening service, we returned to our room, changed into our pajamas and shared girl-talk into the wee hours of the morning. As the week progressed, so did our stories.

I developed a crush on a tall, good-looking boy from Erie named Bob. His soft brown eyes, freckled face and sweet smile attracted me immediately. Martha liked a boy from Youngsville, named Tom. During the day, Martha and Tom walked everywhere together. Tom always wore his Kodak camera around his neck, prepared to take pictures of the scenery and on-going events.

At the end of one very busy day, JoAnne and I hurried into our room to get ready for dinner and the evening services. JoAnne was in the shower, and I was getting dressed, when I noticed some movement in front of the window. I lifted my head and saw Tom standing there with his camera poised to take a shot. Clad only in my slip, I screamed and ran into the hall. I was standing there telling the girls what had happened, when Miss Johnson, our camp counselor, strode down the hall. The crowd around me quickly dispersed. She apparently overheard our conversation because she pointed at me and sternly said, "After you finish dressing, come to my office." I was scared to death. I quickly dressed and ran to her office. When I tapped on the door, she told me to enter.

Before she could say a word, I blurted out, "Miss Johnson, thank you for inviting me to your room. I can explain everything." I hurriedly went on to tell her that Martha had rushed into the building when she heard me scream. Apparently, she and Tom had been debating about which one of them had the messiest room. To prove her point, she invited him to peek through our bedroom window. Tom didn't realize JoAnne and I were back in our room dressing for dinner when he peered into the window through the lens of his camera.

Thank heavens Miss Johnson believed me. If she hadn't, she would have called my parents and sent me packing. Imagine being kicked out of church camp! I would have been mortified. It was hard enough to avoid the whispering girls and the snide remarks from some of the boys for the rest of the week. By week's end, the true story came out, and I was exonerated from my crime of 'stripping-in-front-of-the window'.

The evening services were the most peaceful time of the day for me. As I sat there attentively listening to each spiritual message, I tried to figure out how it fit into my life. During the service, I prayed, thanking God for all of the gifts He had bestowed on me. The more I prayed, the more I felt His presence and longed for His blessings. I asked Him to guide me as I struggled with my family problems. I left each service feeling calm and fulfilled.

On Friday night, the last night of camp, a very soft-spoken, yet dynamic preacher presided over the final weekly service. I was drawn to his every word. At the close of the service, he stood at the pulpit and invited anyone who wanted to welcome God into their heart and into their life to come forward to pledge their life to Him. As I closed my eyes in prayer, a warm, comforting feeling spread throughout my body. I slowly rose from my seat, stepped out of the pew and walked toward the altar. Drawn by the beautiful refrains of "Just as I Am, Without One Plea," I knelt down at the altar and offered my heart and soul to God my Savior. I beseeched Him to accept me 'just as I am.'

I have recalled this spiritual moment whenever I have faced a crisis. It has provided me with the faith and strength I needed to persevere. In my darkest hours, I have felt the presence of God's love. I am eternally thankful for that very special evening.

After the service, we changed into khakis and sweaters and joined the others at the big bonfire down by the lake. We sat before the raging fire singing popular camp songs, sharing funny stories about the week and roasting hot dogs. I was sitting at the back of the crowd when Bob quietly approached and asked if he could sit beside me. While staring into the blazing fire, he reached over, gently lifted my face and softly kissed me. It was my first real kiss; I was completely smitten by this good-looking boy from Erie. The next morning, as we prepared to leave, Bob handed me a note with his address and phone number. He'd also written a question, "Would you like to be 'Bobby's Girl?"

My family only attended church on Easter, and after a time, we didn't even do that. My grandmother Conklin was the person who provided my sisters and me with our religious training. Whenever we spent time with them, we would always go to Sunday school and church at the United Methodist Church in Warren. I was proud that my grandparents each taught Sunday Schools and were pillars of their church. Granny C also paid my church camp fees. It was because of her influence that I attended Immanuel Lutheran Church on my own for three years while I was taking confirmation classes. It was at this time that Reverend Gerald Daniels entered my life and became a strong mentor on whom I could depend.

CHAPTER 16

Flying High

1962-1963

ALTHOUGH THE SUMMER had been great, I couldn't wait for school to start in the fall. Lincoln had become a safe haven for me; a place to escape the problems at home. The best part of my day was meeting my west side friends each morning. We'd laugh, joke and sometimes break out in song as we trekked up the hill to school.

One morning when I arrived, the girls were in the middle of a discussion about Delta Zeta, an established sorority at Lincoln Junior High. This week, bids were being offered to a select group of eighth-grade girls. They were all buzzing about who would and who wouldn't get a bid. The conversation went something like this-

"I don't think Mary Jane will make the cut," Sue commented. "Why not?" JoAnne asked.

"Because her grades aren't very good."

Someone else added, "I know Sharon won't be asked because she's running with a pretty wild crowd."

Hearing those words made me grateful I had opted out of the hayride. They also made me fearful I wouldn't get a bid. Knowing the criteria for being selected for DZ, I didn't think I'd make the cut—I lived on the wrong side of the tracks. I mentally prepared myself for disappointment. Friday was the day the invitations to join DZ were being passed out.

That morning, while crossing the bridge on my way to meet my friends, I rehearsed the congratulatory speech I'd prepared for those who were accepted. I wanted it to sound sincere while hiding my personal disappointment if I wasn't chosen.

Throughout the day, a ninth-grade member of Delta Zeta approached the new candidate by tapping her on the shoulder and handing her a formal invitation to attend the next meeting. When I walked into my first period class, JoAnne ran up and waved the white and gold envelope with her bid enclosed. I hugged her and recited my speech. At lunch, several other girls in our group announced they had received bids. Again, I repeated my congratulatory speech.

Before the lunch period ended, I excused myself from the table, stating I needed to interview someone for next week's column. Instead, I went into the girls' lavatory and cried. When the bell rang announcing the start of the fifth period, I splashed water on my tear-streaked face, held my head up high and went to class. I was sitting there for a few minutes, when I felt a tap on my shoulder. I looked up to see Marianne's smiling face as she handed me the treasured envelope. Omigod! I had officially been invited to join Delta Zeta! My school week ended on a high note, while my weekend would probably start on a low note.

About eight-thirty, every Saturday morning, my mother would holler, "Diana Lynn, it's time to get up. We've got a lot of work to do." I'd pull my covers over my head and try to ignore her calls. After the third or fourth call, I dragged my body out of bed, swore under my breath, and went downstairs. I usually found her sitting at the kitchen table with a cigarette burning in the overflowing ashtray. The can of Blatz she was swigging had recently replaced her morning coffee. This particular Saturday, I became more annoyed than usual as I watched her swig her beer.

"Mom, why do I have to get up every Saturday to help you clean the house when you're here all week while I'm slaving away at school?"

"Hey! Don't be sassy, Miss Priss! Ever since you got into that sorority, you've been pretty full of yourself. I'm your mother and what I say, goes," she curtly replied.

I generally backed down whenever we had an altercation, but this morning I could no longer keep my thoughts to myself.

"You don't understand. I do plenty around here. I make supper two or three nights a week while you're out with your friends. I wash the dishes and clean the kitchen every night. I'm always solving problems between Judy and Kim when they fight, and I change Linda's diapers almost as much as you do. It's difficult to do all that and keep up with my homework. I don't understand why Saturday has to be a big cleaning day. None of my friends have to work like this."

She glared at me and screamed, "I don't give a damn what your friends do or don't do in their homes. I'm sick and tired of you bringing up your perfect friends and their perfect lives. It doesn't kill you to help me on Saturdays."

"It wouldn't kill you to stay home a few nights, either. I'm tired of your friends always coming first, and I'm sick of seeing you with beer in your hand first thing in the morning!"

My mother jumped up, walked over and slapped my face. "Go to your room! You can stay there the rest of the weekend."

I stormed out of the kitchen and went straight to my room. While I was lying there staring at the ceiling, Judy came in. She knelt beside the bed and comforted me by rubbing my eyebrows, the same thing I'd done for her when she was upset.

"I'm sorry Mom got so mad at you. I heard her say she was calling Dad at work to tell him about your fight," she whispered.

"Good, let her," I replied.

"Kim and I will try to help you more."

I kissed the top of her head, acknowledging her thoughtfulness. Later that day, I could hear my mother bitching about me to Dad when he came in the door. A few minutes later he tapped on my door and entered my room. "Hey, do you want to tell me about the fight with your mother?"

I sat up and told my side of the story.

He listened attentively and responded, "Diana, you've been taught to treat your elders with respect, especially your parents." Before he could say another word, I quickly added, "But Daddy, that's the point. I don't respect her anymore."

Surprised by my bold comment, he asked, "Why?"

I quickly unloaded the pent-up anger and confusion I'd been feeling for the past year. I expressed my concerns about the changes in my mother. She never seemed to have time for any of us because she spent most of her time on the phone with her friends. When she wasn't talking to them on the phone, she was out with them in the bars. At times, she seemed unreachable. I could not understand why she became angry so easily, especially with him and Judy. I let him know that Judy and Kim were also upset about the changes in Mom's behavior. Although I wanted to tell him I hated the fact that Frank still came around, I didn't. I thought I had said enough.

Dad hesitated before saying, "I've noticed it, and I'm dealing with it my way. I just want peace in this family, and sometimes it's better to ignore the problems, hoping they'll go away."

He suggested that I focus on my friends, my grades, and my extracurricular activities. His last words, before leaving my room were, "Diana, you're too young to be saddled with the responsibilities of this family. Don't worry about the problems. That's my job, understand?"

I took my father's advice and spent as much time as possible away from home. I became active in more school activities, Delta Zeta and my confirmation class at church. I accepted almost every invitation to slumber parties, birthday parties, and other social events. I had also developed a major crush on David, a boy in my classes. His translucent blue eyes were the color of the sky on a bright, sunny day; his blonde bangs fell softly across his forehead, and his cheeks dimpled whenever he smiled. Talking with him in school soothed me.

In the spring, I was honored to be nominated for Secretary of Student Council for the next school year. When I learned David was a candidate for Vice-President, I became even more excited. We spent a lot of time together during this campaign and our relationship flourished. Just before election-day, David asked me to wear his ring. We were officially going steady!

In my spare time, I worked on my speech. The night before the election, I practiced for hours in my room. Later that evening, I gathered my family together like guinea pigs and delivered it to them. Because they were a biased audience, they gave me a standing ovation. I prayed my classmates would do the same.

The day of the election, my heart was racing, my hands were sweating, and my stomach was rumbling as I sat there listening to the other candidates. To bolster my confidence, I silently recited- "You can do this... YOU CAN do this...YOU CAN DO THIS!"

I proudly stood when my name was called and marched up to the podium. Standing before hundreds of my classmates, I took a deep breath, looked out into the audience and delivered my heartfelt speech with a powerful voice that projected my confidence. When I finished, the applause carried me like a magic carpet back to my seat. At three o'clock that afternoon, the results of the election were read over the PA system. I breathlessly waited to learn who had won the secretarial position. Hearing my name was one of the happiest moments of my life. I had won!

CHAPTER 17

Learning the Truth

1962

THE SUMMER OF 1962 was much like the summer of 1959, only stormier. The ugly clouds that hovered over our lives in '59 slowly dissipated, only to return in '62 with a vengeance. This was the summer I finally learned what I had suspected was the truth— my mother was having an affair with Frank.

Mom continued bowling and spending more evenings in bars with her circle of friends. She jumped at any opportunity to go out. Having a built-in teenage daughter to babysit and a non-confrontational husband made this easy to do because she knew we would take care of everything.

Remembering Dad's comments about keeping peace in the family, I avoided the subject of Mom's frequent absences and tried to suppress the outrage building inside of me. There wasn't anyone I could talk to about the situation, and I never shared these feelings with my friends.

One afternoon, Mom went grocery shopping. I was babysitting when our neighbor, Gina hollered, "Hello, anybody home?" Gina had recently moved into the duplex apartment next to us and frequently dropped in. She looked seductive with her long, curly, black hair pulled into a bun and her sleek, model-thin body. Her face was expertly made up; her dark brown eyes were black from heavily applied mascara and eyeliner. She was appealing until she opened her very loud mouth. The sound of Gina's husky, smoky voice made the hair on the back of my neck stand on end. She was my least favorite of Mom's friends.

"I'm out here making lunch for the kids," I hollered from the kitchen. "Oohh- aren't we the domestic goddess today? Where's your Mom?" she asked as soon as she entered the kitchen.

I pointed the peanut butter-filled knife in her direction and retorted, "Shopping. Where did you think she was?"

From the expression on her face, I knew she was put out by my sarcastic reply. Her demeanor quickly changed. "Sorry. I thought she was here. We were supposed to go to Smokey's today for a pool tournament."

Smokey's, a local bar on the corner of Third and Lafayette, had become Mom's favorite watering hole. Dad sometimes accompanied her, but most of the time she went with Gina. They often drank for free because Gina's boyfriend, Harry, owned the place.

"Didn't she mention the pool tournament when she left?" She asked.

I shot her a disgusted look and tersely responded,

"Are you kidding me? She rarely tells me what she has planned. Since when did my mother become an avid pool player?"

She ignored my comment. "A little touchy today aren't we? Sounds like you need a friend to talk to. Join me in the other room after you've fed the girls." She reached into the refrigerator, helped herself to a can of beer and walked into the living room.

Considering Gina as a friend was the furthest thing from my mind. But I desperately needed someone to talk to and decided she was the perfect person. She was aware of some of our family problems and might be able to answer some of my questions.

While trying to light the cigarette dangling from her magenta lips, she asked out of the side of her mouth, "So, honey, do I detect a little anger coming from you? Are you mad about something?"

Her encouragement was all I needed. I spoke non-stop for about five minutes, expressing how upset I was with the changes in Mom lately and the problems these changes had caused. I complained about my mother getting home later and later at night; Frank stopping in more often and the constant upheaval in our lives because my parents always argued. Though I tried very hard to hold back the tears, they gushed uncontrollably from my eyes. Gina quickly moved beside me on the couch and held me while I cried. When she noticed Judy and Kim standing in the doorway, she shooed them away with a wave of her hand.

When I finally composed myself, Gina calmly addressed some of my concerns. She revealed that my mom was going through a rough time and went out to escape her problems. I could relate to her need to escape because I'd been doing the same thing.

Gina hesitated before saying, "Your Mom isn't happy with your Dad anymore, Diana."

"What has my father done to make her unhappy?"

"It's very complicated for a young girl to understand. Sometimes, people fall out of love for no reason," she explained.

This is what I needed to hear to get to the root of my deepest fear. "You mean she's fallen in love with another man, don't you? It's Frank, isn't it?"

Gina didn't have to say another word; the expression on her face said it all. My hunch was correct. Mom *was* having an affair with Frank. I fled upstairs to the bathroom and vomited into the toilet—purging my heart, soul and stomach of the acidic truth. Ignoring Gina's pleas to come out, I silenced my sobs by burying my face in a towel. I had fallen asleep on the bathroom rug and didn't hear my mother when she entered the room a short time later.

"Diana Lynn, we need to talk," she tenderly said. She moved forward and tried to stroke my face. I slapped her hand away, stood up, looked directly into her eyes and screamed, "Mother, I hate you!"

Running into my bedroom, I locked the door and refused to respond to Mom's knocks and demands for me to come out. I was determined I wasn't leaving my room. I couldn't stand the thought of looking at her or seeing Dad's face when he came home and was confronted with the truth.

Later, I knew my father was home from the sounds of my parents' violent argument. They were shouting words I hadn't heard them use before—"Screw you, you fucking bastard!"—"Shut up you slut!" Suddenly, I heard the sound of a plate or glass shattering against the kitchen wall.

Alarmed by the commotion, Judy began pounding on my door. I opened the door and welcomed my younger sisters into the safe-haven of my room. I cuddled them into my arms and tried to comfort them. I couldn't explain to them what was happening. I still wasn't certain if I entirely understood it. When they finally fell asleep, I carried Linda to her crib and tucked her in. Judy and Kim were too heavy to carry, so I snuggled next to them as they lay sleeping on my bedroom floor.

The loud noises coming from downstairs and my intense nervousness made it impossible to fall asleep. I lay there remembering some of the events leading up to the problems my parents were arguing about now. One of their worst fights took place on New Year's Eve in Modesto when they fought about Joe and Mom. Then I recalled the night I caught Mom and Frank together in the bathroom on Stowe Street. I also remembered the day my mother called Judy a liar for accusing Frank of spending time in the house down the street. I thought about the many late nights when I went to the kitchen for a snack and found my father, staring up at the ceiling while the wisps of smoke from his cigarette curled slowly into the air. I could hear Grandpa Woodard's words when he told me he didn't think Mom would ever be happy because she thought the grass was always greener on the other side of the fence. Although I'd strongly suspected that my mother and Frank were having an affair, reliving these experiences forced me to face the reality of the situation.

Eventually, I drifted off to sleep. I was awakened by the sound of Mom's best friend, Shirley, pounding on the bathroom door and yelling,

"Bonnie, for God's sake, OPEN UP THIS DOOR!"

I leaped out of bed and ran into the hallway. "What's wrong with Mom? Where's Dad?"

Shirley put her finger to her lips and in a hushed voice said, "Go back to your room and stay with the girls. Your dad called and asked me to come because your Mom locked herself in the bathroom. You take care of the girls, and I'll take care of your Mom."

Hearing Linda crying in her crib, I picked her up and carried her to my room. I gathered all of the girls into my bed, it wasn't long before I heard Dad's heavy footsteps as he charged up the stairs. He began knocking on the bathroom door, urging Mom to open it. "Damn it, Bonnie, if you won't open the door, I'll break it down!" And he did! The crash of the door was followed by a scream and a loud gasp. I couldn't restrain myself any longer; I had to know what was happening. I instructed Judy to stay with Kim and Linda in my bedroom. I ran back down the hall to the bathroom.

I was horrified by the sight of the dark-red blood spurting out of my mother's arm up to the ceiling and onto the walls. I watched as Shirley took charge of the situation by holding a towel tightly to Mom's wrist and instructing Dad to call an ambulance. As he rushed past me in the hall, I saw the fear in his eyes. Oh my God, my mother's dying!

Mom slowly opened her eyes and found me standing there. She cried out, "I'm so sorry, honey. I'm so sorry". I wrapped my arms around her and sobbed, "Mommy, I'm sorry, too, I don't hate you. I'm sorry I said that. Please don't die, we all need you,"

Dad watched from the bathroom doorway. He gently approached me, took my hand and led me downstairs. While we waited for the ambulance, he explained I needed to remain calm and take care of my sisters while he and Shirley went to the hospital with Mom. He promised Mom would be okay once she got to the emergency room. I silently nodded my head.

After they had left, I went upstairs and told Judy and Kim that Mom was sick and had to go the hospital. I promised them cookies and cocoa if they stayed in my room a while longer. Then I went about the business of cleaning Mom's thick, sticky, dark-red blood off the bathroom walls and the floor. I was unable to reach the ceiling and prayed my sisters wouldn't notice the sprays of blood. After putting the bloodied towels into the washer, I made cocoa for the girls. While they were snacking at the kitchen table, I fabricated some story about Mom's sudden illness. It was about three in the morning when I finally got them settled back into bed. I never slept a wink the rest of that night.

In the past, I had tried to bury my suspicions about my mother and Frank, hoping they weren't really true. At thirteen, I wasn't ready to accept the truth. But after this night, that was no longer an option. I understood I had no choice. However, no matter how bad things had become, I still loved my mother very much. The beauty and kindness of the mother I had known as a child, occasionally shone through. The part that hurt the most was watching as it destroyed my father.

After Mom recovered from her first suicide attempt, Dad and I avoided discussing it. Once again, we tried to maintain some type of normalcy in our home. Although Mom continued to go out with her friends during the week, she and my dad started going to Smokey's together on Saturday afternoons. If I had plans, my parents took the girls with them. Judy and Kim were delighted by the attention given to them by the bar patrons. People sitting at the bar would buy them pretzels and candy and give them quarters to play the jukebox. They loved to dance to the loud country-western music blaring from the speakers. Sometimes Linda toddled out and joined them on the dance floor. Uncle Kenny and Grandpa Woodard often stopped in, making it a family affair. I was glad that I had other things to do. It embarrassed me to go into Smokey's when I was summoned to come and take my sisters home.

One Saturday afternoon while walking downtown to go shopping with a group of my friends, I noticed a tall, heavy-set man in a baseball cap and blue jeans staggering around out front of Smokey's. As we got closer, I realized it was my grandfather. I was horrified. I moved to the outer edge of the group, hoping he wouldn't see me. When we passed him, he yelled, "Hey Diana, where are you going?" I just kept walking.

"Was that man calling you?" one of my friends asked. I shook my head and said, "No. I have no idea who he is."

The memory of that experience has haunted me for years. I loved my grandfather very much and knew he adored me. One of the most beautiful things he had ever given me was a trip to Modesto, California to visit my aunt, uncle, and cousins.

I was only ten years old, and the memory of that vacation is etched in my mind. Many times, over the years, I've asked myself how I could have walked past him and not acknowledged him.

As an adult, I've come to terms with the choice I made that day. At the time, I was running as fast as I could to distance myself from my abnormal family. I never shared anything about my home life with them. At thirteen, the opinion of my peers meant more to me than hurting and insulting my grandfather. Grandpa Woodard never mentioned it to me, and I've always hoped he was too drunk to realize I had purposely snubbed him. I have prayed many times that if he did see me, he forgave me.

As the fall settled in, so did things at home. My mother went out with her friends less frequently, and occasionally, I saw my parents share a kiss or a hug. This blessed peacefulness ended on a Saturday afternoon in October. I was babysitting while Mom, Dad and Gina spent the day partying at Smokey's. Hearing a loud commotion outside, I peeked out the window and saw my mother and Gina staggering out of a taxi parked in front of our house. After they stumbled through the front door, all hell broke loose!

Because Gina seemed to be more sober, I asked her what had happened. Before she could answer, Mom said, "Your Dad's a bastard, Diana. I know you think he walks on water—but he's a bastard and a drunk." I could barely understand her slurred words.

Her words pierced my heart. I knew Dad was drinking more, and I also knew he sometimes became nasty and jealous when he drank whiskey. One time when he and Mom came home from a party, he became so enraged with her that he punched a hole in the wall with his fist. He stopped drinking for a while after that incident.

Assuming he had been angry like that today, I asked for more details. This time, Gina answered, "Frank came into Smokey's today and he and Stew got into an argument. It turned into a mess. Your dad said something to Frank your mother didn't like and she scratched your dad's face. Then he ran out of the bar."

I tried picturing this chaotic scene. I disgustedly asked, "When is all of this going to stop? I can't stand it anymore. Mom, you and Dad have to stop drinking—you're destroying all of us."

Gina shot me a nasty look. She started walking towards me, pointing her finger in my face as she screamed, "Shut-up! You're just a kid and don't know what you're talking about."

That was all it took for me to come undone. I screamed at her, telling her to get out of our house and our lives because she was a big part of the problem. I pushed her towards the door and said, "Get out and don't come back. You're not welcome here!" Then I slammed the door and locked it.

By this time, Mom had passed out on the couch. I covered her with a blanket. As usual, I took care of my sisters. When I tucked them into bed, Kim asked, "What's going to happen to us? Where's Dad?" Not knowing how to answer that question, I hugged her and promised her everything would work out.

Dad returned later that evening. He was sober when he came through the door. Obviously, the long walk home on this brisk fall night had done some good. His appearance shocked me. His eyes were red and swollen from too much drinking, and there was a deep scratch running down his right cheek. He looked wretched.

"I made some coffee. Do you want some?"

He nodded and followed me into the kitchen. We spent the next few hours talking about everything that had happened over the past few months. It felt good to be able to confront the ongoing problems, rather than continuing to dodge them. I saw relief flood Dad's face as he openly shared his thoughts about Mom and the situation. Before we called it a night, my father calmly said, "Snookey, I have given this a lot of thought while walking around tonight. I've decided to find a small apartment and move out for a while."

My stunned look prompted him to keep talking. "It's the only way for now. You're all at the ages when you need your Mom. If I move out, the fighting will end, and everyone will be better off. It won't be forever. Your mother and I will stay separated until we sort things out."

Although Dad and I shared a lot that night, he was still unable to admit that my mother was in love with Frank. I think he believed if he never said those words, the problem would eventually go away. It was his way of dealing with a tough situation, and a solution I could never understand.

Dad moved out the next day. He rented a two-room apartment on 6th Street, only three blocks away from our house. I often visited, taking the food Mom prepared and making sure he had the things he needed. Judy, Kim, and Linda accompanied me on many of these visits. We shared our school papers with him and told him about the things we had been doing. As promised, he called every day and came over once or twice a week to visit. On some of these visits, he and Mom quietly talked in the kitchen over coffee, not beer.

He returned home before Thanksgiving.

Our Thanksgiving celebration was a repeat of 1961. After the grace had been said, my father stood to make his annual toast. He proudly announced that Mom was expecting a baby in June. When he finished, dead silence filled the room; you could hear a pin drop. I observed everyone's reaction. Grandma Conklin's eyes were a much darker shade of blue; Grandpa Conklin stared down at his plate, and Great-Grandma Smith pursed her lips and loudly snorted 'Humph!" I understood her disapproving reaction because I had witnessed it before whenever one of us did something inappropriate while visiting. Their expressions mirrored my feelings—'Just what we need, another baby.'

CHAPTER 18

On Top of the World

1963-1964

My ninth-grade-year at Lincoln Junior High was the best year of my life. I excelled in school and enjoyed my experiences as a school journalist. I completed my confirmation classes at Immanuel Lutheran Church and was confirmed in April. I was elected Class Secretary of Student Council and Treasurer of Delta Zeta. My highest honor was receiving the 9th Grade Citizen-of-the Month Award in November.

While my friendships flourished, my romance didn't. I experienced my first heartbreak when David broke up with me mid-way through the year.

As the end of ninth grade approached, I was somewhat depressed. I was already missing Lincoln Junior High, my teachers and all of the significant events of the past three years. Participating in so many of these activities had enabled me to build my self-confidence. For the first time, I seriously thought about college. I considered several professions—journalism, teaching, law or social work. My desire to pursue a career was intense, and I knew somehow, I would find the money to finance my education.

Lynn, one of my closest friends, was hosting an end-of-school party. The girls she invited were supposed to bring a date. I was in a quandary over who to ask when another classmate, Brenda Cook, approached me in the hall.

"Diana, do you have a minute?"

Although Brenda and I had shared some classes, we didn't run in the same circle of friends. I considered her friends to be a little wild. However, I was curious about what she had to say. "Sure," I replied.

"Did you know Randy broke up with me?"

Of course, I knew. Everyone at school had been talking about it.

Brenda had dated Randy Sharp, the star running back of the football team, for three years. I nodded my head.

"Well, Lynn invited me to her party, and I thought maybe I could ask David and you could ask Randy. After the party gets going, maybe we could swap dates."

This idea seemed insane to me, but I told Brenda I would give it some thought and get back to her. After considering it for a few days, I agreed to go along with this crazy scheme. The problem was finding a way to invite Randy to be my date; I barely knew him. I had seen him walking across the Third Street Bridge a few times, on his way home from school. A couple of days later, when I spotted him on the other side of the bridge, I crossed the street and joined him. While mustering the courage to ask him to be my date, I realized he was quite cute. Randy was about five-eight with an athletic build— big shoulders and strong arm muscles. His slightly slanted, long-lashed eyes were almost as black as his hair. His smile was warm and inviting. Although I was excited about the prospects of getting together again with David, maybe spending the evening with Randy wouldn't be so bad.

The night of the party, Brenda and David never showed up. However, Randy turned out to be an enjoyable date. At the end of the evening, he asked for my phone number. After that, he called me every day. I finally invited him to my house to meet my parents and sisters. My parents immediately liked him. My three sisters were shy and hid behind me to peek at him. Randy won them over by teasing them whenever he came to visit. Linda bubbled with laughter when he carried her around the house on his back. Judy and Kim soon fell in love with him; it took me a lot longer. We spent many evenings sitting on my porch talking about the upcoming football season, our families, and our mutual friends. His visits made me happy because my parents were always on their best behavior whenever he was around.

In the middle of June, my mother went to the hospital to have the baby. My sisters, and I anxiously awaited Dad's call announcing the baby's birth. Dad finally called and announced he was the proud papa of five beautiful girls. I mouthed the word 'girl' and my sisters went wild. We couldn't wait to welcome Lisa Jean into our lives. I immediately bonded with Lisa the first time I held her in my arms. She was a beautiful baby with big, brown eyes and soft, light brown hair; she looked a lot like Linda. With her soft, little fingers clutching my pinky, I smiled her tiny face and silently promised to protect her for the rest of my life.

This was my fourth and final promise to a sibling.

The highlight of that summer was the day I received an invitation to a rush party sponsored by Theta Gamma Society. There were three active sororities at Jamestown High School, and they all held rush parties at Long Point State Park on Chautauqua Lake before the start of the school year. These parties enabled the current sorority members to meet some of the incoming sophomores and decide which ones would receive a bid in the fall. I attended that event with my closest friends from Lincoln, who like me, were hoping to get a bid to this coveted sorority.

The first days of school at JHS were a bit overwhelming with over two-thousand students flooding the halls. Once I became acclimated to my schedule, the new faces in my classes, and the layout of the school I was more comfortable.

Football season was in full-swing and Randy had been selected to be a starting half-back. I attended every game with my friends, cheering until I nearly lost my voice. The crisp fall air, the intense excitement of watching Randy run with the ball, the half-time music presented by the JHS Band and the vivacious cheerleaders all added to the party atmosphere that filled the stadium on Saturday nights. It was exciting to be dating the star player.

Following the games, dances were usually held at the YMCA.

Occasionally, a high school fraternity or sorority sponsored a dance at Hill Top Hall. Those dances were popular because they were not chaperoned. One Saturday night, while waiting for Randy and the other football players to arrive, I stood with my friends observing several couples as they slipped out the door and headed to their parked cars to make-out and drink beer.

As soon as Randy came through the door, he grabbed my hand and led me to the dance floor. After we had our fill of dancing, we quietly exited the back door into the parking lot. While walking through the lot, I noticed the steamed-over car windows and smelled the cigarette smoke floating through the night air. The sound of music coming from the car radios and the sight of empty beer cans scattered on the ground, added to the evening's excitement. We climbed into the backseat of a friend's car and instantly started to make- out. When things became too intense, I sat up, straightened my hair and rumpled clothes, and led the way back to the dance hall. Randy was frustrated while I was relieved.

At this time, I wasn't sure exactly how I felt about Randy. While he was sweet and considerate, I often felt smothered by him. Although his athletic prowess made him popular, he preferred spending most of his time with me, rather that his friends. Like my father, he was a loner. I still needed the support and companionship of my girl friends and it sometimes created problems in our relationship. I broke up with him on a couple of occasions, only to go back with him a few days later. I felt as if I were being torn between two worlds. His world finally won.

In early October, the sororities and fraternities sent out their bids. It was all my friends and I could talk about that week. Would we or wouldn't we get a bid? In a class of over six hundred students, half of them girls, the likelihood of receiving one of the fourteen bids offered by Thete seemed slim. Once again, I realized my closest friends from Lincoln had the criteria this sorority looked for—girls from well-established, middle-to-upper-class families. This was something I felt I lacked and worried I would not be selected. When I arrived home later that week, my mother met me at the door waving an envelope. My heart soared! My name, Diana Lynn Smith, was beautifully scripted in gold calligraphy on the front. I was elated when I ripped it open the envelope to find my invitation to join the Theta Gamma Society!

As an adult, I've often thought back to those days and why receiving this bid was so important to me. Because my family had moved so frequently during my elementary school years, I desperately needed to belong with a special group of friends. My membership in Delta Zeta and Theta Gamma provided me with the opportunity to bond with some wonderful girls who came from what I perceived as 'perfectly happy homes'. Joining these two sororities filled that void and helped bolster my self-confidence and belief that I was going somewhere in life. At the time, it was my life- line.

CHAPTER 19

Giving In

1964-1965

ON A WARM Saturday night in July, the seemingly calm conditions at home swiftly unraveled when my parents became embroiled in a horrific argument. Earlier that day, Dad, Mom, and Gina went to Smokey's while I babysat for my sisters. About nine o'clock that evening, I heard a car door slam and looked out the window to see them all staggering out of a taxi.

Anticipating a problem, I corralled my sisters and sent them upstairs. While sitting with them in my bedroom, I heard the sound of a loud slap, and my dad shouting, "You drunken slut!"

"Get your hands off of her, you bastard!' Gina screamed.

"Get the fuck out of my house, you bitch. This is none of your business," he shouted back.

"I'm not leaving Bonnie alone with you," she retorted.

The shouting continued. Suddenly the front door slammed shut. I went into the hall and saw my father running up the stairs in his stocking feet. When he reached the top, he slipped and fell backward. The loud sound of his head cracking against the newel post and the violent thud when he landed at the bottom of the steps, terrified me. Judy had heard the commotion and followed me down the stairs. I sat beside my father's listless body and checked his breathing.

"Is he dead?" Judy wailed.

"No, thank God, but I think he's unconscious. Keep the girls upstairs while I get some ice for his head."

While holding the ice pack on his head, I could see my mother passed out on the couch. Her mouth hung open, she was snoring loudly and she had a slight bruise on her cheek. The shrill sound of a siren and the flashing streaks of red lights coming through the windows startled me. I rushed to answer the loud knock at the door. When I opened it, I found Gina and two police officers standing there. I let them into the house.

By this time, Dad began to come around. When one of the officers examined him, he found he wasn't seriously hurt. Gina had obviously called the police and told them about the fight. Against my father's protests, they hauled him off to jail!

The commotion awakened my mother. She gratefully accepted the cup of coffee and cigarette Gina provided. Mom's hands trembled as she struggled to light her Tareyton. Inhaling a deep drag of her cigarette appeared to calm her. In her drunken state, she had no recollection of what had transpired.

I listened as Gina recounted the events leading up to Dad's arrest. According to her, the afternoon started out okay with my parents singing along with the jukebox and playing pool. As they continued to drink, they began to squabble. When the conversation turned to Frank, their dispute turned into a full-fledged fight. Overhearing this argument, some guy at the bar spoke up and said, "Everyone in town knows Bonnie is Frank's whore. Why don't you, Stew? Are you an idiot?" Dad jumped up from his bar stool and tried to grab the perpetrator around the neck. That's when Gina called the taxi and dragged them both out of the bar.

With a look of disgust on her face, Gina said, "You gotta' make Stew move out of this house, Bonnie or the next time he might kill you."

All of my pent-up anger erupted. "You're telling my mother to kick Dad out? Why? He's not the one who started this; she is!" I pointed at my mother.

Glaring holes through me with her steely black eyes, Gina shouted back, "Get off your high-horse. You're living in a fantasy world because you run around with all of your stuck-up friends!"

"I'll never get off of my high-horse you bitch! It's my ride out of here.
I never, ever want to be like you or my mother." I paused before adding, "Gina, get out of this house. You're nothing but a meddling, trouble maker, and you're a big part of the problem. LEAVE NOW!"

I locked the door behind her vowing never to let her back again, no matter what Mom said. My mother buried her head in her hands and moaned, "What have I done? What have I done?"

I sat beside her while she sobbed. When her crying subsided, I said, "It's time for bed, Mom. We've had enough for one night. We'll figure it out tomorrow." She slowly stood up and put her hands out to me. I led her upstairs to her bedroom.

Dad was terribly disheveled, downtrodden and ashamed when he returned the next morning. After giving each of his daughters a big hug, he walked into the kitchen and talked to Mom. Then he went upstairs to shower and pack. He was moving out again.

In about a month, Mom and us girls were moving out, too. Once again, my parents had fallen behind in the rent and we were forced to find a new place. Shortly after school started, we moved from our Seventh Street house to Boniwood, a small area on the outskirts of town. The large, four-bedroom house was run down but Mom encouragingly stated a little elbow grease and paint would make the world of difference to the place. Then she nonchalantly added, "By the way, did I mention Dad's coming with us?" Those words were enough to convince me the move was a good idea.

Although Dad had only been gone a month, we all missed him.

Part of me was saddened to be leaving our house on Seventh Street. Living in the same house for three years was a record for our family and had enabled me to attend Lincoln throughout my junior high years. I was grateful for the stability. The other part of me couldn't wait to leave the horrible memories behind.

We quickly settled into our new home. The picture window in our large, paneled living room reminded me of our house in Modesto. The breakfast nook in the kitchen provided a cozy place to enjoy our evening meals. My parents slept downstairs in a small room off the living room while my sisters and I had bedrooms upstairs. As the oldest, I was given the largest room. It didn't take long to fill my spacious room with memorabilia. A large bulletin board covered one wall while posters and photos decorated the other three. A pretty new bedspread with tiny pink flowers adorned my bed, and matching curtains hung at the windows. Mom justified the newly purchased items by explaining a teenager needs a beautiful room with plenty of privacy to entertain her friends.

I loved my new room and talked on my pink Princess phone with Lynn and JoAnne as often as possible. Because Randy's nightly visits took up most of my time, these conversations with my friends kept me in the loop. My parents treated Randy as if he was part of our family, dropping their guard when he was around. This gave him a bird's eye view of my life. I began opening up to him about my family problems. It wasn't long before he learned about Mom's constant drinking, Dad's frequent moodiness, my parent's financial woes, and my mother's affair with Frank. He became my confidant, offering words of support and suggestions. The more comfort Randy provided, the closer we became.

Before moving back with us, my father took a new job working the night shift at Blackstone Manufacturing in Falconer. He left home about three- thirty each afternoon and returned after midnight, tired and hungry. The nights I was still up when he came back, I had a fresh pot of coffee brewing on the stove. We sat at the kitchen table munching Ritz crackers slathered with peanut butter and talking. We talked about my school day, what the girls had been doing and trivial things. We seldom talked about Mom's drinking or Frank. Those topics were taboo.

One night, my father seemed extremely depressed as he gazed out the kitchen window, waiting to see the headlights of our old Ford shine through the window. I felt his pain. I hesitated for a moment before asking a question that had been on my mind for a long time.

"Dad, why do you stay? Mom keeps hurting you again and again. Why don't you move out and start life over?"

It only took a second for him to respond. Reaching across the table, he took my hand in his and softly said, "I won't leave because of you girls; you all need me. I know people are saying Linda and Lisa belong to Frank, but I choose not to believe that. They're my daughters, just like you. I'm the one raising them and tucking them in at night and that's all that matters. I love you all too much to ever leave you. That's why I keep coming back." I pretended I didn't see the tear trickling down his cheek.

I stood up, walked over and put my arms around him. "I love you very much, too. You're my father, and I don't know where I'd be without you. Thank you." After giving him a kiss on the cheek, I went to bed and prayed to God, thanking Him for sending Stew to be our father.

There were many nights when Judy tip-toed into my bedroom and crawled into bed with me. "My head hurts. Will you rub it, please?" she often asked.

I would pull her close and lightly massage her temples. Lying together gave us a chance to talk. Judy loved to hear stories about my friends and Randy. That night, my ten-year-old sister asked me why Mom and Dad were always fighting and why Mom drank so much beer. I answered as honestly as I could. There was one question she asked I could never correctly answer.

"Why does Mommy love Kim more than me?" "Mom loves you. She just shows it in different ways."

Not satisfied with my answer, Judy emphatically replied, "I know she doesn't love me! Whenever Kim tells her she feels sick, she gets to stay home from school and spend the day with Mom."

I explained that Mom tended to fuss over Kim because she almost died when she was born and had health issues when she was a baby.

Judy quickly retorted, "Remember when I used to get pneumonia? I have asthma, but she doesn't fuss over me. I beg her to let me stay home and spend the day with her by myself. I promise her I'll be good. I even tell her I'll help her clean the house and make her lunch, but she always says NO."

How could I answer that question? At the time, I didn't understand Mom's attitude towards Judy. As the years went by, my mother openly expressed her resentment of Judy. By the time Judy was sixteen, she began retaliating. Some of the battles between her and my mother turned physically and verbally violent.

Although the same pattern of resentment sometimes emerged with Mom's attitude toward Linda, Linda retreated rather than argue. As an adult, I've come to believe my mother was jealous of both girls because, at the time of their conceptions, Mom was deeply in love with each of their fathers. Emotionally unstable, my mother felt threatened by Judy and Linda because they received the attention she thought should be hers.

Randy enjoyed coming to the house in the evenings when Dad was at work, and Mom was out with her friends. He entertained Linda and Lisa while I assisted Judy and Kim with their homework. After the girls had gone to bed, he helped me clean the kitchen. Then we would cuddle on the couch to presumably watch television. It didn't take long for him to push me over on the sofa and start making out with me. At sixteen, Randy's testosterone levels were soaring. The more often he came to my house the heavier these sessions became, usually ending in a wrestling match. Holding him at bay was not an easy task. I felt it was my responsibility to keep things under control. When I wouldn't let things go any further, he often left angry and frustrated.

It went on like this for a long time, until one Sunday afternoon in early March. My parents and my sisters went to Warren to visit my grandparents. I had a history project due and opted to stay home. Not long after they left, I heard someone rapping on the back door. I peeked through the curtain and saw Randy standing there with a bouquet of fresh flowers in his hands and a sexy smile on his face. Whoa. A little voice told me I shouldn't let him in. I ignored that voice and opened the door.

As soon as I closed the door, he pulled me into his arms and began hungrily kissing me. He suddenly stopped, took my hand and led me to my bedroom. Neither of us said a word as he pulled me down on the bed. His tender kisses became more demanding and his hands traveled over parts of my body they had never touched. Afraid and excited at the same time, I tried to resist. I closed my eyes, quieted the little voice in my head and finally relented.

The Road Back to Hell

When he finished, Randy stepped out of bed and went into the bathroom, I lay there asking myself why I gave in. Filled with shame and remorse, I turned my face into my pillow and let my tears fall.

What have I done? Why? Where were the bells and whistles I read about in Mom's *True Story* magazines? Where was the magic? What's next?

The experience wasn't pleasurable as I had dreamed it would be; it was painful—both physically and mentally.

Randy returned from the bathroom and found me lying in a fetal position, huddled under my covers. He lay down beside me, apologized and promised everything would be okay. His assurances fell on deaf ears. I believed he was sorry, but I did not believe everything would be okay.

My voice was weak as I whispered, "You don't need to apologize. I'm as much to blame as you. I should have been stronger. Now we only have one choice."

"What?" he anxiously asked.

"To pray."

CHAPTER 20

Morning Reality

Spring 1965

SCALDING TEARS STREAMED down my cheeks onto my pillow as I lay in bed listening to the sound of my mother's nagging voice calling me to get up. Paralyzed by the terror in my heart, I could not force my leaden legs to move from the comfort of my bed. I realized the moment I put my feet on the floor, I would have to face the stark reality I'd been avoiding for over two months.

Mom's wake-up call wasn't necessary; I didn't sleep most of the night. In fact, I'd spent many sleepless nights the past few weeks. The rising sun casting its bright rays through my bedroom window annoyed me. I yanked the shade down to shut it out. How can the sun be shining when my heart and head are filled with so much pain?

Realizing I could no longer avoid the inevitable, I reopened the shade and let in the sunshine. Maybe it would help.

By this light, I was able to see my bulletin board filled with so many reminders of happier times—the dried flowers from the Spring Gala; a certificate for Citizen-of-the-Month from Lincoln Jr. High School; articles I'd written as a journalist for the local paper and my bid from Theta Gamma Society. I gazed at a photo of a young girl with a dazzling smile, dressed in a floor-length, emerald-green satin gown as she proudly stood next to a good- looking guy. I stood there remembering the wonderful time we'd had at the Snow Ball Dance in the Crystal Ball Room of the Hotel Jamestown. The next picture was Randy in his football uniform, looking proud as captain of the team.

In another photo posted on my board, I'm sitting with JoAnne and Lynn on the fifty-yard line of the Warren-Jamestown game, cheering the team on. Would I ever have happy memories like those again? I forced myself out of bed and wandered around my room picking up pieces of memorabilia. Each item, I held in my hands, evoked another beautiful memory. I donned my plaid Scottish Theta Gamma tam and looked into the mirror. I saw the reflection of a proud young girl the day she opened her bid to Thete. My stomach churned as I thought about my sorority sisters. They were my closest friends. What would happen to our friendships when they found out? Would they be as ashamed of me as I was of myself? Would I lose the respect of these treasured friends?

I was flooded with remorse when I lifted the Bible Granny C had given me on the day I was confirmed at Immanuel Lutheran Church. How would I be able to tell her what I had done? Unstoppable tears of shame flowed down my cheeks. I knew I would be hurting and disappointing everyone in my family when I finally told them I was pregnant.

It was painful to look at the eight-by-ten colored photo of me surrounded by my four beautiful sisters. I had arranged to have the picture taken in December as a gift to my parents on Christmas. It had been a hassle to get four young girls dressed in their Christmas outfits, walk them to the studio and keep them still for the sitting. But the hardest part was keeping it a secret from Mom and Dad.

I'm fifteen-years-old in this picture. My mid-length brown hair is styled in a flip; I resemble my mother through the eyes. I'm proudly smiling as I sit in the center with little Lisa on my lap. The light-brown curls tumbling onto her forehead accentuate her big, brown eyes. Linda is three in this photo and is standing beside me. She's wearing a red pinafore trimmed in white rick-rack and a white, puffy-sleeved blouse. Her hair is pulled into a ponytail, and her long, dark brown bangs draw attention to her pretty brown eyes. Both girls resemble Frank.

Kim is standing directly behind Linda. She chose to wear her favorite hunter green dress with a white, embroidered inset. The faint smile on her lips and the shape of her eyes show her resemblance to Granny C. Judy is standing next to me on the right. She is dressed in a dark-green jumper and a blouse covered with Christmas designs and is almost a head taller than Kim. If her shoulder-length hair was short and her horned rimmed glasses were removed, she would look just like Dad at ten. There's no question about where the familial traits shared by Judy and Kim come from—they are definitely Dad's.

Surrounded by my darling sisters, I look like their mother. I am usually the one they come to when they fall and get hurt, the one who has to solve their battles, the one who tucks them into bed many nights and listens to their prayers. I am the thread that binds us all together; but maybe not for long.

After studying this picture, I set it down and knelt on the floor by my bed. I prayed, "Dear God, please forgive me. How could I let myself get into this situation? My family will be so disappointed and hurt when they learn the truth. I can't think about the baby growing inside me. It's too painful. How can I bring an innocent child into this world and this life; a life I've been trying so hard to escape? What will become of my four sisters if I have to get married and leave home? Please help me find the answers." Prayer calmed me. I was ready to face the day ahead.

The night before, I had called Mom's best friend, Shirley, and asked if I could come to her house after school. I explained I had a personal problem I needed to discuss with her and asked her not to mention it to my mother. I grudgingly went to school. Throughout the day, I watched the ticking clock as time slowly passed. When the dismissal bell rang at three o'clock, I hurried to a phone booth in front of the school and called a taxi. During the ride to Shirley's, I silently rehearsed what I would say when I arrived at her house. She was waiting for me on her front porch. When the taxi pulled into her driveway, she ran off the porch, wrapped her arms around me, and walked me into her welcoming kitchen. Gesturing me to sit at the kitchen table, she retrieved a Coca Cola from the refrigerator, handed it to me and bluntly asked, "What's wrong?" I broke down. My sobs prevented me from speaking.

Shirley, a registered nurse, worked for Dr. Chambers & Dr. Carlson, two local obstetricians. Finally, able to compose myself, I blurted out, "I'm pregnant, and I need your help." I felt like an enormous weight had been lifted from my shoulders when I got those terrible words out in the open. The only friends I had shared this secret with were Randy, JoAnne, and Lynn. I desperately needed an adult to help me make the right choices. Shirley took a long drag off her L&M, and softly asked me what I wanted to do.

"I've thought and prayed about this every day since my last period. After seriously thinking it through, I've decided to have an abortion."

"Why?" she quietly inquired.

"Shirley, you know what my family life is like. My mom and dad are always fighting about Frank; my mother drinks like a fish and Dad isn't far behind. The girls are lost because of the separations and attempted suicides. There's barely enough money to care for us. How can I possibly bring a child into this environment?"

"How far are you along?" Shirley inquired.

"About three months."

Shirley laid her head in her hands, as she contemplated how to reply. She lifted her head and said, "Honey, are you here to ask if I can help you get an abortion?"

I reluctantly nodded my head. She reached out for me. I walked into her waiting arms as she whispered, "I wish I could, but it's too late for an abortion. If you had come to me when you first thought you were pregnant, I might have been able to help you. Now there's nothing I can do. I'm sorry."

Crestfallen by this news, I sat there digesting her words. I could hear the 'little voice in my head' assuring me everything would work out. I realized if I had an abortion, I would never have been able to forgive myself; nor would God. Bolstered by this thought, I replied, "I understand. The next step is to tell my parents. Will you go with me?"

I was filled with dread when we pulled into our driveway. Before leaving the house that morning, I lied to my mother and told her I was going to JoAnne's house after school. She was shocked when I walked into the kitchen with Shirley following closely behind.

She frowned and asked, "What's going on?"

"Bonnie, grab your jacket, we're going for a ride," Shirley replied in her no-nonsense, take-charge voice.

Shirley pointed to the door, and I followed her outside. My mother came rushing out the door as if this was an emergency. From the driver's side window, Shirley told Mom to sit in the back with me. She sped out of the driveway. She drove around the back roads for about an hour while I poured my heart-wrenching story out to my mother. Mom cradled me in her arms and tenderly stroked my hair, just like she had when I was younger. The comfort of her love pouring into me was something I desperately needed.

When I finished talking, my mother said, "Diana Lynn, everything will be okay. Daddy and I will help you through this, and if you decide you don't want to get married, you and the baby can live with us."

I sat upright, looked into her eyes and softly said, "Mom, I love you and appreciate your understanding, but I've decided adoption would be best for my baby."

Her profound shock, disappointment, and anger were revealed through her eyes. She turned her head away and firmly replied, "We'll talk about it later. Right now, you need to tell your father."

Telling my dad was the most difficult part of that long day and the thing I dreaded most. I knew telling him I was pregnant at sixteen would destroy his hopes for my future. I could feel the pain of the knife as it plunged into his heart. The blood on that blade would be on my hands forever.

When we pulled into our driveway, I pleaded with my eyes for my mother to come with me. As if reading my mind, Mom said, "This is something you need to do on your own. Your dad loves you very much, and he needs to hear it directly from you. Go on. Shirley and I will wait in the kitchen."

My leaden feet carried me from the car into the house. Dad was sitting on the sofa when I walked through the door. He opened his arms and beckoned me. I rushed into his waiting arms and began to wail. "Daddy, I'm pregnant and I'm so, so sorry."

"Snookey, don't say another word. I've known for a while. I've been waiting for you to come to me," he whispered into my ear. Shocked, I lifted my head from his chest and asked, "How did you know?"

"I've noticed a change in you. You've been nervous and out of sorts lately. It's not like you to behave that way which made me wonder if you might be pregnant. I love you and we'll get through this together. Don't think about it anymore, you've been through enough for one day."

"Thank you, Daddy. I love you very much and I don't know what I'd do without you."

I let out a big sigh when I realized my worst fears were over, and my family would support me through the rough months ahead. Having been aware of several girls who became pregnant out of wedlock and whose parents were not supportive, made me thankful for my parents.

Mom woke me up at two o'clock in the morning and announced she was taking my dad to the hospital. The pain from his hemorrhoids had become unbearable. I got out of bed, kissed him good-bye and wished him luck. After pouring myself a cup of coffee, I began to laugh.

"Thank goodness," I chuckled to myself. "I thought I was Dad's biggest pain in the ass!"

CHAPTER 21

Moving Forward

Summer 1965

I WAS GREATLY relieved after telling my parents about my pregnancy. But before I talked to anyone else in my family, I needed to speak to Randy. He came to my house and we sat on the porch quietly discussing our plans for the future. Our conversation went something like this-

"I've given our situation a lot of thought and decided I should go away to a home for unwed mothers until the baby is born."

He appeared shocked by my decision. "Don't you want to get married?" he asked.

"Do you?" I countered.

"Not really. I'd have to quit school and get a job, and that would end my chances of getting a football scholarship."

"Exactly," I replied. "That's one of the reasons I've decided to go away. If we get married, we'll be doing it for the wrong reasons. How could that work? You'd eventually feel trapped, and we'd probably start fighting, like my parents. I won't raise a child in that environment. Our child deserves a better future." I was not as confident about this idea as I sounded.

I had sent an inquiry to The House of Hope, a home for unwed mothers, located in Buffalo, New York, a two hour drive from Jamestown. They sent me a brochure explaining the fees, housing availabilities and the counseling assistance they offered. They also included the procedures they followed when selecting prospective parents. It wasn't a perfect solution, but at the time, it seemed to be the only one.

Before leaving, Randy told me he loved me and said we'd get through this together. He promised to tell his mother as soon as he got home.

It wasn't necessary for me to tell my sister, Judy; she already knew. A few days before my parents found out, Judy had walked into my bedroom and found me struggling with my girdle.

"Need some help?" she asked. "Yeah, I think I do."

"You're skinny, why are you going to wear this thing?" She asked as she tugged at my girdle.

What should I say to my eleven-year-old sister? Should I lie or tell her the truth? Because my parents would soon know, I decided to be frank with her. I sat down on my bed and motioned for her to sit beside me.

"Judy, I'm going to tell you a big secret and you have to promise not to tell Mom and Dad, okay?"

After she had agreed, I spent the next half-hour explaining my dilemma. I told her I made a big mistake, one that would hurt everyone. I shared my shame and fears. Because I was her older sister, Judy had always respected and admired me. I apologized for letting her down. When I finished my story, Judy grabbed my hands, squeezed them tightly and told me she loved me more than ever for telling her the truth. As she walked from my room, I realized she had just experienced an important 'growing-up moment'. By sharing my secret with her, I had treated her like a young adult. She seemed a little more confident when she walked out the door.

Grandma and Grandpa Conklin were next on my list. I was heart-sick on the ride to Warren. My grandparents had invited me to go the World's Fair in New York City later that summer. They thought we were coming to discuss the trip. Although they would be disappointed when they learned I wasn't going on vacation with them, I knew they would be heartbroken when they learned the reason why.

When I told Granny C, she reacted as my father had, accepting and supportive. She took me by the hand and led me into the privacy of her bedroom where she shared her secret with me. She had been pregnant with my father when she married Edwin Smith. Through sharing her secret, at the time I needed it most, we formed a special bond that lasted as long as she lived.

I wasn't worried about my mother's family because Adeline and Bonnie were both pregnant before they were married. In essence, I was following in their footsteps. This was not something I had planned to do nor was I proud of it. The reason I was reluctant to tell Grandpa Woodard and Uncle Kenny is because I worried they wouldn't keep it a secret. I was adamant that no one except my family and my two best friends, JoAnne, and Lynn know the truth. Keeping my pregnancy a secret had been one of the main reasons I planned to go to Buffalo.

Although I loved my mother for the support she had so quickly offered when she learned I was pregnant, part of me thought she was a little pleased with my predicament. She had watched me strive to rise above the dysfunction in our lives, and I sometimes felt she resented that. My major misstep had brought me back into the reality of our lives. I believe my mother was happy I was back 'in-the-fold'.

It was difficult, but I kept my secret hidden deep inside my heart.

Mom and I spent hours talking about my plans to go to Buffalo. She was dead- set against it and repeatedly said I should remain at home. Her opinion didn't sway me; I was determined to go to the home for unwed mothers.

An unexpected opportunity presented itself when my cousin, Mary, called my mom. She and her husband, Jim lived with their one-year-old daughter in a lovely suburb of Buffalo. Jim worked for IBM, which afforded Mary the opportunity to be a stay-at-home-mom. Mary kindly suggested I spend a week at their house before entering the home which would give us an opportunity to bond. During my stay at the House of Hope, she said she would visit me and occasionally bring me to their home on weekends. My mother was comforted knowing Mary would be close-by if I needed anything. After mulling it over for a few days, she finally consented to my decision to move to Buffalo until the baby was born.

One major dilemma I faced was explaining my absence to my friends when school started in the fall. I planned to tell my friends I was going to spend the summer in California with my aunt and uncle. I contacted Uncle Jerry in Modesto and told him everything, including my plans to give my baby up for adoption. Remembering his tumultuous childhood made it easy for him to support my decision. My primary objective in calling him was to seek his help. I devised a scheme to send him manila folders containing addressed, stamped letters I had written to my friends in Jamestown. Once he received the envelope, he would remove the letters and drop them into the mailbox.

My friends would then receive my cheerful letters bearing a California postmark. He readily agreed to it.

I approached my parents with rest of my plan. I wanted to have a going-away party at the beginning of July. I invited over forty friends, some of them Randy's pals, to the party. The guys had to leave by eleven, but the girls would be spending the night. JoAnne and Lynn were still my only friends who knew the truth about my trip. As my closest friends, I knew I could trust them to keep my secret.

My spirits soared while planning this party. However, they started to plummet when I thought about the days and months ahead.

The night of the party, a steady stream of cars drove in and out of our driveway as parents dropped off their daughters and sons. The girls hauled their sleeping and overnight bags into the living room while the guys threw footballs back and forth in the front yard. As the sky began to darken, music blared from the stereo speakers sitting on the front porch. The sounds of the Beach Boys, The Four Seasons and the Beatles could be heard all over the neighborhood. The girls danced in the firelight while the guys gathered more sticks from the nearby woods for the bonfire. We were high on Coca-Cola. In 1965, that was enough; the drug scene had yet to reach Jamestown.

When the party was in full-swing, I slipped away for a moment of solitude. I stood in the darkness of a wooded area in my backyard, praying for forgiveness for lying to my friends. While I understood it was wrong to lie to them, I also realized I couldn't stand up and boldly announce I was pregnant. In 1965, unwed mothers were scorned. I convinced myself it was better for my friends to think I was enjoying myself in sunny California, rather than pity me. It was better for Randy, too. He had a big football season ahead.

A short time later, I returned to the party. After the boys had left, the girls made their nests inside. I spent the rest of the night laughing, talking, singing and dancing with my high school friends. I hoped the memory of this night would sustain me during my hiatus.

The next week, I started to prepare for my stay in Buffalo. I packed some of the regular clothing I was still able to wear, along with a few maternity outfits my mom had purchased for me. Watching my stomach grow was a painful reminder of the tiny baby inside me. I stayed as busy as possible so I wouldn't have time to think about it.

As the time neared for me to leave, the atmosphere at home became more tense. My mother came into my room at least twice a day, begging me to stay home. Although my dad acted aloof, I knew he was hurting. My sister, Judy broke into tears at the mere mention of my departure. At nine, I don't think Kim realized what was happening. Linda and Lisa were lost in their world of pretend and noticed nothing amiss. I visited with Gussie and Grandpa Elmer promising to write them while I was away. Granny C and Grandpa Conklin stopped by to see me before they left for New York. Granny C was still trying to convince me to join them, but I just couldn't. I felt unworthy of going on their special vacation with them.

The night before I left, Randy came over. We spent the entire evening walking the back roads by my house and talking about the future. We pretended everything would be okay after I did 'what I had to do'. We both knew it was a farce. Nothing would ever be the same again.

On a Saturday morning at the end of August, Mom and Dad drove me to Mary's house in Buffalo. My parents admired the beautiful homes as we pulled into the cul-de-sac of their housing development. After we'd parked in their driveway, Mary and Jim came out to greet us. Mary was my mom's first cousin and Christmas Eve and summer picnics were the only times we'd spent together. Consequently, I didn't know her very well. She was also six-years older than me which meant we had little in common. I was nervous about my week's stay. *What would we talk about? Would I annoy her? What would I do while I was there?* I almost turned to

Mom and said, "Forget about it, I'm coming home." But I didn't. I made this decision, and I was sticking with it.

While Mary served refreshments, Jim carried their daughter, Sandy, into the kitchen to meet me. When she gave me a big, toothy grin and held her arms out to me, I immediately relaxed. If Mary and I had problems communicating, I knew I'd get along just fine with little Sandy.

After visiting for about an hour, Dad announced it was time to go. My heart sank. *Please don't go so soon.* He went to the car, retrieved my beat-up, borrowed suitcase and carried it into the room where I'd be sleeping. I followed him. As soon as he put my bag down, he hugged me and promised everything would be okay. He said if I got too homesick, I could call him and he'd come and get me right away. I was relieved by his words. Faking a big smile, I replied, "Dad, I'm strong. I'll be okay."

Mom stood in the doorway waiting to kiss me good-bye. When she grabbed hold of me, she started to cry. I comforted her and repeated the words I had said to my dad. She made me promise to call every day. Before leaving, she handed me a bag, instructing me to wait until they left to open it.

Later, when I opened the bag, I found a copy of "Gone with the Wind." My mother had taken me to that movie years before. She remembered how much I loved it and bought me the book. I was moved by her thoughtfulness and read that book every chance I had. By the time I left Mary's, I had finished it.

Mary and I worked together on the daily chores. I enjoyed entertaining Sandy and talking over coffee with Mary. She told me how she and Jim had met; their plans for the future and their desire to have more children. Because of the uncertainty of my future, I found it more pleasant to listen than to participate in these conversations. If these discussions had taken place six months earlier, I would have shared my desire to attend college to become a journalist or a teacher. I may have shared my dreams of meeting my perfect mate in college; obtaining a job in my field; eventually marrying and having children, and living happily ever after. Isn't that what every sixteen- year-old wants?

At night, I lay in bed thinking about Randy, my family and my friends in Jamestown. Sometimes, I would touch my belly and wonder about the little child inside. Is it a boy or a girl? Will it be happy and healthy? When these thoughts became too much to bear, I would bury my head in my pillow and say a prayer. Then I'd cry myself to sleep.

Although my week with Mary was enjoyable, I was ready to leave on Saturday. I needed to get on with my journey. The anticipation of what lay ahead overwhelmed me.

My cousin, Suzie, and my mom came to get me around ten o'clock on Saturday morning. They had a quick cup of coffee with Mary while I loaded my suitcase into Suzie's car. Mom apologized for being in such a rush to leave by explaining she was anxious to check out the 'home.' After thanking Mary for her hospitality, we promptly left.

We drove around downtown Buffalo looking for the House of Hope. When I spotted it, Suzie found a space and parked out front. The turret in the corner of the large, red-brick building reminded me of a castle. The grounds leading up to the entranceway were beautifully landscaped and the leaves on the maple and oak trees were slightly turning color. I remember thinking, *"If the inside is as nice as the outside, I believe I'll like it here."*

"Diana Lynn, we're taking your suitcase inside and reporting to the front desk. Then we're going to lunch before we sign you in." Mom firmly stated.

"Sure, Mom, whatever you say," I replied from the back seat.

Suzie insisted on carrying my suitcase while Mom and I tagged behind. When I started up the front steps, my legs began to tremble. Not wanting my mom to notice my fear, I freed my hand from hers and bravely strode through the front door. The brightly lit lobby was filled with casual chairs covered in soft green and blue fabrics and a flowered sofa with end tables on each side. It felt homey. I breathed a sigh of relief.

Before I could say a word, Mom marched up to the front desk and announced my arrival. The woman behind the counter smiled and welcomed us. My mother told her she was taking me to lunch and we'd register when we returned. Although the receptionist appeared to be surprised by this, she politely responded, "That's okay Mrs. Smith. We'll get Diana registered when you return. Enjoy your lunch." We left my suitcase by the door.

Suzie was sitting in the driver's seat with the engine running when we got to the car. She drove about two blocks and stopped at a Howard Johnson's Restaurant. Mom seemed a little jumpy when she got out of the car. She waited until the waitress took our order before she started her speech.

"Diana, you can't do this! I'm your mother, and I know you better than anyone. If you stay there for three months, you'll be a changed person. They'll fill your head with crazy ideas, and if you decide at the last minute you want to keep your baby, they won't let you. You have to come home."

My head was spinning. She went on like this for fifteen minutes. She said most of the girls staying there were not like me; they were probably wild and would ruin me with their city ways and bad habits. "You'll end up hard and bitter if you stay there. I've talked to a lot of people and I know what I'm saying is true."

Talked to a lot of people? Who told you these things, Mom? The drunks you meet in barrooms?

Every time I tried to speak up, my mother interrupted me with another reason I shouldn't stay at that home in Buffalo. Suzie, who had been quiet during my mom's tirade, began nodding her head in agreement with most of the things Mom was saying. The longer Mom talked, the more confused I became.

"You tell her, Suzie. Tell her about your friend."

Suzie looked at me and in her husky voice said, "It's true. The sister of one of my best friends stayed there when she was pregnant. She gave her baby away, and she's never recovered from it. Maybe you should listen to your mom." Suzie, my favorite cousin and friend, was telling me not to stay! I couldn't believe it.

We hadn't touched the lunches sitting before us. I couldn't think. I couldn't speak. All, I could do, was cry. Finally, I quietly spoke up. "All right, you win. Let's go home."

Mom slapped a fistful of cash on the table, and we abruptly exited the restaurant. Suzie drove to the House of Hope. My mother ran into the lobby, grabbed my suitcase and jumped into the car. She didn't stop to tell the receptionist I wouldn't be staying.

We sped off like thieves in the night.

CHAPTER 22

The Hiding Place

Fall 1965

ON THE RIDE home, it felt like a tennis racket was bouncing a myriad of questions back and forth inside my head. What would I do about school? How could I hide at home for three months? Would I be able to find a loving couple to adopt my unborn child? What would Randy say when he learned I was back? Overwhelmed by these unanswerable questions, I decided to wait a few days before making any serious decisions.

Dad and my sisters were delighted when they saw me get out of Suzie's car. Linda and Lisa rushed up and clung to my legs while Judy and Kim wrapped their arms around me. They made room for Dad to join in the group hug. His eyes lit up when he told me I had made the right decision by coming home. I wasn't convinced. I called Randy as soon as I went inside. He sounded shocked and a little disappointed. Later that day when I heard Mom talking to our relatives, I prayed they would keep it a secret.

Next morning a car raced into our driveway. After it had come to a complete stop, my cousin Mary stepped out. Mom and I rushed out onto the porch. The anger in Mary's eyes leaped out at us. She was livid.

Before she reached the porch, she began screaming "Bonnie, what in the hell are you doing? Why did you bring Diana home?"

Startled by this unexpected confrontation, my mother stiffened her posture, crossed her arms over her chest and retorted, "What do you mean?"

"How could you do this? Diana wanted to get away so she could have a future and a better life for her baby. And now you've brought her back to this?" she exclaimed while twirling her hands in the air, pointing to our shabby house and yard.

"Just who in the hell do you think you are, Mary, to come to my home and tell me what to do with my daughter?"

"I'll tell you who I am! I'm an intelligent woman who understands Diana's baby doesn't stand a chance-in-hell if it's raised in this household!"

Although I appreciated Mary's support, I didn't try to stop my mother when she moved forward and pushed Mary onto the front lawn.

Mary stood up, brushed the dirt off her pants, shot Mom a look that could kill and headed back to her car. Her car tires squealed as she drove out of the driveway.

Mom was visibly shaken when she went back into the house. She opened the refrigerator, pulled out a Blatz and drank half of it in one gulp.

"No one is going to stand in my yard and tell me how to raise my children," my mother ranted. "NO ONE!"

I had stood on that porch and watched in disbelief as Mary and my mother argued about what I should do. What about my thoughts? I had the biggest stake in all of this— my future and the future of my baby. Why couldn't anyone understand? I poured myself a cup of coffee and asked Mom to join me at the kitchen table. We needed to talk.

During our talk, we settled a number of things. Mom promised to call the high school, explain my situation to the principal and find out if I was eligible for a tutor. She also offered to make an appointment for me with Drs. Chambers and Carlson and she vowed to keep my pregnancy a secret, if I promised to stay home. I agreed to the deal only if my mother fulfilled her promises. If she didn't, I told her I'd get my suitcase and find another ride to Buffalo. Emotionally drained, I went to my room.

Mom had always been a drama queen, and this latest episode provided her with a great story to share with Gussie and Mom's two best-friends, Shirley and Arlene. After our discussion, she slugged down the beers while she called them to tell them what had transpired. By mid-afternoon, she was soused and staggered when she came into my room.

Apparently someone in the family had told her Mary was hoping to adopt my baby, and that is why she was angry I didn't stay at the Hope House. This news surprised me. During the week I had spent at Mary's house, she never indicated any interest in adopting my child.

When Dad got home from work, he found Mom passed out on the couch and me standing over the stove making supper. Things were back to normal in the Smith household. After dinner, we talked over coffee.

"I'm sorry, Snookey. I know you thought going away was best, but maybe in the end it wasn't. I have to agree with your mother. I worried about the effects the environment at the home might have on you. We'll just have to make your plan work here."

And we did. We made the most of a very difficult situation.

Randy, JoAnne, and Lynn were the only friends I communicated with during my self-imposed exile. With this limited number of personal contacts, I was stunned one evening when my mother announced someone was here to see me. Who? How did anyone know I was here?

I reluctantly walked into the living room and into the waiting arms of Pastor Daniels. Holding my face in his large hands, he looked down at me and said, "You're going to be fine, Diana. With the help of God, you'll get through this."

"How did you find out?" I quietly asked.

"Your mother called and asked me to come."

He sat beside me on the couch and listened as I shared the entire story. When I finished, he calmly said, "I understand how you feel. I'm sure this has been quite an ordeal for you, but you're a strong, driven young woman with a deep faith in God. He'll be with you through your trying times and He'll guide you when the time comes to make a decision about the baby."

Pastor Daniels had encouraged and supported me during my confirmation classes. During this time, he learned about many of the conflicts I was dealing with at home. I had the utmost respect for him; his words calmed me more than anything else had over the past few months. Why hadn't I reached out to him before?

As promised, Mom made arrangements with the school for a tutor to come to our house three days a week. I desperately missed school and was anxious to start my studies. I was relieved to learn the principal had emphasized that my tutor must comply with the confidentiality rules, and under no circumstances, could she or he reveal my pregnancy or my identity to anyone.

My instructor arrived the next week, carrying an armful of textbooks, papers, and notes. She was a pleasant looking, middle-aged woman with short, dark-brown hair and a slightly chubby face and body. I was reassured by her warm smile. She introduced herself saying, "Hello, Diana, I'm Mrs. Cook, and I'll be your tutor for the next few months."

I wanted to run from the room. Brenda Cook was Randy's former girl friend and I was terrified she may be Brenda's mother. "Are you Brenda's mom?" I asked.

"Yes. Do you know her?"

"I had a few classes with her at Lincoln but I don't see her much at the high-school. You're aware that no one in school is supposed to know I'm pregnant and staying home, right?"

"Of course I am. As a teacher, I have to honor the privacy code. You don't have to worry, your secret's safe with me."

I had no choice but to believe her. We sat down and got to work. I began to look forward to her visits. My daily assignments provided me with something productive to do during my home-stay.

That evening, I called Randy and told him Brenda's mother was my tutor. He expressed some concern and promised to keep his ears open for any rumors. Next I called Lynn. I felt better when she reminded me her father was the president of the JHS school board. If Mrs. Cook broke the privacy code, she would probably lose her job. That should keep her quiet.

Lynn's and JoAnne's parents were very supportive of my situation. Several times, Mom drove me to Lynn's house to spend the night. We left after dark so no one could see me riding in the car. As an extra precaution,

I'd lie down in the back seat of our big, black '57 Ford. There was one occasion when I thought my well-kept secret might blow up in my face.

One Saturday afternoon in September, Lynn invited me to her house.

I was hesitant to ride in the car during daylight hours, but Mom told no one would see me lying in the back seat. I climbed into the back seat with Linda and Lisa. We were about a mile from our house when the engine started to sputter. We came to a dead stop in front of a small service station directly across from the Foote Avenue Plaza. My heart sank. *Now what?*

My mother started to swear. She stepped out of the car and shouted, "This is just great! I don't have a dime on me and here we are stuck on the highway. Get out of the car, we have to walk back home."

"No," I announced from the back seat. "What?"

"I said no. I'm not getting out of this car and parading down the street where everyone can see me. I refuse. Please call Grandpa, he'll come and get me."

After arguing for a few minutes, Mom finally relented and marched into the service station to call Grandpa Woodard. She came back to the car and told me my grandfather was on his way. She berated me for my righteous behavior, grabbed the girls by the hand and proceeded to walk over a mile back to our house. When Grandpa's car pulled into the service station, I put a towel over my head and crawled into his back seat. He burst out laughing. He laughed even harder when I told him what Mom had said.

"You two are quite the pair."

He dropped me off at Lynn's. That evening, after darkness descended we went to 7/Eleven to buy some snacks. Lynn retrieved her brother's hunting jacket from the closet and tossed it to me. Although I looked ridiculous in his hunting cap and coat, it did the job. It was exciting to be incognito as we snuck through the alleys and side streets to the store. We spent the remainder of the night laughing about our 'reconnaissance mission'. Her parents kindly drove me home the next day. They weren't upset when I lay down in the back seat, they understood.

During the day, I was busy with my tutor, doing homework and helping Mom with the household chores. I spent my evenings entertaining Judy, Kim, Linda, and Lisa. Dad was at work, and my mother was usually out somewhere. At eleven, nine, four and two, the girls needed me. In turn, I needed them.

One night when I was reading my younger sisters a story, Linda poked my protruding belly. "Mommy said you have a baby in there. Can I see it?" How do you answer that question?

"Honey, it's impossible to see the baby because it's inside my tummy." She squinted at me through her big, brown eyes, and asked, "When it comes out of your tummy, can I hold it?"

"We'll see." Those were the only words I could think to say.

How could I tell her none of us would be holding this child because I'm not going to keep it? The thought of never looking at my baby or holding it, was more than I could bear. At night, when I was in bed, I would sometimes feel a faint kick reminding me of this beautiful unborn child and the decision I felt had to be made. Those were the most difficult nights of my pregnancy—the nights I would cry myself to sleep.

On another evening, I was walking into the kitchen and caught Judy pushing Kim around while trying to get her pen back.

"Give me that pen back, you brat, it's mine," Judy hollered as she rushed at Kim and knocked her to the floor.

I yelled, "Judy, that wasn't necessary! Help Kim get up and apologize to her."

"No!" Judy retorted as she ran to her room.

Kim was lying in a heap on the floor, bawling. Trying to calm her, I knelt beside her and stroked her hair. I told her Judy had done something wrong, and she would be punished for it.

"Good," Kim uttered. A little surprised by this adamant statement, I asked why she felt that way.

"You always take Judy's side. You love her more than you love me." Her words made me stop and think. Do I always take Judy's side? I pondered this statement before responding, "Kimmie, I love you as much as I love Judy.

Sometimes I do protect Judy, too much, but it's because Mom is always protecting you and I feel like Judy needs someone to be on her side. Can you understand that?"

"I guess so," Kim replied.

I helped her up from the floor and led her into the living room. We sat on the couch discussing the situation and resolving some serious issues. I realized it was the first time my nine year old sister and I had ever had a heart-to-heart talk. It was comforting sharing our feelings and thoughts.

Through the years, Kim and I never shared the same closeness as I had with my other three sisters. She usually went to Mom with her problems and the other three came to me. As adults, a situation transpired which left us estranged for many years. In 2001, when our beloved Grandmother Conklin was dying, Kim drove to Warren, PA from North Carolina, and I drove up from Brookville. We spent a week together at Granny C's. By spending this time together, we were able to talk, laugh and cry about our life experiences. The pain of losing Granny C enabled us to heal the pain we had caused each over the years and we forgave each other.

Saturday nights were the loneliest night of the week for me. I'd sit in my room listening to the high-school football games and wondering if all of my friends were there watching it. I missed going to the games more than anything else. I remembered the thrill of standing in the bleachers or on the sidelines cheering Randy on as he rushed towards the goal post. One night, as I listened to the game on the local radio station, I heard the announcer say, "There he goes folks! Sharp's heading towards the thirty… the twenty….the ten. He's over the goal line! Touchdown!" I began to feel sorry for myself thinking, *I should be there, too. This isn't fair.*

Self-pity disgusted me. I tried to avoid it by reminding myself that I put myself in this position. I allowed it to happen. After my small pity-party, I usually got over it. But that night my self-pity turned into anger, verging on rage. Our house in Boniwood was directly across the road from Hill Top Hall where most of the dances were held after home games.

I became really upset thinking about Randy across the street dancing with some other girl. It was all I could do to keep myself from donning my oversize jacket, crossing the street and walking up the hill to the dance. I envisioned myself walking through the door, seven months pregnant, opening my coat to reveal my big belly and shouting, "Has anyone seen Randy Sharp?"

I started to laugh as I pictured this scenario. Laughing was much better than crying.

Even though my due date was only about a month away, my mother and I avoided discussing my decision about my baby. She couldn't understand why I believed giving my child away was the best option. One day, late in September, she had the opportunity to explain why she was adamant I keep my baby.

We were on the way home from my doctor's visit when she turned onto Maple Street. Since this wasn't the way home, I asked where we were going. "You'll see," she replied.

She slowly drove down the street and parked the car. Mom pointed to a two-story, light-blue, clapboard house. "See that house?" I nodded. "Your brother lives there."

My brother? What in the world does she mean? I don't have a brother.

Her eyes misted over as she said, "I've never told you this before, but I think it's time I do. Before I met your dad, I became pregnant and had a baby boy. You and I were living with Grandpa and Grandma Woodard, I wasn't married, and my parents were struggling to take care of the two of us. The only choice open to me was to give him up for adoption. It broke my heart, but I did it for him and for you."

Minutes passed before I grasped what she was telling me. I sat there as she shared her experience. His name was Denny, and he didn't know any of us existed. She had promised the adoptive parents she would never contact him until he was at least twenty one. Over the years, she had learned that his adoptive parents were kind and loving. Knowing Denny had a nice life provided my mother some peace, but she thought of him every year on his birthday and on the holidays. She said she'd parked the car on this street a couple of times, hoping to get a glimpse of him. When she finally saw him, it was all she could do to keep from jumping out of the car and running to him. After that day, she never stopped again. When she finished her story, I was speechless.

"I hope you understand why I'm dead set against you giving your baby away. I don't want you to suffer as I have."

I looked at my mother through different eyes after she shared this with me. When she was a young girl, what had her life actually been like? How could she have been pregnant out of wedlock two times? Where were her parents through all of this? How much had she suffered? Was this one of the reasons she turned to alcohol? Who was I to judge her? It's taken me almost fifty years to come to terms with it, and I still don't have all of the answers.

On the ride home, I found the courage to ask her something I'd been thinking about for a while. "How do I get in touch with Don King?"

Surprised by this question, she pulled over once again. "Why on earth would you want to contact him?" she asked.

"I need information about my family genetics before I have my baby. I want to provide the adoptive parents with a complete history of the health issues in our family," I answered.

My mother hesitated before speaking. "There's no sense in trying to reach Don King because he isn't your real father."

This was the second whammy in the last half-hour.

"I was born Diana Lynn King, so he has to be my father." In a meek voice, I added, "Doesn't he?"

Once again, my mom revealed a part of her life I knew nothing about. When she was fifteen, she had a relationship with one of Kenny's friends and became pregnant. He refused to marry her. I later learned that her brother Kenny paid Don King to marry my mother so I would have a name.

She revealed my father's real name and told me a little about him. She cautioned me that if found my birth father and communicated with him, Stew would be deeply hurt. That sentence ended any further thoughts about finding my natural father. Stew was my dad, and I'd never intentionally hurt him. I dropped the subject. Marrying Stew and allowing him to adopt me was the best gift my mother ever gave me. Stew's love for me was unconditional. We didn't need blood to bind us. We were bound together by our love, faith and trust in one another. He was my rock. I loved him with all of my heart, as he loved me. I miss him every day.

Dad usually came home from his night shift about twelve-thirty in the morning. If I was still awake, I'd brew a fresh pot of coffee and set out a snack. We'd sit at the kitchen table and talk. Whenever I had a problem, I'd discuss it with him. His wise insights often helped me keep things in perspective.

"Dad, have you always known about Denny?"

After swallowing his last bite of pie, he slowly responded, "Yes. Your mother shared that with me just before we were married. She made me promise to keep it a secret. It's been rough watching her suffer all these years."

"She's still suffering?" I innocently asked.

"Of course, she's still suffering. Giving your child away is something most women can never get over."

"Ever since Mom told me about Denny, I can't stop thinking about it. One day I believe I'm doing the right thing by finding a wonderful couple to adopt my baby, and the next day I wonder if it will be a big mistake. What if the people aren't kind? What if they don't love him or her like I would?"

"I know your mother told you about Denny because she doesn't want you to make the same mistake, but we'll support whatever decision you make."

"Thanks, Dad. That means a lot to me. I'm luckier than a lot of girls in this position whose parents don't give them the chance to make up their own minds. Where would I be without the support of you and Mom?"

At the time, I didn't actually know anyone in my position, but I had heard stories about girls who were immediately sent to homes for unwed mothers when their parents learned about their pregnancy. While I was very grateful my parents were behind me, no matter what choice I made, I realized that the final decision would ultimately be mine to make. I thought about it every night and worried that I might make the wrong decision— a decision that would affect my unborn child and me for the rest of our lives.

"What does Randy think you should do," my father asked. This question startled me because I honestly didn't know what Randy thought.

When I went to bed that night, I remembered Pastor Daniel's words. I got down on my knees and asked God to be with me when the time came to decide.

The next week, I went into labor, three weeks before my due date.

CHAPTER 23

Survival of the Fittest

Fall 1965

While struggling to wake-up from the effects of the anesthetic, I looked around the room trying to figure out where I was. All I remembered was a flurry of activity involving nurses, a doctor asking my name and someone telling me to count backward from one hundred. When the fuzziness in my mind started to clear, I opened my eyes. A big man with curly, graying hair, heavy-lidded eyes and a beatific smile was sitting beside me holding my hand. I looked into the eyes of Pastor Daniels and asked, "Is it over?"

He gently squeezed my hand and nodded. We sat in silence as he witnessed the tears slowly dripping from the corners of my eyes.

"Where's my mother?"

"She stayed with you from the time you came into the hospital until after the delivery. She was exhausted. Fifty-four hours is a long time to sit in a hospital. I suggested she go home and get some rest."

"What day is it?"

Pastor Daniels looked at his watch. "It's ten-fifteen in the morning on Friday, October 22nd."

The memory of the past few days came flooding back. I recalled having sporadic labor pains on Tuesday afternoon. When my mother called the doctor, he instructed her to keep me at home until the pains became more regular. My parents took me to the hospital about ten o'clock that night. I vaguely remember lying on a hard, uncomfortable bed for a long time. My pains were close enough that they wouldn't send me home. At one point, I requested a television. The nurse laughed and told me they didn't have TVs in the labor room. When I complained I was starving, she said I could only have broth. I must have dozed off from boredom and starvation because I couldn't recall much else, including the pain.

Now it was over. My belly bump was gone along with a part of my heart. I knew my stomach would heal, but I wasn't sure if my heart ever would.

"Where do I go from here, Pastor Daniels?"

He held my hand in his and said, "I have faith you'll make the right decision. The answer lies with you and God. Let's pray." We did.

After being settled into my private room, I was finally alone, which gave me the chance to sort out my feelings. I lay there wondering if my baby was healthy, whether it was a boy or a girl, what color hair and eyes it had and which nurse in the nursery was holding it. Was she tenderly kissing my baby and holding it close to her heart? I wanted to rush out of bed to the nursery and grab my child from her arms. But I knew, once I held my baby, I would never be able to do what I had to do. I pushed these thoughts from my mind by convincing myself my decision to give up my child was the only way he or she would have a chance at a better life.

My thoughts were interrupted by my parents entering my room. We shared tears, hugs, and kisses, but we didn't discuss my pending decision. As much as I needed some guidance, I needed their understanding and support even more. They stayed with me the remainder of the day and didn't leave until seven that evening. Before leaving, they told me they would support whatever decision I made.

In 1965, having a child out of wedlock was a disgrace to the girl and her family. Her child was considered a "bastard". Most girls were encouraged, and even forced to go away during their pregnancy to either a home for unwed mothers or to stay with a family friend or relative. After the baby was born, they generally gave them up for adoption. I was very fortunate because my parents were allowing me the right to make my own decision. Although they wanted me to keep my baby, they understood my reasons for giving my child a better chance in life through adoption.

Shortly after they left, Uncle Kenny and his wife, Eileen came in to see me. Eileen was a beautiful, heavy-set, redhead with a very outgoing personality. She was Kenny's third wife, and I believe, his best. My family thought she was a great influence on my uncle. Uncle Kenny proudly announced they had just purchased a new Singer sewing machine for me as a gift because they knew how difficult the past few months had been. Their surprise lifted my spirits until they told me the real reason for their visit.

My uncle cleared his throat and asked, "Gogi Lynn, are you still planning to give your baby up for adoption?" (When I was a baby, he had nicknamed me Gogi, and he called me that for the rest of his life.)

I sighed. "Yes, I believe I have to."

With her smiling Irish eyes, Eileen looked into my saddened Irish eyes and said, "Kenny, and I have been talking about this for a long time. I'm sure you know I'm not able to have children, and we both desperately want one. Would you consider allowing us to adopt your baby?"

Wham! I felt like someone hit me with a hammer! Although I loved my uncle very much, I didn't respect him. He was a heavy drinker, an unreliable worker, and he had been in and out of trouble all of his life.

Why can't anyone understand? I do want to keep my baby, I just can't bear to raise my child in the environment my sisters and I have lived in all these years. I'm too young to raise my baby alone, and I don't think Randy and I should get married. All I want for my child is a happy, safe life with two loving, respectable parents.

I started to cry. I couldn't talk.

"I'm sorry, Diana. We didn't come here to upset you. We just wanted you to know how we feel. Will you think about it?" Eileen asked.

I slowly nodded. They kissed me good night and left.

Shortly after they left, the nurse came in to give me my meds and check my vitals. When she'd noticed I'd been crying she said, "Here, honey, take this pill, it will help you sleep. You've had a tough day. Tomorrow you'll feel better, I promise." She closed the door when she left the room.

I was comforted by the silence of the room. I closed my eyes and let my mind drift back to better times. I remembered when I was a toddler following my mom around like a puppy. I pictured Stew's smiling face the day he adopted me. I could almost feel the strong, love and devotion my parents felt for each other when I was a young child. If our home life were still like that, I wouldn't be considering giving my baby away. I would keep it.

I prayed, asking God to guide me through the night and lead me to the right decision. The social service officials would be bringing the adoption papers for me to sign the next day, and I had to be ready.

After a while, I turned on the television above my bed. Emotionally drained, I was in need of a distraction. I chose one of my favorite shows, Slattery's People. I enjoyed watching Richard Crenna in his role as a state senator, as he tackled societal problems in the courtroom. That night, the show merely provided background noise until I heard the words 'foster child'. From that moment on, I focused all of my attention on this show.

The premise of this episode dealt with the difficulties many young foster children incur when placed in unsuitable homes. It focused on one young boy who'd been lost in the system. This young boy had been moved from home to home where he was often treated badly. In this particular episode, the young boy had to testify in court about the physical abuse he had suffered at the hands of his current foster parents. Every word in this program spoke directly to me.

What if this would happen to my child? How can I be sure that the parents who take my baby will provide the kind of love and security my child will need?

After mulling these questions over for a long while, I found my answer and the peace I'd been seeking for months.

Early Saturday morning, the nurse came into my room and woke me up. I asked her when my doctor would be in to see me. She said he made rounds about eight o'clock. The clock on the wall read seven. I had a long hour ahead of me.

Shortly after eight o'clock, Dr. Chambers nonchalantly strode into my room. "Let's see how you're doing today," he commented as he physically examined me. "Everything looks great. Has anyone told you about your baby?"

Seeing the shocked look on my face, he quickly reiterated, "Oh, that's right, they didn't tell you because you're not keeping your baby."

"But I am keeping my baby, Dr. Chambers. I thought about it all night and decided I can't give my baby away!" I retorted.

"That pleases me. I'm never in favor of adoption if it can be avoided, but it's not my place to say anything. The final decision rests with the mother. I think you made the right choice, young lady."

"What's wrong with my baby, Dr. Chambers?"

"Your child was born with a cleft palate. It's not a life-threatening problem and can be repaired with surgery. Don't worry about it now, you can deal with it later."

I had no idea what a cleft-palate was nor did I care. All I wanted was to hold my baby in my arms. Learning about this condition further convinced me I had made the right decision.

A little while later my parents walked into my room carrying a bunch of balloons and some flowers. Dad leaned over, kissed my forehead and said,

"We thought these might cheer you up, Snookey."

Mom leaned over the other side the bed, took my face into her hands and said, "Diana Lynn, your dad and I have something we want to tell you."

Before she could say anything else, I blurted, "No, Mom. First, I have something to say. I'm keeping my baby!"

My mother was crying when she said, "That's what we were going to tell you! We talked all night and decided keeping your baby was the right decision for you, your baby and all of us!"

Making that joyous announcement helped lift the immense tension I had been feeling for the last nine months. We started laughing, crying tears of happiness and talking all at once. Dad's next comment stopped us in our tracks, "Is it a boy or a girl?"

Oh my God. I hadn't asked Dr. Chambers the gender of my child! Dad helped me out of bed as my mother grabbed my robe. Together, we walked down the hall to the nursery. There, lying in an incubator was my five-pound, four-ounce beautiful baby! The sign on the bed read Baby

Boy Smith. I stared at his tiny fingers, the soft, dark fuzz on top of his head and his beautiful eyes as he slept. I desperately needed to hold him. The nurse motioned for me to enter the nursery. She carefully picked him up and placed him in my waiting arms. I'll remember that moment forever.

A lot happened during the remainder of my hospital stay. I called Randy to tell him I had decided to keep the baby and assured him I was prepared to care for him on my own. After a few moments of silence, he said, "Boy, this is quite a shock. I need some time to think. Will you call me when you get home?"

I named my son Todd Stewart Smith, his middle name in honor of my dad. My parents were thrilled to have a baby boy in our family. I was immensely encouraged by their enthusiasm and love, and prayed things would all right.

The only visitor I had, outside of my immediate family, was my best friend, Lynn. She volunteered as a Candy Striper at the hospital and came into my room on the days she worked. She fully supported my choice to keep my baby and told me her parents were buying a crib for Todd. It would be delivered to my house before Todd and I went home.

The next bit of news she shared was unsettling. Lynn told me she had heard through the high-school grapevine that Brenda was telling her friends I was pregnant. Upon hearing these stories, she had followed Brenda into the girls' restroom where she accosted her about the situation.

"I know you're responsible for starting the stories about Diana, so don't deny it. You'd better tell all of your friends you made that story up or my father will make sure your mother is fired. As President of the Board of Education, he can do that. Do you understand?"

Shocked by this encounter, Brenda weakly replied, "Okay. I'll fix it. I'm sorry." Soon after their discussion, the story died.

I laughed as I pictured Lynn shaking her finger in Brenda's face and threatening her. Lynn wasn't a high-school brawler, but when angered she became one of the most sarcastic people I knew. I admired her for protecting me and treasured her friendship even more.

Another upsetting incident occurred while my parents were visiting. On Sunday evening, a man we had never seen before pushed his way into my room. He was a tall, heavy-set man with a receding hairline and fierce eyes. He stared at me from the bottom of my bed and shouted, "You are a sinner! You're damned to hell for having a child out of wedlock!"

When my mother saw the fear on my face, she jumped into action. She stood up and forcefully said, "I don't know who you are, mister, but get the hell out of my daughter's room right now. Our pastor is giving her spiritual support. He knows her; you don't. How dare you judge her?"

Before he could say another word, Dad grabbed the guy's arm and pushed him out the door. It took us a few minutes to recover from his unexpected outburst. We later learned from one of the nurses he was an evangelist who made it his job to spread what he perceived to be God's word. The hospital received complaints about him quite often. Mom declared that he didn't have the right to act as my judge, jury, and executioner, and she certainly would be filing a complaint.

I was released from the hospital a few days later. My sisters were waiting on the porch when we got home, anxious to meet their little nephew. It was hard to believe my two-year-old sister, Lisa, was his aunt.

After everyone had held him, I carried him into my parents' downstairs bedroom and laid him in his crib. I was surprised to see the stack of baby clothes and packages sitting on the bed. Waving my arms in the air, I asked, "Where did all of this come from?"

My parents, family members and family friends, including the Ottosons and Lynn's folks, had provided these unexpected gifts. What a blessing. While in the hospital, I worried about getting Todd all of the things he'd need. I was grateful for their generosity and kindness.

As promised, I called Randy. He told me his mother was anxious to see the baby and asked if they could come to my house the next evening. I spent that night wondering how Randy would react when he saw his son for the first time.

The next night, when Randy entered our house, he went directly to the bedroom and peered into the crib at his beautiful sleeping son. He softly touched his little face. I lifted Todd from the crib and placed him in Randy's waiting arms. His eyes filled with love as he held him. After holding him for a few minutes, he gently passed him to Marion. At that moment, I realized whether we married or not, the Sharps would always be part of Todd's life.

As planned, I had sent letters to my friends (via Uncle Jerry) informing them my aunt was ill, and I was extending my California visit to assist her while she recuperated. Although I was ashamed to be lying to my friends and creating a non-existent illness for my lovely aunt, I believed I had to do it so I would be able to hold my head high when I returned to school. This fabricated story helped keep the rumors at bay. Before my return to school, JoAnne and Lynn announced I was home from California. When I went back to school two weeks after giving birth to Todd, my friends warmly welcomed me. It was wonderful to be back in the classroom and spending time with the girls during lunch. But when the bell rang at the close of the school day, I couldn't wait to get home to my baby.

During that week, some of my friends asked if I would be attending the upcoming football game and if Randy and I were getting back together. Had he broken up with Cheryl now that I was home?

How the hell did I know? Who was Cheryl? When had he started dating her? After fielding these questions, I decided not to attend Saturday's football game. Instead, my friend Debbie persuaded me to go to the Co-ed Club at the YWCA that evening. Co-ed Club was a place where most of the sorority and fraternity members hung out after school. They sat around drinking cokes, listening to the jukebox, playing ping-pong, gossiping and smoking.

On Saturday afternoon, while I was caring for Todd and doing chores, I pondered my decision to go to the Y. During my first week in school, I only encountered a handful of friends. How would the others react when they saw me? What would I do if Randy was there with Cheryl? I considered staying home, but my mother encouraged me to go to the Y. She thought an evening out would be good for me. I spent an unusual amount of time getting ready for my first social outing. Thankfully, I hadn't gained much weight during my pregnancy, so my slacks and sweaters still fit. When I glanced into the mirror, I was surprised to see a young teenage girl with sparkling eyes and an innocent smile staring back at me. My outward appearance was one of confidence while inwardly I was a wreck.

Dad dropped me off at Coed Club about eight o'clock that night. From the top of the steps, I could hear the sounds of laughter and the band tuning up for the dance. I was terrified as I walked down the short stairway into the club. The dim lights made it difficult to see. I was thinking about leaving when one of my sorority sisters spotted me standing in the doorway. She rushed over and embraced me. She beckoned my other friends, "Hey girls, look who's here!" Surrounded by some of my Thete sisters, I began to relax. They dragged me to their table and bombarded me with questions. I smiled and joked about my made-up adventures. Their warm laughter comforted me.

After the high-school football game, loads of other kids came into the club. Feeling a little claustrophobic, I decided to go outside for some fresh air. On the way up the steps, I came face-to-face with Randy. His arm was draped over Cheryl's shoulders, and he was whispering into her ear. They were as shocked at encountering me as I was at seeing them. I cast my eyes downward, ran up the steps and out the door. I rushed up the street to the Prendergast Library.

I sat on the big, stone wall in front of the library, buried my face in my hands and cried. After I had composed myself, I walked to the phone booth and called home. When my mother answered the phone, I began crying again. "Mom, please send Dad to get me."

"Honey, what's the matter? Are you hurt? Where are you?"

I stopped crying long enough to let her know I was okay but needed to come home. I told her my location. About fifteen minutes later, Dad drove the car into the lot and parked it. He walked up to me and cradled me in his arms while I wept.

We sat there for a long time while I expressed my feelings. I explained that I felt like an outcast, even though most of my friends had been happy to see me. My pregnancy had changed me; I didn't fit in anymore.

Although I'd been excited about attending the dance, I began to feel lost and lonely after I got there. I missed Todd and needed to get home. The reality of seeing Randy with another girl upset me more that I cared to admit. How could he have a new girlfriend? I felt dirty inside and couldn't imagine dating another boy. Who would date an unwed mother? When I finally quit rambling, Dad talked me through most of my doubts.

These are the most important words he spoke that night. "Diana, you've always been a people person. I've been a loner. Do you know why?" When I didn't answer, he continued, "I was popular in high school, just like you. But one day my best friend, a fellow basketball player and someone I'd grown up with, betrayed me by dating the girl I thought I was going to marry. The break-up with Sally, and the betrayal of my friend, hurt me very much. In fact, I never got over it. That experience taught me one of life's great lessons. It's wonderful to have friends, but in the end, the only person you can ever count on is yourself. You have to believe in yourself because there's no one else to depend on when the chips are down."

He ended with, "It's called survival-of-the-fittest. No one will ever be more interested in your well-being than you. Always remember that, and you'll be okay. I promise."

I will always remember my father's wise words and the comfort he gave me on the night when I needed it most. Through the years, I have treasured my special friendships and found our relationships to be very rewarding. I have also learned to depend on myself when it comes to solving life's problems. It has helped.

CHAPTER 24

A Family United

Winter 1965

IT WAS AN unusually warm day in mid-November, and I was sitting on the porch swing holding Todd while I watched Linda and Lisa playing in the yard. Suddenly, Judy came running out of the house to tell me a man was on the phone who needed to talk to Mom right away. I handed Todd to her and hurried into the kitchen. When I lifted the receiver, I sarcastically asked, "Who is this and what do you want with my mother?" I assumed the man calling was someone Mom had met in a bar.

"Your mother needs to get to the hospital right away. Your Dad cut his hand off!"

Dad. Cut. His. Hand. Off. What? It took a moment to digest his words. My sarcasm turned to fear. "What are you saying? What happened?"

The caller's voice was shaking as he described what had happened. The machine Dad was operating had failed, causing my father's hand to be crushed by a five-thousand pound press. The man on the phone had been next to him. When he noticed blood pulsing out of Dad's right wrist, he removed his belt and used it as a tourniquet to control the bleeding.

"Thank you so much. It sounds like you've saved my father's life. My mother will be at the hospital very soon," I promised him before hanging up the phone.

I quickly dialed Smokey's. Gina answered. When Mom came to the phone, I told her about Dad. Thank God she was sober. She started to cry and said she'd ask someone to drive her to the WCA Hospital immediately. I hung up. My legs trembled, my hands shook, and my heart pounded like a jackhammer. I collapsed into the nearest chair. When I'd settled a little, I walked outside to tell Judy and Kim. I put my arms around them, drew them near and said, "Girls, Dad was hurt at work today, and Mom is on her way to the hospital to be with him."

Judy started to cry and Kim stared in disbelief. I hugged them tightly and emphasized that while Dad's injury was serious, it wasn't life threatening. I asked them to watch the two younger girls while I made some calls. Judy wiped her tears and runny nose on her sleeve before heading towards Linda. Kim grabbed Lisa and took her inside to watch TV. I lay Todd down in his crib.

Recruiting Judy and Kim to babysit provided me with the time I needed to organize my thoughts. I didn't want my sisters to know how upset I was.

Dad's hand had been crushed; so had my heart. Would the doctors be able to save his hand? Could he bleed to death? What would he do about a job? How would we pay the bills? He might never be able to play the piano again.

During the five-hour operation, the doctors were able to save his badly mangled hand. However, he faced a long and arduous recovery. Mom stayed in the hospital with him all night. When she walked through the door the next morning, her eyes were puffy and swollen from crying and lack of sleep. I poured her a cup of coffee, and we sat at the table talking. I finally convinced her to get a bath and go to bed.

The days that followed were a blur. Mom cared for Todd while I went to school. When I arrived home at three, I took over so she could visit Dad. The outpouring of support from family, friends and Dad's co-workers was fantastic. Every day, someone brought us a prepared meal or called to ask what we needed. I don't know how we would have made it through this ordeal without them.

Dad was released from the hospital two weeks later. Judy, Kim and I stayed home from school to welcome him back. At the first sight of our old Ford, we ran outside to greet him. Mom had warned us to be careful of bumping into Dad's injured hand, so we hugged his legs and softly patted his left arm. When I saw the determined look in his eyes, I knew eventually he'd be okay.

Life had abruptly changed in the Smith household. Dad was on a medical leave of absence for an undetermined about of time and he went to physical therapy several times a week. Mom got a job in a dress shop and I began working weekends at a local nursing home. My dad split the household duties with Judy and Kim.

As bleak as things seemed, these drastic changes brought hope. Our family was working together as a team for the first time. The future looked brighter.

My fondest memory of this ordeal was of my father caring for Todd during the day while I attended school. With the use of only one hand, he devised a way to bathe Todd on the kitchen counter and change his diapers. He gently cradled Todd in the fold of his right elbow while feeding him a bottle with his left hand. He amazed me!

In mid-December, Randy called to tell me his brother, Tom, and his wife, Sue, had invited us to their home for dinner. Earlier in the month, Sue had given birth to their first son, William Joseph. I was nervous about meeting the Sharps for the first time, but the moment I walked into their charming home, any uncertainty faded away. Tom was a strikingly handsome man, with dark hair, dark eyes, and a winning smile. Randy resembled his older brother. The warmth and beauty of Sue emerged through her friendly, smiling eyes. I was then introduced to their darling daughters, Stephanie and Laurie.

Stephanie, the older of the two, looked like a beautiful porcelain doll with curly dark hair and almond-shaped eyes. She appeared to be shy like her father. Laurie reminded me of a fairy princess with blonde hair, sparkling eyes like her mother, and a pretty smile. These little girls stole my heart, just as their mother had.

After dinner, Sue and I sat on the couch, holding each other's son.

We laughed about the things our boys would probably do as they grew older. Todd provided our first family memory when he peed all over Sue's couch while I was changing his diaper. Through our conversations,

I realized Sue assumed we were getting married. Randy and I still hadn't come to that conclusion. By the end of the evening, I found myself wishing Todd and I could become part of this beautiful family. We needed them. My desire for a normal, loving family grew even stronger when I met Randy's sister, Janet and his brother, John.

Through the years, Sue and I became best friends. I was drawn by her warm personality, witty sense of humor and loving heart. Over the years, we have shared many happy, sad and traumatic experiences. Randy's sister Janet, his brothers, Tom and John, and his mother, Marion, all touched my life in special ways. I have been blessed to be part of their family.

As December 25th drew near, the excitement of Christmas filled our house. My sisters understood there would be fewer gifts under the tree this year. We all realized we had a lot to be thankful for— our parents were happy, Dad was getting better every day, and there was a new baby in the house.

We were blessed.

CHAPTER 25

The Truth

1966

My parents were unable to keep up with the rent and we were evicted from our house in Boniwood shortly after Christmas. Mom rented a three-bedroom duplex on Broadhead Avenue. On a cold, blustery winter's day in January, Grandpa Woodard, Uncle Kenny and several of their barroom friends moved us into our new home. We'd moved so many times over the years, we'd become efficient packers and un-packers. Sometimes we'd be completely settled within twenty-four hours.

My personal life drastically changed. I attended school every day and went to my monthly sorority meetings. I talked on the phone to JoAnne and Lynn and occasionally spent time with Randy when he came to visit Todd.

After that fateful night at Co-ed Club, I avoided social events whenever possible. However, there was one social opportunity I couldn't resist. Every day in biology class, I sat beside a good-looking guy with a great sense of humor. Although we teased and flirted with each other during class, I was surprised when John asked me to a school dance. I didn't immediately accept his invitation. After mulling it over for a few days. I finally agreed to go.

The night he came to pick me up I was very nervous. After introducing him to my parents, I rushed him out the door so he wouldn't hear Todd's cries or see the bassinette in the dining room. On the way to the dance, I struggled to make conversation. Everything in my life had changed, and the trivial things we talked about seemed inconsequential. While he was talking about basketball, I was thinking about Todd. When we were dancing and he pulled me close, I gently pulled away. High-school dances no longer excited me. My pregnancy had caused me to mature much more rapidly than my peers. On the ride home, I chided myself for my duplicitous behavior.

What would he think if he knew the truth? I felt dirty inside. At the end of the evening, he walked me to my door and kissed me good-night.

"Thanks for going to the dance with me, I had a great time. Can I call you again?"

"Sure," I replied. "Thanks for taking me."

As he walked away, I realized he was a great guy, one that I didn't deserve. I really wanted to date him again, but I couldn't. How would he react when he learned I had a three-month- old baby at home? I convinced myself he would hate me. Every time he called and asked for a date, I made up an excuse. I finally quit taking his calls; he got the message.

I never again attempted to date anyone in high school. Because Randy continued to come to the house to see Todd about once a week, it was only natural that we would start seeing each other again. We were still uncertain about marriage, and agreed to keep our relationship under control. Sometimes it was difficult, but we never had sex until the day we married.

While my self-confidence had plummeted, Todd's birth had been a blessing for our family because my parents were doing their best to provide a healthy environment in which to raise my son. Everyone benefited. Mom and Dad stopped arguing. My father was finally able to return to work. Judy was enjoying school. Kim demonstrated her artistic skills by drawing cartoonish characters and hanging them all over the house, and Linda and Lisa became perfect companions for Todd.

It delighted me to see Linda and Lisa fussing over Todd. They raced to be the first one by my side whenever I fed or changed him. I'd been worried they may be jealous of him, but they loved him like a brother.

Two issues continued to cause problems. The first one was Mom's drinking. Now that Dad was working again, she quit her job to stay home and care for Todd. She waited until I got home from school to open her first beer. On the nights she stayed home she consumed six to eight cans before going to bed. The nights she went out with her friends continued to cause friction between my parents.

The second issue was Frank. He'd stopped visiting when we lived in Boniwood. As Mom put it, Frank and my dad were on the 'outs'. When he found out about Dad's accident, he came around again, offering his friendship. Although I couldn't understand it, they'd apparently resolved their problems.

Frank still created excitement in the neighborhood whenever he parked his ice cream truck in front of our house. Sometimes he came bearing gifts—big banks for Judy and Kim; trinkets for Linda and Lisa and a baby gift for Todd. I reluctantly accepted it.

During the day, my mother once again played her stereo. While working around the house, she sang along with her favorite artists —Doris Day, Dinah Washington, and Patsy Cline. When we were younger my sisters and I learned the words to most of Doris's songs. Our favorite was, "Que Sera, Sera-Whatever Will Be, Will Be," and we occasionally entertained our parents with our Smith Sisters rendition. Mom's new favorite artist was Patsy Cline. She played "Crazy" so often I thought I'd go crazy.

My sister Judy spent a lot of time with Mom's friend, Shirley.

Recognizing Judy's middle child complex, Shirley gave Judy her undivided attention whenever she could. Like my dad, Judy had a lovely singing voice; Shirley encouraged this talent. One afternoon, Shirley called my mother to tell her she'd discovered an amazing young girl who sounded just like Patsy Cline. Holding the receiver close to her ear, I watched Mom's facial expressions change from nonchalance to disbelief.

"Omigod, Shirley! Who is singing? She sounds like a young Patsy Cline!" Mom commented.

"Don't you recognize your daughter's voice, Bonnie? It's Judy." Unfortunately, my mother didn't believe it was Judy singing. My sister would always remember my mom's unforgivable slight.

The newly found peace our family had been enjoying came to an abrupt end in early March. Judy was sent home from school because she was sick. When she arrived home and couldn't find Mom downstairs, she went looking upstairs. On the way up the steps, she heard strange noises coming from my parents' bedroom. Judy pushed open Mom's bedroom door and saw my mother naked in bed with Frank straddling her. She screamed, ran into her room and locked the door. She squeezed her eyes tightly shut, trying to erase what she had just witnessed.

Mom pounded on Judy's locked door and begged her to open it. Judy refused. She screamed, "I hate you! You're nothing but a pig and I'm telling Daddy what you were doing!"

"Your dad has been through enough, Judy. If you tell him what you think you saw, it will kill him," Mom said as she walked away from the locked door. Those words were enough to persuade Judy to keep it to herself, for a while.

Tuesday nights were my mother's bowling night, and it was the weekly tradition for Judy and Kim to go to the store for ice cream. After they had returned, Judy followed Dad into the kitchen. No longer able to keep what she'd seen to herself, Judy began to cry and told Dad about what she'd witnessed the week before.

The house was completely lit up when I arrived home from my job at the nursing home at eleven that night. The loud shouts coming from inside the house filled the air. The first thing I noticed upon opening the door were the things strewed all over the living room— pictures, books, couch pillows, knick-knacks and empty beer bottles. Cigarette butts from the tossed ashtrays littered the floor. I found my mother sitting at the table, sobbing. Her black mascara was smeared under her puffy eyes, and her neck bore red scratch marks. She slurred her words when she yelled, "I'm not in love with Frank! Judy lied. She did it to make you hate me! Judy is jealous of me. Why can't you see that?"

I had never seen my father so angry. The color of his eyes had darkened, his face was covered with red blotches, and his hands were trembling. Hatred oozed out of him as he rebutted, "You drunken whore! I'm not letting you sit there and call my daughter a liar! You're the liar. You always have been." Tears streamed down his face as he rushed past me on his way out of the kitchen.

I left my mother sitting there while I ran upstairs to check on the kids. I found them huddled together in Judy's room. Todd was wrapped in his blanket safely sleeping on the bed with Linda and Lisa snuggled beside him.

Judy and Kim were sitting with their backs against the wall, crying. Kneeling before them, I asked them to tell me what had happened.

Judy cried uncontrollably as the words gushed from her mouth. She had been afraid to tell me what she'd witnessed with my mother and Frank. This eleven-year-old girl kept the secret locked tightly in her chest for over a week. Tonight, as she watched Mom walking out the door, she realized Mom wasn't going bowling; she was meeting Frank. That's when she decided to tell my father what she had seen.

I held her while she cried and listened to every word. Then I pulled Kim close to me and wiped away her tears. After both girls had calmed down, I carried Todd back to his crib. I left Linda and Lisa asleep in Judy's bed. On the way downstairs to confront my mother, I noticed the bathroom door was closed. I assumed my dad was in there.

My mother hadn't moved from her perch at the kitchen table. Her hands shook as she attempted to open another beer. I crossed the room, slapped her face and took the beer from her. I proceeded to the refrigerator and removed the remaining six-pack. As I was heading outside, Mom hollered, "Hey, where are you taking my beer?"

"I'm pouring it down the sewer where it belongs!"

Mom ran after me hollering, "Diana Lynn, you can't do that. It's mine!"

I dumped the beer in the backyard and returned with the empty cans. "It's not your beer any longer. It's time to make a choice, Bonnie Jean. You have to choose between the beer and Frank or your family."

She glared at me as she screamed, "How can you talk to me this way? I'm your mother!"

"My mother? What mother? She left us all a long time ago!" I spun on my heels and went to check on the kids.

When I reached the top of the steps, I smelled a faint odor. It took a second before I realized it was natural gas. Frantic, I ran to the bathroom and tried to open the door.

"Dad, open this door now!" No response." You have to open it. If you're attempting to kill yourself, you'll be taking us all with you!" I shouted. He opened the door a crack and solemnly said, "The gas is off. I turned it off as soon as I realized the girls were upstairs."

It was my father's first and last attempt at suicide, his call for help. I sat on the bathroom floor while he propped himself against the wall. We talked in hushed whispers for a long time. He told me he'd come close to choking my mother to death for calling Judy a liar. He believed he had failed my mother as a husband and felt his only redeeming quality was his faithfulness to his daughters. He announced he was moving out the next day and promised to seek counseling.

After checking on my sisters, I lay awake waiting to feed Todd his bottle. He usually woke up about two every morning. I desperately needed to hold him in my arms.

I spent the rest of the night devising a plan of action. My mother's affair with Frank had taken its final toll, and I was determined to do what I could to end it, once and for all. At five o' clock in the morning, I tiptoed downstairs and took the car keys from Mom's purse. It was still pitch black when I started the car and drove downtown to an all-night coffee shop. I didn't have a driver's license, and I didn't care.

My mom had once mentioned that Frank came to this coffee shop about six every morning, so I waited inside the parked car until I saw Frank's truck pull into a parking space across the street. I gave him time to get a cup of coffee and sit down at a booth before I strode into the restaurant.

The shocked look on his face when he saw me approaching his table was priceless. He didn't have to say a word; the expression on his face said it all. Guilty!

I parked my ass in the booth across from his and stared him down. He squirmed. Knowing he was uncomfortable brought me great joy. To hide his discomfort, Frank turned on the charm. He put on his Casanova grin, winked at me and said, "What brings you out this early in the morning?"

No answer.

"Want a cup of coffee?"

"Not a good idea. If you bought me a cup of coffee, I'd throw it in your face, you dago bastard!"

"Whoa. Is that any way to talk?"

"I'll talk to you any way I want to. You're the reason I'm out at this time of the morning. I've been awake all night waiting for this place to open up so I could tell you, face-to-face, to stay away from my mother. Stay away from my sisters and stay away from our house. I hate you for destroying our lives. You called my sister a liar. She's not the liar, you are! You've degraded my dad by using him as a friend the whole time you were screwing his wife, and you've turned my mother into an alcoholic!"

He was speechless for a moment. Then he sarcastically shot back, "I didn't turn your mother into an alcoholic, she was an alcoholic when I met her." His last remark was totally untrue. Before meeting Frank, my mother only drank when she went out socially with my father. It was after they started their affair that she had begun to drink more often.

Noticing the cup of coffee sitting in front of me, I picked it up and flung it in his face. "Stay away from my family you bastard!" I walked out, started the car and drove home.

CHAPTER 26

The Wedding

1966

THE NEXT DAY, Dad rented a room at the YMCA. He came to the house to pack his clothes and say goodbye. Mom hid upstairs in her room. The events of the night before had taken their toll. My father was a broken man and looked like he'd aged ten years. He gathered all of us in the living room and told us why he was leaving.

"Girls, I love you with all of my heart but I need to go. It isn't good for you to see Mom and me fighting like we did last night. Mom loves you; she just doesn't love me anymore. It will be much calmer for everyone if I move out. I'll come to visit, I just won't be living here."

Linda and Lisa became very emotional when they saw Judy and Kim start to cry. Although the older girls had been through situations like this many times before, they were still heartbroken.

"I won't be far away. I'm staying in a nice room at the Y. I'll call you every day and come over a couple of times a week. Diana will bring you to visit me as often as you want. There's a big piano in the lobby, and I'm going to try to play again."

It comforted me knowing Dad was going to attempt to play the piano again. He kissed us goodbye and carried his suitcase to the waiting taxi.

After Dad had moved out, my mother put on her smiley-face and paid a great deal of attention to us. I continued to give her the cold shoulder. With Dad gone, Judy saw an opportunity to get some much-needed attention from Mom. As always, Kim remained loyal to Mom. Linda and Lisa were happy as long as they had their cereal, cartoons and were able to play with Todd.

Dad kept his promise and called every day. Mom went out on the nights he came to visit. Those evenings, he played with the younger girls and helped Judy and Kim with their school work. He held Todd on his lap while we talked over coffee. He usually had left before Mom came home.

Frank never darkened our door again. No more ice cream man. One night, Dad called and asked me to bring my sisters to the Y on Saturday afternoon because he had a big surprise for us. The enthusiasm in his voice lifted my spirits.

On Saturday, Mom dropped us off at the Y. My father was sitting at the piano when we walked into the lobby. His smile broadened when he saw us in the doorway and he motioned for us to sit on the sofa. Then he turned, faced the piano keys and began to play.

It was amazing to hear my father playing the piano again! Goosebumps covered my arms, and my eyes welled with tears of joy. The prospects of him ever playing the piano again had been slim. The accident had caused him to lose parts of his index finger and thumb on his right hand. It was astonishing to watch his fingers deftly flying up and down the piano keys. When he began singing, many of the visitors and residents of the YMCA came into to the lobby to listen. The room filled with applause when he finished, the loudest coming from his proud daughters.

Listening to our father play the piano once again was one of the best gifts he ever gave us. When I was very little, we had bonded while sitting together at the piano at my grandmother's house. I'd missed hearing him play. My sisters and I were extremely proud of Dad that day because we realized what a struggle he had overcome.

Mom was waiting in the car when we left the Y. Judy ran up to the window yelling, "Mommy, Daddy can play the piano again!"

My mother's eyes lit up and instead of crying as she had for weeks, she smiled. "That makes me happy. I prayed someday he'd play again."

I turned to wave goodbye to Dad. He was standing on the steps, smiling too. He had heard her.

The next time Dad came to visit, Mom stayed home. Before he left that evening, Mom invited him into the kitchen for a cup of coffee and a piece of chocolate cream pie. Their coffee-klatches continued every time he visited. On the nights Dad came to our house, my mother made sure she looked stunning. She never opened a beer while he was at the house. His stays became longer, until one night. That evening he never left.

Our lives were much better with Dad back home. Each time my parents reunited, they acted like newlyweds. Unfortunately, this never lasted very long.

As I was doing family research for this book, I realized how much our lives had become like my mother's when she was a young girl. It seemed we moved whenever my folks got behind in the rent, just like Adeline and Elmer. My parents were arguing more often which sometimes led to physical abuse. The one thing I could not get an answer to was whether or not Adeline had affairs or if she was an alcoholic. If I believe what my Mom and my great-grandmother told me about her, I don't believe she did. Maybe someday I'll be able to find out more about my mother's childhood. I think it would shed a lot of light on how our family environment changed from fairly normal to extremely dysfunctional.

I felt some trepidation about Dad's return and worried about what would happen to my sisters when it all turned sour again. I also worried about my small son. Todd was very attached to my father and I believe he had felt his absence.

Mom obviously had the same thoughts about Todd because one morning, shortly after Dad's return, she told me she wanted to talk with me. Then she shared a recent discussion she and Dad had about Todd's future. She explained that while they loved us living with them, she and Dad thought it was time for Randy and me to get married. She stressed the importance of Todd being raised by his mother and father together, in their own home.

Randy and I had recently talked about it, too. While agreeing that marriage was best for Todd, we also realized the problems we'd be facing. Randy had one more year of high school and was counting on receiving a football scholarship to help pay for college. We had no idea how we could afford to get married at this time.

After opening her fourth beer, Mom became exasperated by our concerns and indecision about marriage and shouted, "Diana Lynn, it's time to shit or get off the pot!"

So we did. Randy and I agreed to be married on August 6, 1966.

Randy planned to work for his brother-in-law, Dan, during the summer while I continue to work at the nursing home. We'd get our own apartment as soon as we'd saved enough money. Waiting until August to get married would give us about two full months to accomplish our goal.

Delighted by our decision, my mother quickly shared the news with family and friends. She offered to make all of the arrangements for the wedding while I attended school and worked. I had two requests. My first request was to get married in Immanuel Lutheran Church by Pastor Daniels, and my second request was to wear a wedding gown. The wedding dress was questionable because I obviously wasn't a virgin. We compromised by having my dress dyed ice-blue. The wedding dress was important to me. Because I wouldn't be wearing a cap and gown to receive my diploma with my class in June, 1967, I felt I deserved this one concession.

The other problem I faced was how to tell my sorority sisters about Todd and my upcoming wedding. The day of the next sorority meeting, I invited the President of Thete, Julie to my house. After she had arrived, I told her to follow me upstairs. When I opened my bedroom door, Julie was shocked to see a small child sitting in a crib playing with a stuffed animal. It took a moment before she fully understood. "Oh, Diana, he's precious! He's yours, right?"

JoAnne and Lynn were still my only friends who knew about Todd. It was a very proud moment when I was felt confident enough to introduce my son to another friend. Julie was dumbfounded when she heard my story. She held her arms out to me and together we cried. She reached into the crib and took Todd into her arms.

"I can't believe you could keep this beautiful baby a secret all of this time. I don't know how you did it!"

Because I needed time to compose myself before facing my sorority sisters, I asked her to go to the meeting ahead of me and tell them my story. I was uncertain about their reactions. When I arrived at the meeting and stepped out of my parked car, the muscles in the back of my neck began to tighten, and the acid in my stomach pushed up into my throat. Before I got to the front door, my sorority sisters rushed out to greet me. I welcomed their embraces and words of support. The pains in my legs and stomach vanished.

Before the wedding, Randy and I encountered one major set-back we hadn't anticipated. Jamestown High School had recently hired a new football coach. Eager to establish his authority, Coach Ferraro's first order of business was to make the entire varsity football players get buzz cuts. Word quickly spread that he was a tough, kick-ass coach with one thing on his mind— winning. His second order of business was calling the star half-back into his office to inform him he would NOT be getting married in August.

Unbeknownst to us, there was a clause in the school by-laws prohibiting married students from participating in extra-curricular activities.

The downtrodden look on Randy's face, as he walked through our front door, told me something catastrophic had happened. He shared this unsettling news.

"Are you kidding me? They won't let you play if we get married?"

"That's about the size of it."

"We'd better tell my mother, right now."

Randy stood beside me and watched as Mom threw an absolute fit.

We suggested postponing the wedding, not canceling it, and stressed the importance of Randy possibly receiving a football scholarship to college. Our words were wasted. Mom wouldn't bend.

"I don't give a damn about football. I want my daughter to get married and give my grandson a legitimate name! The hell with what this coach has to say, I won't postpone the wedding," she shouted loudly enough for our next door neighbors to hear. "Besides, the invitations have already been sent out. What will my friends say?"

That sentence pretty well summed up my narcissistic mother. She was more worried about what her friends would think if we postponed the wedding than she was about our future.

Next day, before practice, Randy told the coach we wouldn't be canceling the wedding. Coach Ferraro refused to be bested by a woman. With Randy's permission, he called my mother and set a meeting to talk about the situation. He was meeting with her at my house the following evening. Randy and I paced the sidewalk in my backyard while awaiting coach's arrival. Mom was on her own because Dad was working. I wasn't sure how this meeting would work out.

It was a sweltering evening at the end of June when Coach Ferraro arrived. The dining room window was wide open to let in a little breeze. It also let out the sound of their voices. Randy and I crouched beneath the bay window listening to their conversation. They started out with the usual pleasantries between two strangers meeting for the first time. He refused Mom's offer of a beverage and got right down to the reason for his visit. He wanted Randy to play ball—end of story. My mother wanted her daughter to get married—period. The longer they sparred, the louder they got. Mom finally ended the argument by yelling, "I don't give a damn who wants Randy Sharp to play ball. He's marrying my daughter on August 6th, and that's that! Now get the hell out of my house!"

I slowly slid down the siding beneath the window and shook my head in disbelief. Randy peered through the branches of the lilac tree, watching as the coach climbed into his car, slammed the door and peeled off down the street.

About a week later, Coach Ferraro called Randy into his office to inform him he'd presented the dilemma to the Jamestown High School Board of Directors. They had voted to amend the ruling. Randy would be the starting half-back in the fall! Heartily laughing, Coach Ferraro said, "Can you believe it? I convinced an entire school board to do something I couldn't convince a five-foot-two, one hundred pound woman to do! That's hysterical." It was also very helpful that Lynn's father was President of the JHS Board of Directors.

We were married on August 6, 1966 in the Immanuel Lutheran Church in Jamestown, with Pastor Gerald Daniels officiating. My bridesmaids, Lynn, JoAnne, and Mary, stood beside me as I took my father's arm. He proudly walked me down the aisle while I smiled brightly as I passed our family and friends. Mom sat in the front row holding ten-month-old Todd in her arms. My four sisters sat in the pew behind her beaming with joy. Our reception took place in a fire hall in Falconer following the wedding. We spent our wedding night in a motel in Falconer, New York, and moved into our new apartment the next day.

Our four-room, first-floor apartment was located on Prospect Street, two blocks from my parents house and one block from Randy's mother, Marion. The proximity of our houses made it convenient for family visits.

Acclimating to our new lifestyle was easier than we'd anticipated. Randy attended classes at JHS in the fall and practiced football each day while I spent my days caring for Todd and my evenings working at the nursing home.

Although I desperately missed attending school my senior year, I was grateful for the opportunity to take my English class in the evenings twice a week with Mr. Green. Taking this course enabled me to receive my high school regents diploma in June, 1967. Unfortunately, I wouldn't wear a cap and gown and walk down the aisle of the auditorium with my classmates.

Instead, I'd receive it in the mail, another price I'd pay for bearing a child out of wedlock.

My social life revolved around occasional visits from my friends and the monthly meetings of Thete. I looked forward to these meetings because it kept me connected to the day-to-day school activities I was missing. This social opportunity ended for me on a fall afternoon in late October.

It was my day off from work, and I had spent the morning cleaning our apartment. That afternoon, I heard someone knocking at my door. I was surprised and excited to see two of my sorority sisters standing on the porch. I welcomed them into my living room and offered them a coke. They politely refused. Soon after they were seated, they explained the reason for their visit.

Apparently, several mothers of some of my sorority sisters had discussed my marital situation over lunch at the local country club. They decided it was inappropriate for a married woman with a child to continue as an active member of Thete. They hurriedly apologized and expressed their regret at being the bearers of this news.

I was speechless. I felt the tears pressing against my closed eyelids, anxiously waiting for release. Rather than let them see me cry, I put my index finger and thumb on the bridge of my nose as if I was thinking. Then I cleared my throat and said, "I was expecting this."

Although they were surprised by my statement, they also looked very relieved. I told them my life had drastically changed, and I no longer fit into their circle. Susan quickly pointed out they were not asking for my total resignation; I could stay on as an associate member. Of course, this excluded me from participating in any of Thete's activities. I said I understood the request and would send my letter of resignation before the next scheduled meeting.

Todd saved me from the awkwardness of this situation by starting to cry. I thanked them for coming to tell me face-to-face and asked them to please leave so I could take care of my baby.

As soon as they walked out the door, I picked up my son and cradled him in my arms. While sitting in a rocking chair feeding him his bottle, I watched the beautiful gold, red and yellow leaves fall gently from the maple tree in my front yard. Each falling leaf reminded me of something in my past slowly slipping away from my life. The thought that these dying leaves would be replaced by new growth in the spring gave me hope.

That fall, the highlight of my week was watching Randy as he led the JHS football to victory. During one game, while sitting in the bleachers with Lynn, the man behind me commented to his wife, "Hey, I heard that Sharp kid is married and has a baby." I glanced over my shoulder and said, "You're right mister. He's married, and I'm his wife." My quick response was good for a laugh from everyone sitting around us.

The amendment made by the school board to allow Randy to participate in sports as a married student paid off. In the 1967 Red & Green yearbook, the leading sentence of the paragraph describing the 1966 season read: "With Randy Sharp's ten touchdowns and 665 yards gained, the Red Raiders swept on to a smashing 7-0-1 season."

The possibility of a college football scholarship was very promising!

CHAPTER 27

The Canary

1967

THE NEW YEAR was brought in by gusty winds blowing across Chautauqua Lake, blanketing Jamestown with wet snow, ice, and bitterly cold temperatures. The bad weather subsided by the middle of the month, allowing Randy, Todd and me to travel safely to Buffalo.

Todd was scheduled for surgery to repair his cleft palate at Buffalo Children's Hospital on Sunday, January 15th. The date is easy to remember; it was the day of the first Super Bowl. The mothers of the children in the surgical ward spent the day keeping watch over their child while the fathers gathered in the waiting room. The men were crammed around a small black and white television watching the game. The silence in the ward was broken by enthusiastic shouts from that room. The only thing Randy remembered about Todd's first day in the hospital, was the score of the game. The Green Bay Packers beat the Kansas City Chiefs 35-10.

I remember my fear and feelings of guilt. Although Todd's condition was not life threatening, the thoughts of my small child being anesthetized were daunting. At our last office visit, our doctor had explained the entire procedure to us. Todd was fortunate because he didn't have a cleft lip. Only his soft palate needed to be repaired. Dr. Clement was hopeful this would be the only surgery Todd would need.

While researching the causes of this condition, I discovered extreme stress during the first ten weeks of gestation could be one of the results. I'd certainly felt stress during the early stages of pregnancy.

Only one parent was permitted to spend the night with their child. I slept on a cot in Todd's room, and Randy stayed at the Ronald McDonald House across the street. He returned early the next morning with a cup of steaming coffee. When it was time for Todd's surgery, the nurse allowed me to carry him to the elevator where she took him out of my arms. Before the elevator doors closed, we kissed him. Then we walked down the hall and into the waiting room. I filled the time by praying. About three hours later, the doctor came into the room and told us the surgery had gone very well.

To prepare us before we saw Todd, Dr. Clement explained Todd had splints on his arms to prevent him from touching his nose and mouth.

When the nurse carried Todd off the elevator, I was grateful the doctor had prepared us. It saddened me to see my little son with dried blood on his face. I spent the night gently wiping his face with warm washcloths, rocking him in my arms and softly rubbing his eyebrows. The next day, Randy returned to Jamestown for school and work while Todd and I remained in Buffalo.

When we returned home, the peacefulness of our apartment was short-lived. I was bombarded by calls from my family. The normalcy my parents had created while Todd and I had lived with them vanished shortly after we moved out. I dreaded answering the phone. It was either Mom calling to tell me about her latest woe and some offense Dad committed or Judy calling about some mean-spirited punishment Mom recently enforced. Several times their neighbor, Caroline, called to complain about the noisy fights she heard through the paper-thin walls separating their duplex apartments.

I didn't need or want this information. Randy and I were trying to build our own lives. I attempted to ignore the drama by taking care of my little family and keeping to myself. It seemed to be working until early one morning when my mother appeared at my front door. I saw her standing on the porch through the window. Her eyes were swollen from crying, her hair a disheveled mess, and she wasn't wearing any make-up; three obvious signs there was a major problem. When I opened the door, she stormed into the kitchen, grabbed an ashtray from the counter, slammed it on the table and pulled an unopened Blatz from her purse. It was seven-thirty in the morning.

The Road Back to Hell

The first words out of her mouth were, "I'm going to kill your father! He's having an affair!"

Although I tried to avoid these confrontations, here she was, crying her heart out to me and looking for sympathy. It was all I could do to keep from lashing back at her, reminding her that she had being doing the same thing for over eight years.

Apparently my dad had been stopping at the Bullfrog, a local bar in Falconer, after work. These occasional stops soon became daily occurrences, which infuriated my mother. When she accused him of having an affair, he denied it. She was waiting for him when he walked in the door at five-thirty in the morning. Not long after their fighting began, Dad admitted he was having an affair with the bartender, Elaine. Mom became hysterical as Dad walked past her and went upstairs to get ready for work. He didn't say a word when he walked out the door.

"You have to talk to your dad. You're the only one he'll listen to."

When I told her I didn't want to get involved, she begged me to talk to him for my sisters' sake.

Get involved for my sisters' sake? Why don't you tug my heart strings a little tighter, Mom?

I finally relented. When I arrived at their house early that evening, I was relieved my mother wasn't home. Without her there, it was easier for Dad to tell me his version of the story. He confessed he hadn't intended to become involved with this woman. Their relationship, which had begun by discussing the problems they each faced with their spouses, soon turned into an affair. He claimed they loved each other, needed each other and were planning on moving in together.

I was astounded by this news. While I had lost a lot of respect for my mother over the years, my dad had remained my idol. Now he was tainted by the same brush, and I looked at him through different eyes. This situation deeply pained one part of me, while another part of me sympathized with him. He had been through hell the past eight years because of my mother.

Maybe he believed he had a right to be happy with someone who seemed to love and appreciate him.

Two weeks later, following another blistering fight, Dad moved out.

Mom was devastated and became deeply depressed. When I discussed the situation with Judy and Kim, Judy informed me she had met Elaine and liked her very much. She described her as a cute redhead with a loving heart. She made me promise not to tell our mother that she had met her. Then Kim shared her story. One Saturday afternoon, she went to Smokey's to get money from Mom. Mom introduced Kim to her new friend, George. Kim stayed for a while and talked with him. She said he seemed like a very nice man and she thought Mom was dating him. I promised her I wouldn't mention it to Dad.

Late one night, I received a hysterical call from Caroline informing me my mother had slit her wrist. When I arrived at the house, Caroline was helping my mother into the front seat of her car. I followed them in my car to the emergency room. While the nurses were caring for Mom, I asked Caroline to please go back to the house and take care of the girls. When Caroline asked if she should contact my dad, I said no. I held my mother's hand as the nurse pushed the gurney towards the operating room. My mom mouthed the words, "I'm sorry". I spent the rest of the night in the chair beside her bed. I asked God to guide me through this latest ordeal.

Early the next morning, Pastor Daniels arrived. He wrapped his arms around me and listened while I relayed the story. A short while later, the doctor peered into the room and summoned me to join him in the hallway.

Because it was not my mother's first attempt at suicide, he strongly suggested I commit her to a ninety-day stay at Gowanda State Hospital—a facility specializing in the treatment of mentally handicapped and addicted patients. When he learned I was uncomfortable making that decision, he told me my mother had refused to admit herself. If I didn't commit her, the doctors would and Mom's stay could be much longer than ninety days. I reluctantly agreed. Pastor Daniels stood beside me while I explained the situation to Mom. It took some persuasion, but she finally admitted she needed help. An ambulance took her to Gowanda State Hospital the next day.

Dad's escape to paradise was short-lived. He moved back home to care for the girls.

Patients were permitted to have visitors two days a week. Randy accompanied me on my first visit. We were shocked by my mother's appearance. She was wearing an old hospital gown and a tattered robe; her hair was unkempt and her face pale and drawn. She slurred her words when she tried to speak. When I asked the nurse why my mother was acting this way, she informed me they were giving her sedatives to calm her nerves and help with her alcohol withdrawal.

Throughout our visit, Mom kept apologizing. I closed her in my arms and promised her this treatment would help her get better. She smiled as she watched me unpack her clothing and make-up. Her eyes lit up when I laid a carton of Taryetons and the current issue of *True Story* magazine on her nightstand. She obviously enjoyed these magazines because she could easily relate to many of the characters in the monthly dramas.

During one of these visits, I met George. This time, it didn't concern me that she was seeing someone else. By then, I realized my mother could not survive without a man in her life. Maybe this last separation would work out for both of my parents and they would each find the peace and happiness they appeared to be seeking.

George was about five-feet, eight-inches tall with curly black hair, flecked with gray, a ruddy complexion, warm, brown eyes, and a loving smile. During our conversations about my mother, I felt George honestly cared about her and would give her the support needed as she recovered.

Every time I visited, she was wearing the same yellow dress. One day I asked her why she didn't wear any of her other outfits. She perkily replied, "It's my favorite dress, and everyone tells me I look beautiful in it."

It wasn't until years later when I was researching the causes of my mother's depression and alcoholism, that I truly understood the significance of her comment.

She had been in Gowanda a little over sixty days, when I got a phone call from her on a Sunday night. "Hi. I just wanted to let you know I'm home."

I was shocked. I had no idea she was being released. Next day, I found out what had happened. After sixty days, patients were permitted to leave the facility on Sunday afternoons. When George had visited that day, she persuaded him to take her out for dinner. During dinner, my mother convinced him she was better and wanted to go home because she needed to be with her daughters. As soon as they finished their meals, they drove to Jamestown. She hadn't been released; she had escaped!

When her fellow patients learned she was gone, they referred to her as "The Canary" because she always wore yellow, and she flew the coop.

Although Mom caused me a lot of anxieties, sometimes she made me laugh.

Dad was doing an excellent job caring for the girls. He worked every day and stayed home every evening, except for Saturday. That was date night for him and Elaine. When my sisters and I met Elaine, everyone liked her except Kim. She remained steadfastly loyal to our mother.

My father was at the house the night Mom unexpectedly arrived home from the hospital. They spent the night amicably talking about the roles they would each play in my sisters' lives. Mom expressed her desire to find another place because there were too many bitter memories in the house on Broadhead Avenue. Dad agreed to help her move. He also announced he was moving back in with Elaine.

The passing of winter and the onset of spring helped lift our spirits.

The sweet aroma of blooming lilacs; the bright, red tulips and yellow daffodils popping up in neighborhood yards, and the sight of the first robin brought a feeling of newness. Perhaps the changes my parents had made would enable them to each have a fresh start in life.

CHAPTER 28

Just Over That Hill

1967

As the date of Randy's graduation approached, we were anxiously waiting to hear from various colleges about the possibility of a football scholarship. He received letters of interest from the Corn Huskers in Nebraska, West Virginia University in Morgantown, a couple of mid-sized colleges on the west coast and Clarion State College in Clarion, PA. Coach Ferraro promptly sent films to all of these schools. Most of the coaches sent letters of rejection after viewing these films, explaining that although Randy was an extremely fast runner, he was too small (only 5'8") for their team. Bill Johns, the Clarion coach, was the only one interested. He came to Jamestown to meet with Randy and extended an invitation to visit the college in early June.

On a bright, sunny June morning, we set out on our eighty-five mile drive to Clarion to meet with the coach and visit the college. As we headed down the long hill into Clarion, the view of the river was breath-taking. The Clarion River appeared to be green, which intrigued us. After we drove up a winding hill, we spotted the college football stadium at the top of the hill.

Randy looked over at me and smiled.

When we finished viewing the campus, we had lunch with Coach Johns while he spelled out our options. It was disheartening to learn Clarion couldn't offer scholarships because it was a state college, not a university.

Coach Johns said he'd help Randy get a work-study job and he'd also investigate other financial opportunities for which Randy might be eligible. At the end of the day, Randy shook his hand and told him we would let him know our decision in a few days. On our drive home, we decided it was doable if Randy qualified for student loans. As soon as he got the loan approval, he notified Coach Johns that he would be reporting for football camp in August.

To save money, we moved out of our apartment in July and stayed with my mother. When Randy started college in mid-August, Todd and I would continue to stay at Mom's until we found suitable housing in Clarion. At the time we made this decision, we were unaware of the tumultuous situation brewing at my mother's house.

The relationship between my mother and Judy had turned violent. Whenever my mother made crude remarks about Dad and his 'whore', Judy would defend them. One afternoon, their fight became physical with Mom slapping Judy across the face and Judy pushing her to the floor. My sister packed her bags and called Elaine to come and get her. Mom was furious.

In the middle of August, I drove Randy to Clarion to begin football practice. Before returning to Jamestown, we looked at several apartments, none of which were affordable. He promised to keep looking and take the first suitable place he found.

On the lonely drive home, I thought about all of the things going on in our life. We were excited about starting a new life in a small town. We understood we would struggle financially at first, but believed things would get better when I found a job. While Randy's spirits were lifted by the prospect of becoming the starting half-back on the freshman team, my spirits were spiraling downwards. I dreaded staying with Mom and listening as she constantly berated my dad and Judy. The soap-opera of their lives depressed me. As soon as I arrived at my mother's, I was determined to declare my independence. It was time for Mom, Dad and Judy to solve their problems on their own.

Mom was sitting on the front porch talking to Caroline when I parked in front of the house. She ran down the steps to the car and proudly announced, "I fixed her!"

"Fixed whom? What are you talking about?" I asked as I stepped out of the car.

"I fixed your sister. I had a long talk with Grandma Conklin about Judy living with that dreadful woman and your dad, and Grandma agreed to let Judy live at her house."

Mom was delighted with her accomplishment. I had no idea she'd even considered taking Judy away from Dad and Elaine. Elaine had been wonderful to my sister; she paid attention to her. It was the first time Judy truly felt special and wanted. Consequently, she had fallen in love with Elaine and my mother couldn't stand it. I questioned my mother's motives. Was she doing this out of revenge or was she genuinely concerned about Judy's welfare? I feared the repercussions. Although Judy and Grandma Conklin were very close, I didn't know if my grandmother was capable of controlling a rebellious thirteen-year-old girl.

Mom and I argued about it the rest of the evening. I spent most of the night trying to decide how to separate myself from all of these problems and get on with my life. The next morning, I still didn't have any answers.

While pouring my first cup of coffee, my mother asked me to drive her to the attorney's office to pick up the legal custody papers necessary to remove Judy from Elaine's home. I refused to do it. Offended by this slight, she recruited Caroline to take her. After Mom had picked up the custody papers, Caroline drove my mother to Elaine's to retrieve Judy. From there they went to Warren. I was grateful I wasn't present to witness the scene.

The next week, I drove to Warren to visit Judy at Granny C's. Judy was calmer than I had expected, but still saddened about leaving Elaine's house. Granny C was a wise woman who understood a lot about life and I looked to her for guidance. After lunch, she sent Judy to do some errands so we could talk alone. She explained that she had agreed to let Judy stay with her because she thought it was improper for her to live with Dad and Elaine. Because they weren't married, my grandmother felt it was an unhealthy environment for a young girl. Although she and Mom had issues over the years, in this case, she sided with my mother. I sat and listened, never sharing my opinion. I wanted to tell her the conditions at home for Judy were even worse, but I didn't.

A week later, my father offered to take me to Clarion to look for an apartment. The two-hour drive gave us the opportunity to talk, something we hadn't done in a while. He shared his feelings about his relationship with Elaine. "Elaine and I have reached a decision. We love each other very much, but we both agree it would be best if I moved back home."

I sat there with my mouth hanging open, digesting what he'd just said. When I asked him why they were doing this, he explained that he and Elaine understood sacrifices have to be made, even when you don't want to. They were both deeply affected by Judy's forced move. He feared Mom wasn't capable of caring for Kim, Linda and Lisa on her own. If he moved back with Mom, Judy might return home, too.

Once again, I was astounded by my dad's unselfishness when it came to his children.

When we got to Clarion, we looked at several places before we found a small, affordable, two-bedroom apartment located above a gas station.

Noticing the empty windows on the second floor, I asked Dad to stop while I went into the station to inquire about it. The manager handed me the keys and Dad and I climbed the enclosed staircase. When we opened the door, we were shocked by the filthy condition of this apartment. A window had been propped open with a beer can; a naked, single mattress was pushed into a corner and ashtrays overflowed with cigarette butts, some littered the bare floor. A garbage bag filled with empty beer and liquor bottles sat on the floor of the kitchen. It smelled like a brewery.

"Wow! It looks like party central. With a little soap and water, this place could be perfect," Dad cheerfully remarked.

After surveying the rest of the apartment, I decided I could make it livable. We went downstairs and told the manager we'd take it. Randy, Todd and I moved in two weeks later. The weekend I moved out of Mom's, Dad moved back home.

While Randy attended classes and football practice, I spent my days caring for Todd. In the afternoons, we often went for a ride. As I drove past the campus, I noticed the guys playing Frisbee on the lush green lawn and the girls, my age, tanning in the bright sunlight. I watched as the students hustled from class to class, each with a load of books in their arms. I wished I was one of them. What would it feel like to be free and a freshman attending college? How exciting it must be to meet new friends and go to parties on the weekends. I pictured myself sitting in a lecture hall mesmerized by the speaker. Then I looked at my sweet son, sitting quietly beside me and snapped back to reality.

I found a job as a waitress in a coffee shop about two blocks from our apartment. Working the evening shift eliminated the need for a babysitter. My new job enabled me to make friends which helped me overcome some of my homesickness.

Attending Randy's football games was the highlight of my week.

Once again, he was the star running back. That ended during his sixth game. His knee was severely injured by a forceful tackle. I watched as they carried him off the field to a waiting ambulance. I followed them to the Clarion Hospital. The injury was more severe than we'd anticipated. It ended his football career and set us back financially because he couldn't work for two months.

Whenever I was feeling down, I called my great-grandmother. Talking to Gussie always brightened my day. While we talked, I could envision her sparkling blue eyes that crinkled at the corners whenever she laughed. Her soothing voice and funny stories comforted me. One afternoon, she called to ask if she could come for a visit on Sunday.

"Of course you can, we'd love to see you, but how will you get here?" I excitedly asked.

It was a logical question because she didn't have a driver's license and had never driven a car. She said her boarder, Mr. Reynolds, agreed to bring her. I was astonished. I could not imagine him driving all the way to Clarion.

At seventy-five, he walked, talked and drove like a turtle. She assured me they would be at my house by one o'clock Sunday afternoon.

I was delighted to be able to prepare a Sunday dinner for guests.

Promptly at one o'clock, a large, gray and white sedan pulled into our parking space. I raced downstairs and threw my arms around my darling great- grandmother. I had missed her almost as much as I had when I lived in California. When I inquired how the trip had been, she gave me a mischievous smile and said, "Ducky- just ducky."

Later that day, I asked how she had convinced Mr. Reynolds to drive over eighty-five miles to Clarion.

"Whenever he asked how much further we had to go, I said, 'Just over that hill," she replied. The eighty-five mile drive to Clarion was mainly rolling hills.

We laughed so hard, tears streamed down our cheeks.

CHAPTER 29

Christmas at Our House

1967-1969

W<small>HILE WATCHING THE</small> fluffy clouds billow through the fall air far above me, I closed my eyes and pretended I was a blue jay swiftly flying away from my nest and into the sky. The miles separating my mother and me provided a temporary respite from the daily soap opera drama of her life. Her problems were no longer the first thing on my mind each morning, nor the last thing on my mind each night. It was refreshing to get out of bed, pour myself a cup of coffee and watch the news before Todd woke up.

Although I didn't miss the problems, I did miss my sisters and often wondered how they were getting along. Judy was starting eighth grade at Lincoln Junior High School, and I was concerned about her. Remembering my trepidation about starting at a junior high where I knew no one, I prayed she'd select the right door.

Mom called me three or four times a week to fill me in on the latest gossip, the girl's activities and her latest problems. When trying to change the subject failed, I held the phone away from my ear and watched whatever was on television. Some days, I didn't answer the phone.

One weekend in October, we went to Jamestown for a visit. My mother and sisters had moved from Broadhead Avenue to a smaller, more affordable house on Cook Street. We slept in the spare bedroom of Mom's new place. Our homecoming was joyous. Linda and Lisa couldn't wait to play with Todd while Judy and Kim greeted us with a peck on the cheek and promptly left to meet their friends. My mother had spent the afternoon making two of my favorite things— her delicious spaghetti sauce and coconut cream pie. After dinner, my mother and I sat in the kitchen talking while Randy entertained the kids in the living room.

She pulled a wrinkled pack of cigarettes from her pocket, stuck one in her mouth, bent over the flame on the stove to light it, exhaled and proudly announced, "You'll never guess what Judy and Kim did last week!"

Before I could answer, she went on to say, "Linda caught them smoking in the bathroom and ran down to tell me. I immediately called them downstairs." She paused long enough to take another puff.

"What did you do about it?" I asked.

"I sent Linda to the store to buy two big cigars. When Judy and Kim came downstairs, I made them tell me what they'd done. It took a while, but they finally confessed. After Linda returned, I handed them each a cigar and made them smoke it." She became animated as she described their reactions. After inhaling the strong cigars, they had both turned pale and started to choke and cough. Judy ran into the bathroom and threw up.

She finished by saying, "I think I've cured them of smoking in the future." I watched as she stubbed out her cigarette and pulled another from the pack.

On Saturday morning, Randy and I took Todd to visit his family. Sue had invited us to dinner, so their house was our last stop of the day. On Sunday morning, we dropped in to see Gussie. She sat in her rocker holding Todd while regaling us with funny stories about her boarders and card club friends. I loved listening to her lively voice and watching her radiant eyes whenever she shared a tale. Visiting Gussie was like a breath of fresh air.

Unlike my mother, she shared cheerful stories, not doom and gloom. When we returned to Mom's for Sunday dinner, I was surprised to see my dad in the kitchen.

We had stopped by his apartment the day before, but he wasn't there. I worried we might not see him before we left for Clarion. I rushed over to him and gave him a hug. He hugged me back and whispered, "I've missed you all so much."

Since he was living on his own again, he had resumed his affair with Elaine. I didn't ask any questions. However, I noticed the saucy smile on Mom's face as she bustled around the kitchen getting ready to serve dinner.

After everyone had left the kitchen, she quipped, "He still sees that bitch, but I'll get him back. Wait and see."

I was always appalled by the way my mother played with my father's emotions. When things weren't going well, she would start a big fight, which usually resulted in her kicking him out of the house. After he seemed to be getting on his feet and possibly finding some happiness, she would reel him in again. Her seductive powers were both amazing and disgusting. The old saying, 'Can't live with him and can't live without him' was certainly true in this case. And what was wrong with Dad that he would let her entice him back again and again? When I recalled the night Dad and I had talked about this in the kitchen and he told me he stayed with her because of us girls. I convinced myself that was the reason.

It didn't take long for Mom's words to come true. When we returned at Christmas time, Mom and Dad announced they were getting back together and moving to Warren. They planned to move at the beginning of January, 1968. None of us were surprised. They both promised to leave their paramours, George and Elaine, behind.

My grandfather Conklin helped Dad get a job at the Forge in Youngsville. They moved into a small house on Fifth Avenue. Once again, the girls would be going to new schools. Judy attended Beatty Junior High School. Kim and Linda attended the local elementary school while Lisa stayed home with Mom.

It's impossible to count the number of times my parent's had moved over the years, but each stressful move was usually caused by failure to pay the rent or another separation. Not only did my sisters have to deal with making new friends in a different school, they also had to readjust to the absence of a parent. Unfortunately, these two situations continued to occur more frequently in the years to come.

During one of our Sunday visits to Warren, we stopped at Granny C's. While sitting at her kitchen table enjoying a piece of her freshly, baked apple pie, I asked how she felt about Dad and his family moving to Warren. Her eyebrows furrowed when she whispered, "Only time will tell." I understood.

In May, Randy and I discussed our future in Clarion. He was disillusioned by his football experience as a freshman and wasn't certain he wanted to return to college in the fall. After several lengthy discussions, we decided to pack everything and move back to Jamestown at the end of the semester.

Sue found an apartment for us on Bush Street, right across from their house. Once I became settled in my new surroundings, I realized how much I had missed my friends and family. Many mornings, I walked across the street and had coffee with her while Todd and Billy Joe played in the living room. It wasn't long before we became best friends.

She began inviting us to dinners, dances and parties at the homes of their friends. These evenings were filled with laughter and fun and for the first time since I got married, I felt like I belonged.

About six months later we moved again because our apartment was too small. Sue was an excellent decorator and helped me paint and wallpaper the dining room and kitchen. I learned to refinish the used furniture I had purchased at second-hand stores. Our little house became a home.

Randy and I considered returning to Clarion at some point but realized we needed to save money to do it. I decided to find a job. Other than working as a nurses' aid, I was virtually untrained. An ad in the local paper for a position at a local ad agency intrigued me. I called and scheduled an interview. I arrived ten minutes early. When the secretary called my name, I stood up and confidently walked into the owner's office. Mr. Jones spent a long time asking me about my life, my qualifications, and my experiences. I assured him I was a very driven woman, and if I didn't know how to perform some of the necessary duties, I'd quickly learn. He grinned and led me into a room with an electronic typewriter. Yikes! Typing was the one class I almost failed. I took it my junior year in high school, every day after lunch. Getting up every night between two and three to feed Todd a bottle interfered with my sleep. Consequently, I slept through most of my typing classes.

After Mr. Jones left the room, I panicked when I saw the electric typewriter—I'd never used one! I thought to myself, "Oh well, here goes."

My finished product looked something like this- TTTTThhhhheee eo-ooooolllldddd gggraaaa aayy ff fox xxx. After ten frustrating minutes, I pulled the paper out of the typewriter, returned to Mr. Jones' office and handed it to him. He roared with laughter! "Honey, you can't type but you sure have guts!" He explained as a typesetter you had to have excellent typing skills and promised to call me if any other job became available. I politely thanked him for his time and walked out.

Next, I interviewed for a position as a personal secretary at Crawford Furniture. Once again, I wore my badge of confidence. While I sat in the reception area waiting to be called, I assessed my competition. Most of the applicants were dressed like me in a starched, white, long-sleeved blouse, a dark mini-skirt, and either a blazer or a sweater. I was inhibited by the attractive brunette with a beehive hairdo, dressed in a navy-blue suit and spike heels. I felt better when I glanced at the plump girl dressed in a slovenly outfit. When the secretary called my name, I held my head up, put on my brightest smile and marched in to meet Mr. Carlson. As soon as he began the interview, I explained I had graduated with an academic degree but had no business training. Once again, I stressed I was an eager learner, a hard-worker and a people person. He seemed impressed by my honesty. After talking to me for about an hour, he expressed his concern about my lack of experience because the available position required someone with excellent secretarial skills. He also promised to call me if anything became available.

When I interviewed for a waitress position in a downtown luncheonette, I was hired on the spot. They were so desperate they asked if I could start in two hours. I did. Three weeks later I received a call from Mr. Carlson. The experienced person he had hired didn't work out. He remembered our interview and decided to offer me the position. I politely said I was highly flattered but had taken another job. I've often wondered what my life would have been like if I would have accepted it.

At least once a month we made the short trip to Warren to see my parents and sisters. Their lives seemed to be going fairly well, which pleased us. But in the summer of 1969, things rapidly eroded when Judy returned from a trip to California with Grandpa Woodard. Before the vacation, she was excited and optimistic, but when she returned, she seemed afraid and depressed. A few days after she had returned, she told my mother that Grandpa Woodard molested her on the trip home. Mom refused to believe it. Once again, she called Judy a liar.

It was difficult for me to accept Judy's story because nothing like that had happened to me when I traveled with my grandfather. Yet, I found it difficult to believe Judy made up that story. The incident planted a seed of doubt in my mind, a seed that would further develop roots by year's end.

We had been living in Jamestown for a year and a half, when we decided to return to Clarion so Randy could pursue his degree in education. We planned to move at the beginning of January, 1970. We had also decided to host Christmas Eve at our house. Since we no longer celebrated that holiday at Gussie's, I invited my parents, my sisters, Grandpa Woodard and his wife, Kate and Uncle Kenny to our house.

It wasn't easy decorating with packed boxes stacked in the corners of the rooms, but I managed. On Christmas Eve day, Todd kept looking out the window and asking when Santa was coming. At four, he could barely contain his excitement. His next question was, "When will Grandma Bonnie and Grandpa Stew be here?"

He ran to the door and greeted my family as they began to arrive on Christmas Eve. Dad carried the gifts and Todd carefully put them under the tree. After all the presents were in place, Linda, Lisa, and Todd sat in front of the tree pondering which gifts belonged to them. The colorful lights on the tree were reflected in their sparkling eyes. You could feel their excitement about opening those brightly, colored packages.

After dinner and before heading into the living room to watch the kids unwrap their gifts, the adults filled their beer and cocktail glasses. When

Linda, Lisa and Todd were finished opening their presents, they took their new treasures up to Todd's room to play. The adults refilled their glasses. It was a typical Christmas Eve.

Kim said she wasn't feeling well and went upstairs to lie down on my bed. A while later, while cleaning up the wrapping paper, I noticed Kim's startled expression as she descended the stairs. She approached my mother who was sitting on the sofa and whispered into her ear. Suddenly, all hell broke loose!

Mom shouted, "Stew, get in here right now!"

Dad had been on the front porch talking to Grandpa and Randy when he heard her scream. He raced into the house to find out what the commotion was about.

My mother was visibly upset. Her hands were shaking, her mouth quivered, and fire streamed from her eyes. I overheard her say, "Kim just told me Kenny came into the bedroom where she was sleeping and started kissing and pawing her!"

"That sonofabitch!" he shouted as he ran out the front door. Kenny was standing on the opposite side of the porch when my dad grabbed him by the shirt and flung him into our front yard. They rolled around in the grass, exchanging punches. Dad threatened to kill Kenny and Kenny shouted back denying any wrongdoing. Randy and Grandpa Elmer joined in the fracas, trying to restrain them. With blood running from the corner of his mouth, and his right eye clenched shut, my father screamed, "If you ever touch one of my daughters again, I will kill you!"

My grandfather wrapped his big, burly arms around Kenny, lifted him up and dumped him into the front seat of his truck. As he was pulling out of the driveway, he opened the window and said, "I'm sorry, Diana. Tell Kate I'll be back to get her." He sped off.

Randy helped my father inside the house while I went to get a bag of ice and a washcloth. When I noticed Linda, Lisa, and Todd peering over the stairway, I said, "Everything's okay kids. Go back and play with your toys."

Mom and Judy were in the living room hovering over a sobbing Kim. When my mother lifted her head, I saw the faraway look in her eyes.

Her look silenced me from asking any questions. I believe she was remembering.

I'll never forget the expression on my mother's face. Whenever I tried to discuss what had supposedly happened to Judy and the incident with Kim, she quickly changed the subject. I regret that I never pursued it at the time, because it may have shed some light on some of the psychological issues my mother had dealt with most of her life. Instead, it seems as if everyone, including my father, eventually 'swept it under the rug'.

CHAPTER 30

The Long Ride Down

1970-1972

THE UPS AND downs of our lives, over the next few years, made it feel as if we were riding the world's fastest roller coaster. I hung on for dear life throughout most of the rides. In 1969, the coaster car Randy and I were riding in slowly moved upward. At the end of the year, as my parents neared the peak, their coaster car rapidly spiraled downward, double-twisting the whole way. Their marriage crumbled under the weight of the abuse accusations.

It was not possible for my mother to accept Judy's accusations that my grandfather had molested her on the trip home from California. After arguing fiercely about it for days, Dad finally relented by walking away from a battle he knew he couldn't win. The incident with Uncle Kenny was another story. My mother reacted much differently and banned Kenny from their home. The emotional toll of each of these occurrences caused my parents to split up again.

Shortly after Christmas, Mom moved back to Jamestown with Linda and Lisa while Judy and Kim stayed in Warren with my dad. Randy and I returned to Clarion.

When Gussie was eighty-four, she had downsized and moved from her thirteen-room house on Seventh Street into an eight-room house on Windsor Street. She still had a few boarders. When Mom, Linda, and Lisa left Warren, they moved in with her. The arrangement worked out well for my younger sisters. Every day after school, Gussie met them at the bus stop and walked them to her house where she had hot tea and something freshly baked waiting for them on the kitchen table. In the evenings, they watched television together and chatted. Gussie was a godsend because she filled the void left by mother's absences. Most days, Mom left Gussie's about noon to search for a job. She ended her day at Smokey's and often didn't return until after midnight. I was relieved knowing that Linda and Lisa were with my great- grandmother.

Years later, Linda and Lisa shared their fond memories of living with Gussie. Lisa loved her because of the amount of time she spent with them, talking, laughing and listening. Lisa hated the hot tea Gussie served every afternoon, but drank it because she didn't want to hurt her feelings. Linda wished they had never left Gussie's house; she felt safe and loved while living with her. For two young girls, aged seven and nine, Gussie's love and understanding provided them with a sense of security, something they had lacked most of their short lives.

My father moved into a three-room apartment above a pool hall in Warren with Judy and Kim. My mother had taken most of the kitchen supplies and furniture, leaving them with very little. At night, I lay in bed worrying. What were Dad and the girls using for dishes? Was the apartment clean? What were they sleeping on? Did they have blankets to keep them warm at night? What types of kids hung out at the downstairs pool hall?

One night, I couldn't sleep because of these worries, so I decided go to Warren the next day to get answers to these questions. Early the next morning, I called my dad and asked him to leave the door unlocked because I was coming to spend the day. I left Todd with Randy and drove to Warren. Parking in front of the five-story apartment building, I assessed the situation. The outside of the brick building didn't appear to be as seedy as I'd envisioned. The shades on the windows of the pool hall were drawn, making it impossible to see inside.

After lugging two bags of cleaning supplies up four flights of stairs, I opened the unlocked door and shuddered. The place was filthy. The kitchen floor was grimy with dirt and grease, the rusty kitchen sink had an inch of scum around it and a few of the cupboard doors were missing. The windows were so dirty you couldn't see through them. I sat down at the rickety wooden table and bawled.

The Road Back to Hell

How can two teenage girls live in this place? How could Dad have rented such a dump? Through all of their many moves, my sisters had never lived in such squalor.

After I had recovered from my initial shock, I set to work. I scrubbed every inch of the filthy kitchen and bathroom. When I finished, I showered and went shopping. My shopping cart overflowed with inexpensive kitchen curtains, some throw rugs, tea towels, dishes, glasses, cups and a few other amenities. I made my second trip of the day hauling bags up to their fourth floor apartment. About three o'clock that afternoon, I heard Judy and Kim giggling as they ran up the steps.

"Holy cow! I can't believe this is the same kitchen!" Kim exclaimed. Judy stood and stared. We laughed and cried while standing there hugging each other. The girls filled me in on their school activities while we prepared dinner.

That evening, my father and I discussed their new situation, how my sisters were doing in school and what rules he was enforcing. He then explained his financial situation.

"I know this place is shabby but it's all I could afford. I'm sending your Mom half of my paycheck every week to take care of Linda and Lisa. That sure doesn't leave much for us to get by. I'm trying to find a part-time job."

Later that night, I snuggled up with my sisters in their double bed. When we chatted about their current living conditions, they both seemed happy. They became very animated when describing their new friends. Judy talked about an older boy she had met. When I questioned her further, she changed the subject. I gave them my 'big-sister' lecture about choosing the right friends and following Dad's rules. Before drifting off to sleep, they promised to heed my advice.

I felt much better on the drive home. The situation wasn't perfect, but when had it ever been? If my dad and my sisters were happy with the situation, who was I to judge?

Over the next few months, my father was unable to find any part- time jobs. Their financial situation worsened, forcing them to move back to

Jamestown. My grandparents loaned Dad enough money to rent a small apartment on Barnett Street. Fortunately, Dad got a good job at a local factory.

With so much disruption in their lives and little supervision from my father, Judy and Kim went wild. They began running around with a bad crowd and experimented with alcohol and drugs. Randy and I were made aware of this during a weekend visit in June.

At one o'clock in the morning on a warm summer night, we were returning from a party when we saw Judy and Kim walking down Third Street with some older-looking boys. Randy drove up to the curb, put the car in park and jumped out. He grabbed Judy and Kim by the arms and shoved them into the back seat. He caught up to a scruffy looking guy who appeared to be the ringleader and shouted, "Stay away from my sisters-in-law! If I see you hanging around them again, I'll personally kick your ass. Do you understand?!" The guy nodded and quickly walked away with his buddies.

Dad's apartment was dark when we arrived. He wasn't home. After accompanying my sisters into the house, we grilled them with questions.

What were you doing out walking the streets at this time of the night? Who were those boys? Where is Dad? How often are you left alone? They sheepishly answered most of them by explaining that Dad worked all day and spent most nights in a barroom. With no parental supervision, they did whatever they pleased.

The situation worsened when Judy relayed a story she thought was amusing. "The night before Easter, Kim and I went to a party with some friends. Someone gave us some acid, and we tried it. When we got home, Dad was waiting up for us to give us our chocolate Easter rabbits."

Kim began to giggle.

"What's so funny?" I sarcastically asked.

Kim was unable to answer, so Judy resumed the story. "The rabbits melted before our eyes. Fat streaks of yellow, blue and orange slowly dripped from the chocolate rabbits onto the kitchen floor. It was weird!"

Randy and I were dumbfounded. With his sternest voice, he said, "Girls, this is serious. Are you crazy? What were you doing experimenting with drugs? You're only thirteen and fifteen, much too young to be on your own. You definitely need more supervision."

Just then, Dad staggered in. He was surprised to see Randy and me sitting there. He slurred his words when he asked, "What's going on?" I jumped out of my seat and hollered at him.

"We found Judy and Kim walking the streets with some hoods at one o'clock in the morning! And we just learned they're not only drinking, they're now trying drugs! Where the hell have you been? Are you blind? You're the parent I've always trusted! How could you let this happen?"

My father plopped down in a chair. Ashamed, he covered his face with his hands. "I'm sorry. I failed. I can't do this anymore."

"That's for sure!" I retorted. "Everyone goes to bed, now. We're leaving, but we'll be back tomorrow morning to deal with this."

We watched the girls as they sheepishly went into their bedroom. I threw a pillow at my father and told him to sack out on the couch.

When we got to Mom's apartment, we stayed up until dawn, talking about what we could do to help Judy and Kim. We considered taking them back to Clarion to live with us but knew we couldn't afford to do it. We were struggling to get Randy through college and this additional financial burden would bury us. When my mother awoke, we discussed the situation with her and she agreed to assume the responsibility of caring for the girls. Ironically, Judy and Kim would be better off living with Mom at this time in their lives.

The next morning, before leaving for Clarion, we went to Dad's house to tell him how we had resolved the problem. It took some persuasion, but Judy and Kim finally agreed to move in with Mom. We loaded their belongings into our car and drove them to her house.

Losing my sisters was the wake-up call my father needed. He stopped going to bars and cut back on his drinking. As it always happened, after a major split, my father soon moved in with Mom and the girls.

In September, Todd started kindergarten at Clarion Elementary.

Although he wouldn't turn five until October, Randy and I thought he needed interaction with other children. There were no kids in our neighborhood and at that time, preschool wasn't an option. My decision was easily made one morning when Todd looked up at me with his big brown eyes and asked,

"Mommy, why don't I have any friends to play with?" His words prompted us to try to have another child.

When we had decided to marry in 1965, it was out of necessity rather than love. During the first few years of our marriage, our relationship grew into one of friendship, respect and love. Although I never felt Randy was my true soul mate or the person I would have chosen under different circumstances, I admired him for the active role he played with my family. Whenever there was a crisis, he rapidly responded. We tried not to let my family problems interfere with our personal life. The Sharps had provided me with the love and stability I had been missing and I wanted to model our family after Tom & Sue's. After much discussion, we felt we were ready to bring another child into the world.

In December, I went to an obstetrician in Franklin and learned I was pregnant. Our baby was due on August 3, 1971. We were ecstatic! This pregnancy was much different than my first one because we had planned for a baby. At twenty-two, I was excited and proud to become a mother again.

In the spring of 1971, I was still working as a waitress. During my sixth-month of pregnancy, I experienced severe leg cramps during the night and at work. The leg pain became unbearable, forcing me to quit my job.

Because we depended on my income, I decided to babysit in my home. We converted the front room of our house into a mini schoolroom. Five families responded to my ad in the Clarion News. Six of the younger children arrived about eight o'clock every morning. After school, their brothers and sisters came to our house, making a total of twelve children in my charge.

I ran my babysitting service like a day care facility by following a daily schedule of planned activities including arts and crafts. While working with the kids, I often wished I'd been able to pursue my dream of becoming a teacher. Randy suggested I take some classes, but I refused. Someone needed to be the full-time breadwinner; I'd wait until he finished college.

My sister Judy joined us early in July to assist with the babysitting. I wanted her to get to know the kids and the daily routine so she could care for them while I was in the hospital. On July 29, 1971 at 7:29 p.m., our baby son was born. This time, my labor was short-lived. My contractions began about 4:30 in the afternoon while I was outside talking to one of the mothers. When Barb noticed me wincing and grabbing my stomach, she asked what was wrong.

"Oh, it was just a little twinge. My doctor told me during my visit yesterday everything was on target, and he would probably see me on the 3rd."

"I think he was off by a few days. You'd better go into the house and call him right now. Sometimes the second baby arrives in a hurry," she said as she walked down the driveway to her car.

When my second contraction occurred ten minutes later, I called the doctor's office. His nurse instructed me to leave for Franklin as soon as possible. My bag was already packed. I grabbed it, kissed Todd good-bye, gave Judy some last minute instructions and headed for the car. Because the Franklin Hospital was thirty miles away, Randy was ready with the engine running when I got into the car. We arrived at the hospital at 6:45 p.m.

While Randy was registering me, the nurse whisked me away in a wheelchair. My water broke as soon as we reached the labor room. After prepping me, they wheeled me into the delivery room, put a mask over my face and told me to count to ten.

I was groggy when I woke up from the anesthetic. Randy was sitting beside me when the nurse came into the room and announced I'd had a beautiful, healthy six-pound, seven-ounce baby boy. At first I was disappointed; I'd been hoping for a girl. Then they laid him in my arms. He was perfect! I touched his tiny, wrinkled red face, kissed his soft, downy head and cradled our second son, Nathan Clifford Sharp, close to my heart.

My parents had driven from Jamestown to Franklin, arriving shortly after ten that night. As soon as my dad saw Nathan, he exclaimed, "Look at the size of his hands and feet. I think he's going to be a basketball player!"

Judy stayed to help me for two weeks after I returned home. When I was back on my feet, she took a bus back to Jamestown. My in-home babysitting service enabled me to stay home and care for Nathan. Todd proved to be an excellent big brother by fetching bottles and sitting on the couch, gently holding his little brother in his arms. Quite often, he entertained the older kids after school by playing ball outside. We happily settled into our new routine.

I spent the remainder of the year focusing on my two sons and pushed aside thoughts of my family in Jamestown. At forty-one and thirty-nine, it was time for Dad and Mom to deal with their own problems without involving Randy and me. Respecting our newly set rules, my mother made it a point to be upbeat whenever she called. She loved listening to stories about her two grandsons rather than sharing her woes. Because Judy and Kim seemed to have settled down and Linda and Lisa were excelling in school, I assumed their lives were better.

My assumption was shattered when my mother called me early in January, 1972. She was livid because she'd just learned Judy was pregnant. She ranted and raved about the baby's father being a good-for-nothing bum, and fell short of calling Judy a slut. A few days later, I received a frantic call from Judy asking if she could take a bus to Clarion to stay with us.

"Are things really that bad at home, Judy?" I inquired.

I could hear her crying on the other end of the line. Between sobs, she caught her breath enough to say, "Mom accused Dad of fathering my baby! I can't live with her another minute, Diana. She's the sickest bitch in the world!"

At midnight, I met her at the bus stop. Randy and I allowed her to stay with us on one condition—she had to enroll at Clarion High School. Reluctantly, she did. She also got a job at a local coffee shop on weekends and comfortably settled into our lives and our home.

The Road Back to Hell

One morning, in the beginning of March, Judy noticed blood on her panties. Because there weren't any gynecologists in Clarion, she made an appointment to see her doctor in Jamestown. I drove her to the appointment the next day. Her doctor suggested ten days of complete bed rest and a return visit in two weeks. She decided to remain in Jamestown with her friend, Debbie until the baby was born.

About three weeks later, my mother called. She was hysterical. My father had apparently punched her in the face and broken her nose. I was accustomed to her dramatic acts and coolly replied, "What did you do to provoke him?" She hung up.

Through the years, I'd witnessed enough of my parents' arguments to know my mother was the provocateur about ninety-percent of the time. While I didn't condone physical abuse, I realized Mom obviously pushed Dad to the limit if he'd hit her in the face. Sometimes, when she verbally abused Dad to his breaking point, his fists came out and he punched holes in walls, dented the refrigerator or broke a lamp or two. But most of the time he stormed out of the door.

While trying to decide whether or not to call her back, the phone rang again. This time it was my sister Judy. "Dad told me to call and let you know he's hitchhiking to your house. He and Mom had the worst fight they've ever had, and he wanted to get away before he killed her!"

Then she told me the story. Debbie, Judy's friend, worked part-time at her parents' bar on Windsor Street. That afternoon, Debbie called Judy and told her to grab a taxi and get to the bar right away, because her father needed her! When Judy arrived, she found Dad slumped over the table with his head buried in his hands, shaking uncontrollably. She put her arms around his shoulders and asked, "Daddy, what's wrong?"

Dad slowly lifted his head, wiped the tears from his cheeks with the back of his hand, and said, "Mom and I were having a huge fight when Linda rushed into the room to try and stop it. The next thing I know, your mom started screaming that Linda isn't my daughter—she belongs to Frank. I couldn't listen to another word, so I pushed past her and fled out the back door."

Judy described how my father took a deep breath, stared up at the ceiling as if looking for some sign, and continued. "Linda came outside and found me on the back steps. She was crying when she asked me if I was her daddy. I wrapped her in my arms, held her close and assured her I was her daddy and always would be. I told her to ignore her mother because she was lying. I kissed her and walked away before anything else could happen. Then I walked down here."

After a few moments of silence, Dad went on to say, "That fucking bastard Frank called here to tell me he is Linda's father!" His face crumbled as he emotionally fell apart. When he looked up a few minutes later, his eyes implored her to tell him the truth. "Linda is *my* daughter, isn't she, Judy?"

Before Judy could answer, she saw Frank come strutting through the door with his chest expanded like a puffed-up rooster. She raced across the barroom floor and confronted him. "What did you do to my father, you asshole?"

"I didn't do anything to him—he did it to himself," Frank proclaimed. The sinister look in his dark eyes was unnerving. "He's never been man enough to keep your mother at home and now he can't face the fact that I fathered your sister!"

Judy kicked him in the balls. "You're not a man, you're a pencil dick!" she hollered.

The bartender helped her get Dad into the waiting taxi. They went back to Mom's to pack his things. While Judy was busy throwing Dad's clothes into bags, she overheard Mom yell, "Stew, Frank's right. You're a sorry excuse for a man! You've never been man enough to keep me home. He fathered both Linda and Lisa!"

Judy looked into the kitchen and saw Dad punch Mom in the face before he stormed out the door. Judy followed him.

Eighty-five miles wasn't far enough to keep me away from my family's never ending problems. I often cursed Alexander Graham Bell for inventing the telephone. Dad arrived at our house early the next morning. When I saw the haunted look in his eyes, his disheveled appearance and a long, deep scratch on his face, I couldn't turn him away. He needed us.

The Road Back to Hell

A small room upstairs we used for storage was easily converted into a bedroom for my father. Within a week, he found employment as a truck driver for Clarion Manufacturing, a local mobile home plant. He was away most of the week hauling mobile homes. On the weekends, he helped with little chores around the house, spent hours playing with Todd and usually spent Saturday nights at the bar at Rhea's Corners. My dad could talk to anyone, from an unemployed guy down on his luck to a science professor. He was well versed in a variety of subjects, especially sports, music and world events. With his outgoing personality and entertaining stories, he easily made friends at this little bar in Shippenville.

One Saturday night, I was in the kitchen heating a bottle for Nathan, when I heard him singing as he passed by the window. He opened the back door, winked at me and said, "I just met the woman of my dreams. I think I'm in love!" The huge grin on his face made him look like a teenage kid coming home from his first date. I was delighted for him until I learned the woman's name. I recognized it. She was married to a prominent business owner in Shippenville. There had been numerous stories about her carousing.

"Dad, you can't date Joan, she's a married woman!" I exclaimed. "I know, and I'm technically a married man. She's not happy and neither am I. So why can't we just enjoy each other's company?"

"Go to bed. We'll talk about it in the morning." I pecked him on his cheek and went upstairs to feed Nathan.

The next morning, over coffee, I expressed my thoughts about his new relationship. It was impossible to convince my father his foolhardiness would result in another broken heart. He didn't heed my warnings. Instead, he began dating Joan on a regular basis.

While the year was ending badly for my mother and sisters, 1972 was ending on a high-note for Randy and me. Randy graduated with a teaching degree from Clarion State College in mid-December 1972. We celebrated by hosting a party for all of our friends. Our house overflowed with well-wishers and partiers who were there to congratulate him. Everyone asked about our plans for the future but we couldn't answer them because our future depended on whether or not Randy could obtain a teaching position.

At the end of the evening, when everyone had left, I found Dad passed out in a recliner. With his elbow propped on his knee and his right hand holding up his head, he reminded me of Rodin's sculpture of "The Thinker". I snapped a picture.

I've often wondered what he was thinking about on that joyous night in December, 1972.

CHAPTER 31

1973- The Beginning

WHILE WRITING THIS memoir, I would often search for items in a box of memorabilia I had stored in my attic. Three months before finishing this book, I was looking for an old newspaper article when I discovered some folded pieces of spiral notebook paper. When I unfolded them, I realized the cursive handwriting belonged to my mother. I was stunned. At the top of the first page, she had written 'My Personal Diary- 1973'.

As I stared at the yellowed pages, I tried to recall when and how these letters had come into my possession. I did not remember ever seeing them before. My hands were shaking as I began to read her words from so long ago. I settled into an old chair and read every page. When I closed my eyes and remembered her, as she had been in 1973, I began to cry. She weighed about one-hundred and forty-pounds; twenty- pounds over her average weight. She had added some blonde coloring to her short, dark brown hair, making her look much older than forty-one. Her face was puffy and she wore more makeup than she had in her younger years. When you looked into her eyes, you could see how the years of upheaval had taken their toll.

Her letters clearly reminded me of how unhappy and conflicted she had been throughout most of her life. Many of the memories I had buried deep in my heart came flooding back. At one point, I began speaking out loud about these things. I could almost feel her presence. I told her how much I had loved her as a small child and how painful it had been to watch as she became addicted to alcohol. When I expressed my bitterness because she had practically abandoned my sisters, especially the youngest two, the dam broke. I sobbed for a long time. After I had purged myself of the pent-up anger, I felt a great sense of relief, and with it, some forgiveness. I looked up at the attic ceiling and said, "Mama, it's over now. I pray that you have finally found peace." I knew she wasn't sitting there before me, but I felt in my heart she had heard me.

I still don't remember receiving this packet of letters. When I asked my sisters about Mom's diary, none of them were aware of it. Instead of pondering the source, I have accepted it as a gift—a gift I shared with Judy, Linda, and Lisa. Her diary provided us with a deeper understanding of Mom's pain, her alcoholism, her strengths, and her weaknesses. Although it provided each of us with some peace, we are still seeking answers to our mother's psychological problems.

Her diary paints a picture of her day-to-day life during the first two months of 1973. It also offers glimpses into the ongoing problems my parents faced throughout their twenty-two years of marriage. I have transcribed the words exactly as she wrote them, to give you, the reader better insight into our family life.

January 1, 1973
Dear Diary,
I suppose for a woman my age, this is rather silly, but I need help and I'm sure I'm the only one that can do it along with the help of God. I've got to make it, and if I write things down every day, and read it, maybe I can improve myself. I've got to stop drinking beer as I do. I know how much I'm hurting everyone I love. First I lost Stew, then Daddy, & now little by little I'll lose the kids love, too. I've got to straighten up. If Mom were alive, she'd die of a broken heart, too. The only time I've ever been happy in my whole life is when I married Stew. Oh God, why did things ever have to go so wrong between us? No matter who's to blame, I've always loved him. I know I've wronged him so, and I'd give anything if I could undo it. But of course, it's all too late now. He doesn't want me anymore. If is a very big word though. But, I'll love him until my

dying day, no matter what I do. I really believe that's why I turned to George. I was so lonely, & he was like Stew in so many ways. But I don't love him. The only reason I've seen him since Xmas is because I got so lonely. But dear diary, I'm going to help myself for my kids, & Mom & Dad. Stew probably won't care by now, but at least my girls & Mom & Dad will know, & maybe respect me & love me again. Oh my loves, I'm sure going to try. I love you & need all of you so.

January 4
Dear Diary,
Kim told me, her and Dan may get married soon. Well, we'll see.
 Stayed home again, but goofed and drank a 6 pack. But that's some improvement. Going to watch TV now.

January 6
Dear Diary,
Kenny and George came down tonight and played Yahtzee. George bored me so much I came in and watched TV. Oh he irritates me. I know he's good to the kids and they love him, but you know Diary, he's <u>not</u> Stew, and I can't help it. I had 4 beers today and one tonite. Nite now, I'm tired.

January 10
Dear Diary,
Sorry I haven't kept in touch, but I've been fighting with George.
 When he calls, I'm going to tell him to leave me alone for good. He took me out last night and I got drunk. But I was miserable. I kept hoping all day yesterday Stew would call to wish me a happy birthday. Guess what! I didn't have one beer all day & only 2 tonite. Stayed home all day, too. See you tomorrow. Nite now.

January 11
Dear Diary,
Guess what! Stew called today and wished me a Happy Birthday. He's coming up tomorrow. Oh God! I know he only wants to see the kids, but he was so nice to me on the phone. I can hardly wait to see him. Careful Bonnie! Don't get your hopes up. Nite now!

January 12
Dear Diary,
Oh, I'm so disappointed. Stew called & said he couldn't make it after all. God I feel so low. I wish I really didn't care anymore. The kids know the truth, but I doubt if he'll ever know. I'd like to get drunk, but I'm not going to. I've had about 4 or 5 beers, but I'm going to sleep now so I won't drink anymore. See ya tomorrow. Nite now.

January 13
Dear Diary,
I turned the 7:30 news on today & got the shock of my life. George was arrested for burglary. Kenny said he'll face about 20 years for this. I'm kinda upset now. He has <u>no one</u> in the world. I know he knows I don't love him, but Kenny said not to say anything now, as there's no telling what he'll do, knowing what he's facing. I suppose I should lie to him & let him think I care, but I don't know if I can do it. I was down to Smokey's today, and of course, I goofed. I'm not drunk, but I drank a little more than I have lately. D--me, anyways. I'm sorry. You know, I'm so tired. Nite.

January 16
Dear Dairy,
Stayed home all day. Had 5 beers, then a couple later. Stew stopped tonite. He had a trip to Dansville. I had spaghetti and chocolate pudding. He could only stay a couple of hours. He

made love to me. God I love him so, but how can I ever prove it, after what I've done? I'd give anything if we could get back together. I cried when he left. If only I could make him believe in me again. We <u>could</u> be happy now, I know. Kim will be leaving soon. Stew said I may as well let them get married. I know if we're alone with just the little girls now, we'd make it. But there I go again. He'll probably never come back. Maybe I <u>should</u> take the kids to Arizona. I can't go on like this. Maybe out there we could make a better life. The kids don't stand a chance here, after what Stew and I have done. But can I do it, alone? I'm scared, but maybe I will. I've lost everything I love here, Mom, Dad, Stew and soon my kids might hate me. Well, I'm going to try to sleep now. Nite

January 18
Dear Diary,
Al drove me up to take George some ciggs. Phil bought for George. I didn't see him, & thank God, I don't want to. What do I tell him? I can lie in a letter, but if he saw my eyes & face he'd know the truth. Last nite, Jessie & Sherry & Al brought me home. Ish, he's a puke! My kids are mad at me, and I don't blame them. Today Al came up & took the little ones & me down to Diana's for Randy's birthday. I didn't eat all day & was feeling it when we got to Diana's. The kids stayed down there. I slept all the way home. He's a creep. I was praying I'd see Stew, but didn't. I didn't do anything wrong but get drunk, but Stew probably would never believe me. But I do have some pride.

January 21
Dear Diary,
Stew & his girl friend brought the kids home from Diana's today.
    Lisa was sick. God but he looked so wonderful. Oh Diary, I love him so. May as well try and forget it, tho. He didn't give

me any money, but said he sent it. Sure hope so. It's so good to have my girls home, I love them so. Only had 3 beers today. I'm <u>still</u> trying. I'm <u>still</u> going to make it Diary, for myself & everybody.

January 22
Dear Diary,
Stayed home today. Kept Lisa home. She has a little fever., but doesn't act to sick. Hope she'll be ok. Didn't sleep much last nite. I keep seeing Stew the nite he came up and I had spaghetti. It was so good to cook for him again. Did real well today, Diary. Only had 3 beers today. Nite now.

January 23
Dear Diary,
Lisa's still sick. Kept her home again. I feel so lonely tonite. I had 4 beers today, but none tonite. The girls seem so happy to be home. I love them so, and God knows I don't mean to hurt them. I'm not going to anymore, if I can help it.

January 27
Dear Diary,
Sorry, I forgot you last nite. Same story, tho. I was home all day, but yesterday, Jan. 26, I went down to get my hair done. I ran into Kenny and never did get it done. Mary Beth & Eddy brought me home. Oh dear, I goofed again. I went downtown late today as the kids weren't home, but I came home at 7:00. Kids said Stew called! He's supposed to call back! Oh God, I hope so. See you later.

(8pm) Stew just called. He's going to try and get Diana's car & come up. He sounds as if he wants to see <u>me!</u> Oh, I'm so excited. I love him so.

January 28

Dear Diary,

Stew just left! He got here about 3pm. It was so wonderful to be in his arms again. We took Nannie to the hospital this morning. She's pretty sick. Then we met Kenny at Smokey's. We had a nice time, but he had to leave early as Diana needs the car, I'm so happy. I love him so. The kids are really happy, too. I know he still loves me, I can tell when he makes love to me. But I think he's afraid, and I <u>don't</u> blame him. If he gives me another chance, I'll never let him be sorry. We seem to be able to talk things out better now. Well, who knows? He said he'll try to come up next weekend. Goodnight, Dear Diary.

February 6

Dear Diary,

Sorry I haven't written, but Stew came home Sat. I went back with him Sun. nite (tho Diana told me she's afraid he'll hurt me this time!) I can't believe it. We had a wonderful time, and he seems as happy as me. I came home on the bus tonite. God I miss him, but he'll be home on Sat. It's going to seem so long till then.

February 7

Dear Diary,

Had so much to do today around here. But only 2 beers. See, I am getting better. I'm so happy, I keep pinching myself. I've waited a year for this, but never had much hope. Of course, nothing's different yet, but after what we've had together lately, I can't believe Diana. All I want in this world is for Stew & I to be back together, and be a family again, as it was years ago. I love him & the girls so. God above me knows this. Well, nite now.

February 12
Dear Diary,
Stew came home Sat. He met me at Smokey's, when his bus came in. I wanted to go home and change, but he wouldn't let me. He said I looked so pretty & told everyone I always look pretty. I was so proud of him. He looked so sharp. We went out for dinner, but then the kids called and we had to go home. We stayed home Sunday & I cooked for him, then Kenny & I took him home. I'll see him next week. Maybe we can go out Sat. nite as we started to last weekend. It was so wonderful to be with him. I dread this week. It's going to just drag. But Friday is Kim's shower, & the guys all have to get their tuxes on Sat., so I probably will be home early. I'm really starting to be proud of myself. Diary, I'm doing good. I want to make Stew & the girls proud of me, and Mom & Dad, too. I know I have hurt Daddy, too, and I'm so ashamed of hurting all of them as I have. Well, nite now.

February 15
Dear Diary,
Went downtown yesterday to get Stew a Valentine & goofed again.
   Got home about 9:00. The kids are upset, but not like they used to be. I'm mad at myself. I stayed home today. I've had about 6 but no more tonight! Gee, sure wish it was Sat. Diana doesn't think Stew's is coming tomorrow nite, but he'll probably be on the early bus, Saturday. Well, night now.

February 17
Dear Diary,
Well, Stew didn't come home. I called him today. He sounds kinda funny & I've got a weird feeling. Oh God, please let me be wrong. I went downtown about 3:00 to see if I could borrow some money. I only have had 21/2 beers & left one. I waited until 7:00 praying Stew would surprise me & come in on that bus, but no luck! I

called Diana to come get me. She came home for Kim's shower. I babysat tonite for all the kids, even Billy Joe. I didn't have one beer. I'm so miserable. Maybe Stew will call me tonite. I'm scared, Diary.

February 18
Dear Diary,
Well, my fears were not in vain. I called Stew today. He doesn't want to come back, after all. He said he's afraid. I found out the truth. Him & Joan had a fight & she was in Florida. Apparently, that's why he's been coming up. Oh god, I can't believe he'd do this to me, although he did it before with Elaine. My kids told me Joan is so bossy to Stew & even her kids say she's mean to him. I think she found out he's been seeing me again, now she wants him back.

Well, if she means more to him than the kids and I do, he can have her. I won't fight. But I'm still going to keep on trying, for the kids sake. I went downtown today, but had to fight tears all day. I feel just like I did when Daddy died. I got the kids some subs & came home at 7:30. I only had 5 beers.

I just opened one, but I don't even want it! Oh Stew, why did you come back & do this to me? Was it for revenge? If so, you surely got it. I feel so bad, but my little girls have been on my lap all nite. At least I've got them. No matter how I hurt, dear Diary, I'm going to be fine. Nite now!

February 19
Dear Diary,
Stayed home today, & washed & cleaned all day. It helps to keep busy.

Tried to watch TV, but kept thinking of Stew & Daddy, so finally gave up. I'm going to Dr., as soon as I can, & get some nerve medicine. I hope I can find a job, but I shake so, I can't even write anymore. Oh God, how much more can I take? I'm trying tho, and won't go off the deep end again. If I do goof once in a while, please forgive me. I'm <u>still</u> going to make my kids & Dad proud of me. I think I'm making a start. I've learned to live without Stew fir a year now. All I have to do is make myself realize it's over. Only this time, I'm going to really become a decent person again. If Stew really wants me, he knows I'm here. If we don't get back together soon, I may as well let the divorce go through. I know this God, that Joan doesn't really love him. She's just using him. Well, it's none of my business, I guess. He said he'd call me this week, but I really doubt it. The kids feel so bad. But they've been hurt so much, too, they're trying to accept it. They know they've got me. I had about 6 beers today. I'm sorry but at least I was home all day. Nite now. See you tomorrow.

February 20
Dear Diary,
Well, I didn't stay home today. Went down to get Kim's invitations, then went to Smokey's. Judy & the baby came in & Vic gave us a ride home. I called Stew, like a fool. He said he's <u>not</u> coming back. He hung up on me and it made me so mad. I called Joan and told her how he's been coming up & all he's said & done, & how upset the kids have been. I don't really care, either. He can't keep on hurting me and not get paid back. No matter how I love him, I'll never trust him again. I'll piece myself together. I've been hurt so much, what difference does it make now? Well, only a short time now before my Kim will leave me, too. She's getting married a week from Friday. I'm so worried about getting things done for the wedding. Stew promised he'd give me money, but all of these things have to be paid, & there's no money for it. I don't know what to do half of the time. I want things so nice for her, but every time I try to do something, it backfires in my face. I'm about

ready to just give up, I've had it! I suppose Stew will really hate me when he finds out I've called Joan. Oh well! She wasn't coming back anyways, so who cares?

God I wish I could find a job. I'd feel so much better. I've got too much time on my hands. Well, nite now!

February 21– Mom's Suicide Note

Dear Diary,

Well, today was another day. I've had it, dear Diary. I've done all that I can, but this is about it. You should have heard Judy and Kim. Stew promised he'd send money for the gas, but he didn't, of course. He never does keep his promise. Diana, I know this is my diary, but I've got to ask you. Please don't ever let Joan & Dad have my girls. Make Dad help you, but please, you take care of them. I couldn't stand it if Joan had them. I just want them to grow up happy. Please, please don't let Dad and Joan have the girls, no matter what happens. All I want is their happiness. I think with all of my heart this is the only way I can give it to them. I want them. I want them to remember "Mommie" & how much they do love me. I don't want them to think of me as you kids do. Daddy's always right, and no matter what, I'm wrong. I love you Diana. I love all of you girls. You've been my whole life.

The gas will be turned off. I tried to tell your Dad, but he didn't believe me and wouldn't listen to me. I don't know why he did this to me, but I'm going to die so he & Joan can live. Don't let them have the girls, please!!

Joan, I've got to say this to you. I don't feel anything about you being with Stew. But if you are any kind of woman, stay away from my kids, please!

Be woman enough for that!

Mom C,. I'm sorry Stew hasn't been around. I tried and I love you. I always tried to make him close to you. I'm sorry for everything. I love you, almost like my own Mom. Well Diary, said about enough for one nite. Please let everyone know how much I love them all. I really and truly do. Nite now.

Diana, I have to say this. Honey, I don't want to put any more burdens on you, but please, please take the girls. They love & need you. It will only be a few years. Everyone else has turned to you. This is the only time I've asked if I could live with you. I never have and never would, but <u>please</u> don't let Dad have the girls. Take it to court if you have to. They'll be grown up soon.

<u>Please</u> keep them honey. Don't let Dad and Joan have them. I couldn't stand that. I want them to grow up right, with you. Honey, this is the only thing I can give them. I'm no good, but please let them know I love them so much, I feel this is the only thing I can do. I don't want them ashamed of me, and I know they are. I'd rather be dead. That's the very best I can give you all. I <u>Love You</u>

February 25
Dear Diary,
I haven't written for a couple of days, but every thing's so mixed up now I don't know what I'm doing. I'm so hurt and confused. I've got to go to Arizona and I'm afraid. I don't want to leave the kids, but Diana thinks this is the only way left for me. I wanted to commit suicide the last time I wrote to you. Diana feels if I go out there for awhile, I can straighten up & make a new life for myself. Well, I don't <u>want</u> to go. I will, because I know this is the only decent thing I can do for Linda & Lisa. They deserve a better life. If I get a job & like it out there, I'm coming back for them. I certainly don't want to give them up. They're all I have. The other kids have lives of their own.

February 25
Dear George,
Hi hon. Wanted to write to let you know how very bad I feel that I didn't get up to see you yesterday. I really tried, but couldn't find anyone to take me. Kenny smashed up his car and I couldn't find anyone else. I got your letter the other day, and was very happy to hear from you.

Honey, I've got some bad news for you. I'm going to Arizona. Diana talked me into it. I'm leaving the kids with Diana, and when I find a job & get settled, I'm coming back for them, altho it won't be until June, when they're out of school. She's afraid I'm on the verge of a breakdown & God help me, I believe her. Maybe it will do me good to get away for awhile. If I don't like it out there, I can come back. I'm letting the kids take my furniture, so at least I'll have it if I do come home. I really don't want to leave them, but I know I have to do this. I'm leaving next Sat. Kim is getting married Fri. nite, and the kids are going to take care of things for me. Oh hon, I'm so scared. I don't want to leave my kids and friends, but I'll never have anything is this town. I want to get up there to see you before I leave Sat. Maybe Diana can bring me up. I'll write to you when I get out there, & let you know where I am and what's going on.

Take good care of yourself hon. I'll see you on Sat. if I can.
Love always,
Bonnie

Last Letter-(no date)
My Darlings,

I wanted to write this letter to all of you to let each and every one of you know how very much I love you. I'm so frightened. Not of going away, but of leaving all of you. I pray to God I will be big enough to do it. But my love for all of you is so deep, I know I <u>have</u> to do this for you. I know it's better for all of you than what I have been doing to you. I don't want to hurt you anymore, and that's all I seem to do, all the time.

I wish I wasn't such a weak person, and been able to hold up under what I've gone through better than I have.

I know I can't be alone. I get too frightened. Maybe if I haven't always had to worry about money all the time, I could have made it. But it's too late now.

Diana, I really did want to work & straighten up. I did try and find a job, but that was even against me.

I know the loneliness that is in store for me. I only hope I can bear it. But when I feel I can't stand it, maybe it will help when I realize how much happier the girls life will be. I don't want Linda to grow up like Judy, and I know if I stay here & keep making her go through all this heartache, she will..

Diana, help Lisa, too. She's going to be so lonely for me. She'll probably get sick, at first. She always does when she's away from me. But please, please let them know how much I really do love them.

Oh honey, there's so much I want to say, but I can't find the right words.

It's going to be so hard to leave you all. I only wish they wouldn't turn my gas off, so I could have all of you with me the last couple of days, especially.

I hate your Father for doing this to me, because actually, he started this with me. I know I've done wrong, but honey, he has, too. I loved him so much. That's why I don't want him & Joan around the kids too much. He'll brainwash them as he always did Judy, especially now when he knows I'm gone. You can tell him, honey, he finally did get his revenge on me. It was about the cruelest way he could, but he did it.

When I come back for the girls honey, I'll be SOMEBODY! that you'll all really be proud of. This I swear to all of you. I will go to a Dr. out there. Shirley will help me, too. I'm going to get a job as soon as I get out there.

Diana, I love Judy, too, but I've never forgive her. I can't take anymore. She doesn't care at all about me, she's proven that. I can't take any more beatings from her or your Father.

Well, my dearest loved ones, I guess that's all. Honey, let Todd & Nathan know how very much Grandma loves them. I'll see you all on Thurs.

Your Loving & Devoted Mom, Always

Kim and Dan were married on Friday evening, March 6, 1973. The next day, Randy and I drove Mom to the bus stop for her journey to Arizona where she hoped to make a better life.

CHAPTER 32

1973-The Middle

AFTER MY MOTHER and I had shared a tearful goodbye at the bus stop, I went back to her apartment. I stayed in Jamestown for a week, closing up her apartment and packing Linda's and Lisa's belongings. Randy picked us up on Saturday. My sisters were saddened because Mom would be so far away, but they were also excited about living with us.

Dad moved out of our house so we could make a bedroom for the girls. I enrolled them in Clarion Elementary School where they quickly adjusted and made new friends. They seemed more like our daughters than my sisters, making it easy for Randy and me to welcome them into our lives.

Mom was having a difficult time adjusting in Arizona and frequently called. Before allowing her to speak to the girls, I made her promise she wouldn't upset them with her problems. They were happier than they had been in years, and I didn't want them disturbed. She kept her promise, saving all of her woes to share with me when we talked. Occasionally I spoke to Shirley, my mother's friend, about Mom's progress. Given time, Shirley believed she'd be able to help our mother quit drinking.

My father was welcome to visit Linda and Lisa whenever he wanted, but I kept Joan at bay as I promised my mother I would. One weekend in late April, I relented and allowed Dad and Joan to take them to Jamestown for the weekend. I knew they were missing Kim and Judy.

Judy never returned to my mother's house once she left in 1972. At the time of this visit, she was nineteen and living in Jamestown with her boyfriend, Corky and small son, Brandon. At seventeen, Kim was living with her husband, Dan in an apartment not far from Judy and Corky. The close proximity of their homes did nothing to improve their relationship with each other. The older they became, the further apart they grew, only getting together for occasional family visits. This was one of those visits.

When Linda and Lisa returned to Clarion on Sunday night, they told me about an incident that occurred while having dinner at Judy's.

Linda and Lisa had spent Saturday night at Kim's house and ate dinner at Judy's on Sunday. Dad and Joan were also invited. Like our mother, Judy was an excellent cook and throughout the meal, Joan complimented her cooking skills. After dinner, Judy asked if she'd like some dessert. When she consented, Linda and Lisa jumped up from the table and retrieved a brightly wrapped gift from the counter.

Smiling, Linda handed Joan the package. "We bought this for you." "It's for me? How sweet of you," Joan commented.

Lisa cowered behind Linda while Joan unwrapped the box of chocolates. "Oh, chocolate covered candy, my favorite. Thank you so much," she said before popping a large piece into her mouth. The expression on her face rapidly changed when she bit into it. "Hmm, this has a very unusual taste and texture. What is it?"

Lisa stepped out from behind Linda and proudly announced, "Chocolate covered bees!"

Aghast, Joan spewed the remaining piece onto her plate, stood up and declared she was leaving. She grabbed her purse and stormed out the door.

My four sisters howled with laughter until Dad yelled, "Whose idea was this?"

Seeing Dad's red face and the fire in his eyes, everyone knew he was furious. After a few moments, Linda and Lisa broke the silence by confessing they were the ones who bought the candies. While shopping with Kim the day before, they had spotted a sign in a store window advertising "Chocolate Covered Insects". They decided this delicacy would be the perfect gift for Joan. Unfortunately, Joan was unable to finish the first bite and never tasted the ants and flies remaining in the box. It was a long, silent drive back to Clarion.

When I shared this story with my mother, she laughed, which was something she had not done in a while. My mother called me about two weeks after the candy incident to tell me my Dad and Joan had split-up.

After spending almost three months in Arizona, Mom had decided to move back to Jamestown. Learning Dad was no longer with Joan obviously played a big part in her decision because she returned home the next week. Although she hadn't completely quit drinking, she was proud of herself for 'keeping it under control'. She appeared to be more emotionally settled. The separation from her family had enabled her to better understand what she needed to do if she wanted Linda and Lisa back. In preparation for their return, she found a small, affordable apartment, gathered her possessions from storage and got a job. She anxiously awaited the school year to end in June so Linda and Lisa could return to Jamestown.

Randy and I were extremely reluctant to take them back and they were sad to be leaving. The girls had thrived while living in Clarion. It was an unhappy day for all of us when we packed up their belongings and drove them home. However, we understood there was no choice. Mom had worked hard to improve her situation and, as their mother, we'd decided she deserved another chance.

The first few weeks after Linda and Lisa left, our lives felt empty. I missed their constant chatter, the sounds of their feet as they chased each other through the house, their laughter, and their love. We had truly bonded during the five months they had spent with us, and I wished they could have stayed forever.

When Randy graduated from college, he had applied for several teaching positions. The only job he was offered was in Fairbanks, Alaska, which we felt was too far away. Since January, he had worked for a masonry contractor from Shippenville, constructing foundations for mobile homes. Many nights after work, he stopped with his boss, John, for beers before coming home. John was an alcoholic, and I feared Randy was following in his footsteps. As his nightly stops at the bar increased, so did our arguments. Our biggest argument occurred on the night he didn't get home until 3:00 am.

The Road Back to Hell

Earlier that week, our Volkswagen had conked out, and we had to replace it. Randy was beaming when he stepped out of the 1967 pea green Chevy Camaro he had purchased in Oil City. He instructed me to call the babysitter so we could go for a spin in our new car. After our babysitter had arrived, I climbed into this sporty car and we sped off. The windows were down, and the radio was blaring as we cruised around Clarion like two teenaged kids. We stopped at Rhea's Corners to get something to eat and to show our new car to some of our friends who worked there. After a couple of drinks and dinner, we returned home. I went into the house while Randy drove the babysitter home. She only lived a few blocks away and I expected him back shortly. When an hour had passed and he hadn't returned, I began to worry. After two hours had passed, I decided to call Rhea's, thinking he may have gone back there. The bartender told me he hadn't seen Randy since we had been there earlier. I paced the floor as midnight turned into 1:00 am. By 2:00 am, I was frantic. When he walked in the door at 3:00 am, I was furious! We argued until he passed out in a chair.

The next morning he apologized. I refused to accept his apology until he told me where he had been for over five hours the night before. He couldn't look me in the eyes. Instead, he grabbed his coffee thermos, brushed past me and said we'd talk when he came home from work. He left me steaming mad.

I was relieved when my daily charges started arriving that morning. Caring for the children kept me busy, and I didn't have time to dwell on last night's fiasco. While the kids were watching television, I gathered a basket of dirty clothes and started to put them into the washer. The navy-blue jacket Randy had worn the night before lay on the top of the heap. As I was going through the pockets, I pulled out a balled-up, crusty, white hanky which I assumed he had used to blow his nose. Then I noticed the dried, flaky, white streaks on the front of his jacket. Next, I checked his underwear. The dried substance was on there, too. At that moment, I realized what had kept him away so long. It was apparently dried semen! I threw up in the sink.

Over the years, I had overlooked his flirtatious behavior but this time was different. I decided I'd get my revenge. I called a friend and asked if she'd meet me for drinks that night, telling her I needed to talk. Randy came home from work about five and was shocked when he saw I was wearing my brown, pinstriped mini dress and high heel shoes. I'd applied fresh makeup and styled my hair into a flip.

"Wow! You look beautiful! What's going on?"

I didn't want to scream in front of the boys, so I got as close to him as possible and in my strongest, non-shouting voice said, "I'll tell you what's going on, you cheating bastard! I found your scummy jacket and hanky when I was doing the wash. It's pretty clear that you were out screwing our babysitter last night! I hope you realize she's only seventeen and you could get arrested for seducing a minor!"

"I can explain," he dismally muttered.

"Don't bother. I'm going out tonight and show you how it feels to wonder where I am and what I'm doing. I fed Todd and Nathan so you should be able to handle the rest of the parental duties. Your dinner's on the table." I strutted out the door leaving him with his mouth hanging open and no opportunity to reply. I wondered how he'd react when he saw the big pile of mashed potatoes topped with meatloaf, peas, tossed salad, and anything else I could find, sitting on his plate, covered with gravy which had coagulated from sitting there so long.

I was shaking when I started the car, and had no idea where I was going. I had an hour to kill before meeting Marlene at the Holiday Inn, so I stopped at the home of an older friend who worked with me at Rhea's. She was a motherly type who would be able to calm me down. Theresa was delighted when I knocked on her door. She was even more delighted that I had reached out to her in my time of need. Feeling much better after my talk with Theresa, I left to meet Marlene.

On the drive to the Holiday Inn, I thought about my objective for the evening—getting even with Randy. How was I going to do it? I would never pick up a guy in a bar and have sex with him. The thought nauseated me. I'd be acting just like my mother. Instead, I decided to drink myself into oblivion, which Marlene encouraged me to do by promising to see I got home safely.

I had a great time belting down the stingers and dancing the night away. At the end of the evening, a local State Policeman joined me at my table. I'd waited on him for years and felt comfortable with his presence. He expressed his concern for the amount of alcohol I'd been drinking and offered to drive me home. *Sure. Why not? He's a cop; it's safe.*

When Marlene returned to our table, I announced that Bill would drive me home.

"Oh no, he won't!" she retorted. "You came with me and you're going home with me. Get your purse, sweetie." Then she guided me out the door. Next morning I called to thank her for saving me from an ugly situation.

After several days of serious talks and many apologies from Randy, I forgave him. What choice did I have? We had two sons who needed both of us. He promised he would never do anything like that again. I believed him.

One of the things we had seriously talked about over the past few days, had been our future. After Randy had graduated, we had considered moving back to Jamestown. My friend, Lynn, said her father would help Randy get a job in the office at Crescent Tool. As generous as this offer was, Randy didn't think he was qualified for that type of position.

When we had first moved to Clarion, I couldn't wait for the day we could return home. But my feelings had changed. I loved Clarion and did not want to go back to the melodrama of my parents life. We decided to stay.

I read an advertisement in the *Clarion News* about a house for sale in Shippenville for $10,000. The owners were willing to accept a rent-with-option-to-buy deal. It was an opportunity we couldn't miss. I promptly made an appointment with the owner to see it. It was a white, two-story clapboard house located on a private back street in Shippenville. There was very little traffic on the road, making it safe for the boys to play outside. It needed some cosmetic work, nothing that a little paint and elbow grease couldn't fix. We signed the sales agreement the next week and moved in two weeks later.

I gave up my babysitting jobs and became a full-time wife and mother. I loved it. The day we moved in, our next door neighbor, Nancy, brought us a hot casserole for dinner. She had a son Todd's age, a husband who loved watching sports and drinking beer, and she enjoyed drinking coffee with her friends. Life was good!

Whenever Dad's job as a driver for Clarion Manufacturing took him through the Jamestown area, he stopped to visit my sisters. I assumed he spent time with Mom as well, but I was totally unprepared for his news. I was outside working in the yard on a beautiful summer day in July when I noticed his truck coming down the road. When he descended from the cab, he had a bright, sunny smile on his face. I smiled back and invited him inside for coffee. I hadn't seen him for a while and wanted to catch up.

As he was preparing to leave, he casually said, "I stopped to tell you that your mother and I are getting remarried in August. We would like you and Randy to come to the wedding."

I froze. "Are you kidding me, Dad? After all she has put you through, you are actually going to remarry her?"

"Diana, I'll always love your mother. I know she's done some pretty awful things in the past, but so have I. I believe she's changed, and we can make it work this time."

Is he crazy? How can he go back to that situation? Why is he putting Randy and me in this position?

"Where will you live?" I sarcastically asked. "We're looking for a place in Clarion."

I was shocked. The smile on my dad's faded when I didn't react positively. All of the horrible scenes from the past rapidly scrolled through my mind. While I loved my family, I couldn't face dealing with all the drama again. Something inside me snapped.

"How can you do this to us?" I cried. "How can you bring Mom down here? Randy and I are trying to escape from the problems. We have built a beautiful life for ourselves in Clarion and now that will all change. We'll be dealing with your problems for the rest of our lives."

My father rarely raised his voice to me, but that day, he shouted, "Diana, I can't believe you feel this way. I never thought you were capable of hurting me so deeply." Tears welled up in his eyes. "Just remember one thing—blood is thicker than water," he said as he walked out the door.

Although my father's blood did not flow through my veins, he was the only father I had ever known, and I loved him with all of my heart. He was not only my Dad, he was often my best friend and confidant; his words made it very difficult for me to stand my ground.

Later that day, when Randy came home from work, he found me crying in our bedroom. I could barely speak. I finally stopped crying long enough to tell him what had happened. I was upset I'd hurt my father. But the thought of my parents living in this small town where everyone would know about the sordid past from which I'd run, upset me even more. This was not fair!

Mom and Dad were married in the Evangelical Methodist Church in Warren on August 26, 1973. The only people in attendance were my Uncle Kenny, who served as best man, and Mom's friend, Vonnie, her maid of honor. A week later Dad, Mom, Linda, and Lisa moved into a lovely, little house in Marianne Estates, two miles from our home.

Looking back, I cannot remember how Kenny had re-entered our lives after the incident with my sister, Kim. But like so many other situations, my parents had obviously pushed it "under the rug".

CHAPTER 33

1973-The End

It was still difficult for me to accept the situation. After my parents had been in Clarion for about two weeks, Randy finally broke the ice by saying, "I understand you're upset because your mother moved here and I'm aware of the problems she could cause. But, I think you're more upset about the fight you had with your dad."

It took me a few minutes to reply, "I am upset about Dad. It's killing me."

"That settles it. Grab the kids, and we'll surprise them with a visit." Todd's eyes lit up when I told him we were going to see Grandma Bonnie and Grandpa Stew. Having lived in their home as a baby, he was very close to them and anxious to see them. At two, Nathan was oblivious to everything. While washing Nathan's face, I told him where we were going. He looked up at me with his big brown eyes and asked, "Linda and Lisa, too?" I pulled him close to my chest and whispered, "Yes, Linda and Lisa, too." He put his small hand into mine as we walked out the door.

My fears and reservations dissipated the moment I entered their new home. Our reunion was joyous. The moment my father came into the living room, I ran into his waiting arms. The strength of our embrace was enough. No words were needed.

The next four weeks were like something out of a fairytale. My mother's transformation was evident in everything she did. She glowed whenever she talked about Dad. She made sure he had a hot meal every night for dinner, and often made his favorite desserts. Every day when Dad came home from work, Mom greeted him at the door with a smile and a kiss. This is not to say she had become a Stepford Wife, but it was a vast improvement over the wife she'd been for the past twelve years. She reminded me of the mother I'd known when I was four. I looked forward to our daily upbeat conversations and listened as she proudly bragged about Linda's and Lisa's progress in school. The girls had been delighted to return to school in Clarion, and reunite with the friends they had made while living us.

Todd spent Sunday afternoons helping Grandpa Stew with chores. He told his grandfather he wanted a mini-bike, so my dad 'hired' him to help with little jobs around the house and the yard. The money Todd earned was put into the Mini-Bike Fund. During our frequent visits to my parents house, Nathan entertained everyone with his effervescent personality. We all gave him our undivided attention whenever he did or said something funny and he soaked it up like a sponge.

One afternoon after work, Dad came to see me. We sat on the porch watching the boys playing in the yard and talked about their new life. As we sat there talking, I noticed significant changes in my father—his face was fuller, his smile was brighter and he was much calmer. When I looked into his eyes, it was evident he was happy. It was one of the most peaceful times we'd ever spent together.

Toward the end of September, Dad's workload had increased due to severe flooding in areas around the Appalachian Mountains in New York. Clarion Manufacturing had been contracted to provide mobile homes to that area, which meant their drivers delivered homes non-stop. My parents were grateful for the additional income the extra hours provided, but Mom was concerned about Dad's health. She told me the past week had taken a toll on him and he was exhausted.

On Thursday evening, I invited my mother to a Tupperware party I was hosting, so she could meet my friends. I was surprised when I heard Dad's truck pulling into my driveway. Just as the demonstrator began her presentation, Dad popped his head inside the front door and motioned for Mom to join him outside. Returning a few minutes later, she told me my father had been called to work to make another delivery to New York. We were both upset. He'd only been home for a short time from his last trip and hadn't had much rest.

About eleven o'clock, the next night, my father called Mom and told her he was in Elmira, NY and on his way home.

At five o'clock in the morning, on September 29, 1973, I was awakened by the shrill ringing of my phone. I lifted the receiver to my ear. Hearing my mother's hysteria quickly brought me to me senses. "Diana, I need you to come over right now. Daddy's dead!"

"What are you talking about?" I anxiously asked.

Her speech was incoherent. When she calmed down a little, she said someone from the State Police barracks called to tell her my father had been in an accident. The officer asked if there was another adult in the house he could speak to. When she told him she was the only one there, he advised her to contact an adult family member and have them call him. She begged me to hurry to her house to call the officer back.

I rushed out the door and started the car. Although I had been able to control my voice, I was unable to monitor the tremors in my legs. On the drive to my mother's house, I drove erratically.

Every light in the house was on when I pulled into her driveway. I ran into the house and found Mom sitting at the kitchen table, weeping uncontrollably. When she lifted her head, I saw the fear in her eyes. "I think he's dead, Diana."

Struggling to control my emotions, I knelt beside her and took her hands into mine. "You don't know that. He must have been in an accident, but that doesn't mean he's dead. Give me the number, and I'll call the sergeant right now."

She handed me the crumpled paper with the phone number on it and I went directly to the phone. My hands shook as I dialed. The phone had only rung twice when a male voice answered, "Pennsylvania State Police, Officer Kahle speaking, how may I help you?"

I swallowed the lump in my throat. "This is Diana Sharp, Stew Smith's daughter calling. My mother told me I was to call about my father Was he in an accident?"

"Just a moment please and I'll connect you to Sgt. Johns." What felt like hours, was only seconds when I heard a voice say, "Mrs. Sharp, this is Sergeant Johns. I need to make you aware of the situation with your Dad.

How is your heart?"

How was my heart? How the hell would your heart be if you were awakened in the middle of the night with a call from a shrieking mother telling you your Dad is dead?

Although those thoughts ran through my head, what came out of my mouth was, "My heart's okay. Please tell me what happened."

I'll never forget his chilling words, "I'm sorry to be the one to tell you this, but your father was killed in an accident."

He explained that the crash occurred at approximately two-thirty that morning just outside of Portland, New York. I was speechless. I felt as it was a bad dream, and I would soon wake up. The reality set in when I felt my mother tugging at my sleeve trying to get an answer from me. I gently shooed her away. I needed to find the strength to continue the conversation.

My next words were, "Tell me what I need to do."

My mother collapsed in my arms when I told her the news. We were devastated. Then I realized Lisa was standing in the living room. She had overheard every word. I gently sat mom in a chair and went to Lisa. She wrapped her arms tightly around my waist and said, "Is Daddy really dead?"

I couldn't answer her. I held her close and let her cry into my bosom.

I held my head up so she wouldn't see the tears streaming down my cheeks and into the crook of my neck.

Within twenty minutes, Randy arrived with Todd and Nathan still in their pajamas. Lisa ran to Randy the moment he walked in the door. Todd rushed to Grandma, and I held Nathan. Even though Nathan couldn't understand what had happened, he knew his mommy was sad. Holding him close brought me comfort. Linda wasn't home. She was spending the night at a slumber party.

About nine o'clock the next morning, Randy and I went to pick-up Linda. Before we left, I had called her friend's mother and shared our tragic news. She said she would wake Linda up and have her ready to go when we got there. She promised not to tell her. Linda looked confused when I went to the door. When we got to the car, I sat beside her in the back seat and held her in my arms while I shared the news of Dad's death. She stared at me in disbelief.

As with any family death, there were calls to family members and funeral arrangements to be made. As the oldest daughter, I was in charge of these duties. Frankly, I was grateful; it allowed me to escape the reality of my father's death.

My first calls were to Judy and Kim. Judy screamed, and Kim kept repeating, "Omigod, omigod." Telling Grandma Conklin she had lost her son was the most difficult call. I could not bring myself to say the words, "Daddy died in an accident," so when she answered I asked to speak to my grandfather. I rarely talked to him on the phone and I'm certain my request alerted her that something was dreadfully wrong. Upon hearing the news, Grandpa's voice cracked, "I'll tell her now, and we'll call you back soon."

The next call I made was to Pastor Daniels. He agreed to come to Clarion to officiate at Dad's funeral and closed our conversation with a prayer. Once again, he was my rock.

At ten that morning, the CEO of Clarion Manufacturing and Dad's supervisor arrived at my mother's house. After expressing their deep sorrow for the loss of my father, they offered any assistance they could provide to our family and gave Mom an envelope with a considerable amount of cash to help with the funeral expenses.

Grandma and Grandpa Conklin arrived around eleven. The shining gleam of her blue eyes had been replaced by a dull gray color; the whites of her eyes were reddened from weeping. With a forced smile, she comforted all of us with her hugs and her presence. As always, she was a stoic lady. They stayed at my house for the duration which gave us a chance to share memories of my father and her son. We laughed and cried a lot over the next few days.

After Judy, Kim and Uncle Kenny arrived, we sat down to plan the funeral. Ironically, the Welcome Wagon lady had stopped at my mom's on Thursday, two days before Dad's death. I was visiting Mom when she knocked on the door. My mother was delighted to see her because through all of her various moves, no one from Welcome Wagon had ever contacted her. We sat at the table while she spread out her bag of goodies. There was one item we laughingly dismissed. It was the first offer we'd soon redeem.

"I'm certain you won't need this anytime soon," the Welcome Wagon lady said as she laid the card for Goble Funeral home down on the table.

"God, I hope not," Mom cheerfully replied.

Spotting the card, still laying on the table, I picked it up and called Goble Funeral Home. I made an appointment for three-thirty that afternoon. Earlier that day, I called my doctor to get a prescription for Mom's stress. I can't remember what he prescribed, but it put Mom in a zone for the next three days. She was so spaced-out, Kim had to help her dress for the trip to the funeral home.

My mother, Grandma Conklin, Judy, Kim and I met with the funeral director. I was in a daze when we selected the casket and set the date and time of the funeral. The funeral director informed us my father's body wouldn't arrive until Sunday evening.

My father's body? Surely he didn't just say that. I think the policemen made a mistake when they identified the body. My dad's going to walk in here tomorrow and ask what's going on.

There was still some hope in my heart that this could actually happen.

My heart was broken on Monday morning when I saw his body lying in the casket.

All day Sunday, calls kept coming in from friends and family wishing to express their condolences. Our Clarion friends provided us with a marvelous array of meals and desserts. The outpouring of kindnesses overwhelmed us. Everyone in the family kept as busy as possible to avoid facing the reality of Dad's death. I volunteered to take his clothes to the Laundromat. One of my sisters asked me why I needed to wash his clothes when he wouldn't need them. I shrugged and said, "It's something I want to do."

As I dropped his soiled clothing into the washer, I lifted a dirty pair of size thirteen socks to my nose and inhaled his scent. My dad's feet were always smelly; these socks retained his odor. Then I lifted his soiled T-shirt to my nose and inhaled the scent of Old Spice, cigarette smoke, and sweat.

When I closed my eyes, it was as if he were standing next to me.

"Daddy," I whispered into his shirt, "I miss you so. What will we do without you?" I carefully put these items into a small bag. When I got home, I hid the bag in my closet. For several months after his death, whenever my pain was unbearable, I retrieved them from my closet and sniffed them. As the odor slowly faded, so did the pain.

The director of Goble Funeral home called Sunday evening to tell us Dad's body would be ready for the family viewing on Monday morning at ten. I had a difficult time sleeping that night. Whenever I closed my eyes, I saw my dad's face—his soft, curly blonde hair, his twinkling blue eyes and most clearly, his mischievous, quirky smile. I pictured him as he taught me to ride my bike, running in the rain with me, talking to me at the Prendergast Library and holding Todd and Nathan for the first time. Restless, I decided to get up. Walking past the bedroom where my grandparents were sleeping, I could hear my grandmother tossing and turning, too. I softly rapped on the door.

"Granny C," I whispered through the crack," Do you want to join me downstairs for coffee?"

"Yes," she quietly replied.

It was four o'clock in the morning when I started the first pot of coffee. I could hear Granny C's soft footsteps when she came into the kitchen. We embraced and shed more tears. Wiping the tears from her cheeks, I said, "No more tears tonight. We're going to talk about the happy times." My grandmother and I talked until the pinkish hues of the rising sun peeked over the horizon, replacing the darkness of the long night.

We met my mother and my sisters outside of Goble's at nine forty-five that morning. Although we all felt and looked like hell, we were able to smile and join hands as we walked through the doors of the funeral home. We stood in silence, mentally preparing to walk up to the casket and view Dad for the first time. It was the most difficult task of the entire three-day ordeal.

Mom was the first person to kneel at the casket and talk to my father. Although her wrenching wails were unbearable, we allowed her to lament for some time. When I could no longer take the sound of her crying, I walked up and gently led her to the sofa. My grandmother was the next person in line. While her cries were softer, I knew she was broken apart inside. My turn came next.

When I saw my father's body lying in that casket, I finally accepted the reality of his death. I could not cry. I just kept mumbling, "Daddy, I'm sorry. I'm so sorry." I prayed to God for the strength to help my mother and my sisters through the next two days. When everything was finally over, I would allow my tears to freely flow.

That afternoon and evening, the funeral home filled with flowers and friends. I was amazed at the number of people coming through the doors to express their grief over Dad's untimely death. I was particularly surprised when the Welcome Wagon lady touched my hand. I kept watch as the people came through the door. I was specifically looking for one person. I'd decided earlier that day if Joan set foot in the funeral home, I would meet her at the door and escort her out. I worried needlessly. She never showed.

The morning of the funeral, I anxiously awaited the arrival of Pastor Daniels. Throughout the past three days, my family had taken turns emotionally supporting one another. Now it was my turn to be comforted by someone I greatly admired. When he entered the funeral home, he walked directly up to me, wrapped his big, strong arms around my shoulders and patted my head while whispering, "It will be okay. He's with God now."

The funeral service was held at Goble Funeral Home. Before the service began, my grandparents and uncle were seated on the left side of the first row, with my mother cradled between Randy and me and my sisters seated beside me on the right. We joined hands as we listened to the moving eulogy Pastor Daniels provided. He extolled my father's many virtues and shared funny anecdotes reminding us of Dad's quick wit and sense of humor. He closed by telling us that Dad's suffering was over. He was now living in the House of the Lord. His words comforted us.

We followed the hearse to the Clarion Cemetery. Once again, Pastor Daniels offered words of wisdom and comfort. Just before the final prayer, he looked at me and my sisters and said, "Always remember girls, your father loved you all equally. You were his number one concern. Although he may no longer be with you in the flesh, he will continue to be with you in spirit." Mom knelt down in the dirt and loudly wept. We were all crying, but Judy's keening affected me the most. Hearing her wail made me shudder; I wanted to put my hand over her mouth and beg her to stop. I couldn't bear listening to her pain. Instead, I gathered all of my sisters together as we said our prayers and goodbyes to our father.

As everyone was leaving, Pastor Daniels pulled me aside. "Diana, I want to share something with you. You've been so strong throughout this ordeal because you were at peace with your father. You'll continue to be strong until all of the duties ahead are fulfilled. But the day will come within in the next two or three months when the reality will hit you. When that day comes, please reach out to me. I'll be there."

His kind and thoughtful words helped me more than anything during this very difficult time in my life.

While September 29th was not the end of the year, it was the end of my father's forty-three years of life and my parents' twenty-two years of marriage. Through all of the ups and downs of those years, I like to believe my father died a happy man. At that time, he and Bonnie were as happy as they had been when they married on May 26, 1951. Their lives had come full- circle.

CHAPTER 34

The Spirit of Christmas

1973

AFTER MY FATHER'S funeral, I assisted my mother with the mounds of paperwork needed for the insurance and social security claims. I also offered her comfort on the days she could barely function. Unable to face the reality of my father's death, I left myself no time to mourn.

There were two very positive outcomes from this tragedy. Tom, the CEO of Clarion Manufacturing, called my mother and told her they were giving her a new mobile home. They invited her to the showroom where she could select any mobile home she wanted. We were amazed by their generosity and relieved that Mom and my sisters would have a permanent roof over their heads. When Mom discovered she was receiving $40,000 from Dad's insurance, she offered Randy $5000.00 to start his masonry business. As pleased as we were with this generous offer, we cautioned her to be careful how she spent this money because she might need it, now that her breadwinner was gone. She insisted on helping us because we had helped her so much over the years. We scheduled an appointment with a local attorney in mid-October to discuss the legalities of starting a business.

When we visited the mobile home lot, Mom was overwhelmed by the choices available to her. She selected a beautiful single-wide home which would be delivered to a nearby mobile home park by the end of October. I was very surprised when she called me a few days later to tell me she bought a brand new car.

"I did it!" she exclaimed. "It's the first new car I've ever had! Wait until you see it—it looks like a race car," she giggled.

Diana Lynn

My first instinct was to object because I feared she was spending her insurance money too quickly, but how do you get a horse back into the barn when the door has already been opened? After everything she'd been through, I couldn't dampen her spirits with my negative remarks, so I replied, "You're kidding me. I can't wait to see it!"

"I was hoping you and Randy would come over tonight, and we could drive it to Rhea's for dinner." My mother had not gone anywhere socially since my father's death, three weeks earlier. I thought it would be good for her to get out for a while, and I readily agreed.

We made plans to meet at her house about seven that evening. It made me happy to hear the enthusiasm in Mom's voice. I drove to Randy's work site to tell him about our plans.

When Randy wasn't home from work by six-thirty, I became concerned. Surely, he wasn't out drinking with John when he knew we had plans to take my mother out for dinner. When he still wasn't home by seven-fifteen, I called the bar he frequented and asked to speak to him. The bartender called him to the phone.

"What are you doing? Did you forget we promised to take Mom out for dinner?"

"I was just walking out the door when you called. I'll be there in five minutes." I could tell by his voice he was drunk.

When he pulled into our driveway five minutes later, I felt like smashing him in the face, but I didn't. Instead, I ordered him to jump into the shower and change his clothes. Although the shower had sobered him up a little, I wouldn't let him drive. He opened the driver's side door and started to get into the car.

"Oh no, you don't. I'm driving. Give me the keys," I demanded. He sheepishly handed them over.

The first thing we noticed when we arrived at my mother's house was the sleek, fire-engine red 1974 Dodge Charger sitting in front of the garage. She was right—it did look like a race car. The thoughts of her seated in the driver's seat zipping down the highway made me shudder.

Linda and Lisa were waiting on the porch for Todd and Nathan. "Doncha' love Mom's new car?" Lisa squealed.

"It's something, alright. I just pray she can handle it," Randy quipped.

Randy plopped on the sofa while I went into the bedroom to get my mother. Mom looked much better than she had the past two weeks. The puffiness around her eyes was concealed by her make-up; her short brown hair was fashionably styled, and her smile warmed my heart. Hugging her, I whispered, "I love you, Mom."

When we walked into the living room together, I noticed that Randy was missing. "Where's Randy?" I asked Linda.

"He said to tell you he went back to see John about something and he'd meet you and Mom at Rhea's in about an hour."

I was dumbfounded. He wasn't in any shape to drive. What was he thinking? Not wanting to alarm Mom, I grabbed her car keys and said, "Let's take your jazzy car for a spin."

Our drive lasted three minutes because my mother lived just over the hill from Rhea's Corners. I hadn't been there since my dad died, so I was a little uncomfortable. As soon as we walked in, Dad's friends rushed up and offered their sympathies. They invited us to join them at their large table.

They entertained us for over an hour with funny tales about my father. He was very well liked in this little, corner bar. When Charlie, one of Dad's favorite drinking buddies, stood up, the group quieted.

He looked like a hillbilly in his bib-overalls and flannel shirt. He cleared his throat, sheepishly grinned and said, "I'm glad you ladies stopped in tonight. I was planning on coming to your house, but now I don't have to. You know, everybody in here loved Stew. We didn't know what to do for ya'll after he passed, but we finally figured it out."

After a poignant pause, Charlie continued, "All Stew talked about the last few times we seen him was how his grandson wanted a mini-bike and he was gonna' see he that got one. Seeing how Stew's not here anymore, we're doing it for him." He reached behind the bar and retrieved a glass jar with a sign that read, 'Todd's Mini-bike Fund.' Mom and I were amazed by this thoughtful gift. Hot tears welled up in the corners of my eyes, and I was unable to speak. Charlie walked over, put his arm around my shoulders and said, "Don't cry little lady. This is something to be happy about." I began to giggle.

It was almost nine and Randy still hadn't come to the restaurant. The knots in my stomach began tightening. Where is he? Why hasn't he called?

Then the phone rang. The bartender answered it and summoned me to the bar. Assuming it was Randy, I curtly replied, "What's going on? Where are you?'

Instead of Randy's voice, I heard my friend, Sandy's familiar voice on the other end of the line. "Sorry, it's Sandy, not Randy. Bob just called from the Shippenville Fire Hall and told me Randy was in an accident. You need to get to the Clarion Hospital right away."

What is she saying? This can't be!

My mother shot me a perplexing look when she heard me ask, "How badly was he hurt?" I held up my hand, halting her questions.

"I don't think it's life threatening, but Bob said he's pretty banged up. I hated to be the one to make this call. I offered to do it because I knew where you were." Sandy and Bob were personal friends, and I'd mentioned we were having dinner at Rhea's in an earlier conversation with her that day.

I hung up the phone. Trying to be as discreet as possible, I announced that we were leaving because the kids were arguing. On the way to the car, I told Mom the truth. She offered to drive, but I insisted I could get there faster.

On the drive down Clarion River Hill, my right leg was out of control just like it had been when I drove to my mother's house at five-thirty in the morning the dad my father died. The pulsating motion of my foot caused the car to jerk forward and slow down, jerk forward and slow down, all the way to the hospital. Five minutes later, we raced into the Clarion Hospital Emergency Room. I stopped the first nurse I saw. "My husband, Randy Sharp was just brought in from an accident. Can you tell me where he is?"

She ushered us into a little cubicle where Randy was writhing in pain. I grasped his hand and asked where he was hurt and how it happened. He was having difficulty talking when the doctor touched my shoulder and quietly told me to follow him. When we were out of Randy's earshot, he described his injuries—some broken ribs, a broken arm, and a broken leg. They'd know more after they took x-rays. I watched as they rolled Randy toward the waiting elevator.

The tables had turned and this time, my mother was consoling me. "It's okay honey. He'll be all right. Have faith."

While we were sitting on the couch in the waiting room, a local policeman approached me and asked to speak to me privately. I followed him into an office. His gesture suggested I take a seat. I was relieved to have a place to plant myself. My relief was short lived. The officer asked, "Mrs. Sharp, does your husband have a drinking problem or take drugs?"

"Not to my knowledge," I lied.

"We have reason to believe he was intoxicated tonight. We'll know more when we get the blood tests back. Along with being charged for driving while intoxicated, your husband could be facing vehicular homicide charges."

I jerked my head up and said, "Did you just say someone was killed in the accident?" *This is not happening. I'm having a bad dream! Is he telling me that someone died in that wreck, and it was Randy's fault?*

"Unfortunately, I am. The victim was a two-year-old boy. He was pronounced dead upon arrival. You may want to consult an attorney as soon as possible."

I sat there in a trance-like state. I couldn't comprehend what this man was telling me. The acid rolling from my stomach into my throat forced me to flee to the bathroom. After I threw up, I wiped my mouth and sat on the toilet seat. I couldn't sit, I couldn't stand, I couldn't think and I couldn't cry. I was numb. Mom came into the bathroom a few minutes later and found me crouching on the floor, staring at the wall. She wiped my face with a wet paper towel, pulled me up to my feet and led me to a private corner of the waiting room. She cradled me in her arms while I sobbed.

Around midnight, I convinced my mother to leave because I needed to be alone. Randy was out of surgery by then and soundly sleeping in his hospital room. I pulled a chair up to the bed and lay my head on a pillow.

Although I was anxious about the charges Randy might be facing, I was more concerned about the devastated young mother lying somewhere in this hospital, mourning the loss of her child. The child my husband accidentally killed. I could not fathom her pain. I prayed for her and her family, asking God to be with them. They needed Him more that I did. I knew Randy and I would somehow get through whatever lay ahead.

At some point during that long night, I remembered our appointment with the Clarion attorney, scheduled for nine the next morning. I phoned Tom and Sue shortly after 6:00 a.m. When they learned what happened, they told me they would be in Clarion by 8:00 a.m. I never asked them to come; they made that gracious offer on their own. My throat constricted, making my heartfelt thank you almost unintelligible. Knowing they were on their way helped me regain the strength I needed to face the day.

Randy woke up early the next morning with questions about his whereabouts and the events from the night before. I considered withholding the information about the fatality until after I received some legal counseling. However, fearing the police would come to talk to him while I was away, I decided to tell him. "No!" he howled. "No!" I'm sure Tom and Sue could hear him as they walked down the hall to his room. I was very grateful when they came into the room.

The three of us met with the attorney at the appointed time. I explained that I wasn't there to discuss my husband's new business venture. Instead, I wanted to talk about my husband's pending charges. I shared what little information I had and answered his questions to the best of my ability. I was hoping he would be able to alleviate some of my fears. Instead, he made them worse.

"Mrs. Sharp, from the information you have provided, I feel reasonably confident your husband will be facing a mandatory twenty-year sentence in the state prison."

Tom and I exchanged looks of disbelief. I stood, thanked him for his time, asked him to send me a bill and walked out of his office.

"Are you kidding me? That man had Randy guilty and convicted before he even knows the facts! How can I hire him?" I ranted the entire way to the car. Next morning I called another attorney who readily accepted the case. After meeting with him, I had a little more hope.

That afternoon, after Tom and Sue had left, I went back to the hospital. Instead of going to Randy's room, I asked the nurse at the desk to please tell me what room Mrs. 'X' was in. I followed the corridor to her room. I stood outside the door, gathering my courage, said a short prayer and walked into the room. She was lying in her hospital bed, staring out the window when I entered. She had a puzzled look on her face as she was trying to place me. After taking a deep, breath I said, "Mrs.' X', I'm the wife of the driver who collided with your truck."

Appearing to be dumbfounded by my admission, she stared at me through glassy eyes.

"I've been praying for you and your family ever since I learned about your loss. I know that the words 'I'm sorry' are probably meaningless to you, but I am sorry, from the bottom of my heart. I cannot imagine the pain you are going through."

She continued to glare at me as I laid a piece of paper on her bed stand.

"I've put my name and phone number on this paper. If there is anything I can do to help you, please don't hesitate to call me," I said. Before walking out the door, I went on to say, "I'll keep you in my prayers."

I cried the entire way to Randy's room.

The thoughts of Todd, Nathan, Linda, and Lisa were the only thing that kept me grounded in the weeks to come. Knowing they needed my love and attention enabled me to face each day and do what needed to be done.

Randy was laid-up for nearly six weeks, which gave us plenty of time to discuss our future.

Mom moved into her new home on October 25th. They had only lived there ten days when Linda's little dog, Lucky, ran out of the trailer and into the path of a car. He died instantly. Linda was devastated. The only positive thing to come from this loss was to believe it was the third bad thing to happen to our family. If there's any truth to the superstition 'bad things come in threes', we were home free for a while.

In November of that fateful year, 1973, I had two very spiritual experiences. The first one occurred one evening while Nathan was in the bathtub. I watched as he kept throwing a ball into the air and catching it. After his final throw, he stared at the ceiling and said, "Got it." Curious, I asked him what he was doing.

"Playing ball with Grandpa Stew," he innocently replied. Overcome with emotion, I lifted his soaking wet body out of the water, held him in my arms and whispered, "You miss Grandpa Stew, don't you?"

He snuggled his little face into my neck and nodded.

Next day, we made our weekly stop at the cemetery. While kneeling on the ground, pulling dead leaves from Dad's recently planted bushes, I discovered a little red rubber ball among the leaves. I mumbled, "Damn kids playing ball in the cemetery," and flung it away. As soon as the ball left my hand, I understood the meaning of that little ball. It was my Dad's way of letting me know he'd be on the receiving end of Nathan's throws; watching over us from afar. I got goose bumps.

The piles of dead leaves covering lawns and walkways were soon replaced by piles of snow, reminding me that Christmas was not far off. How do you celebrate Christmas with a broken heart? You look into the eyes of the children around you and draw your strength from them. I understood if they believed in the Spirit of Christmas, then so must I.

My mother and I did our best to make a nice Christmas for everyone.

She bought a truck-load of gifts in hopes the myriad of presents would ease some of our pain. I made cookies with the kids and helped them write their letters to Santa. Linda and Lisa laughed when I made them join in. Assuming the first wish on their list would be to have their daddy back, I called them into my bedroom to talk about it. We sat on the floor and laughed about the funny things Dad had done with us over the years.

"You see? Daddy's not gone. He's still in our minds and our hearts." I hoped my words would help them.

I did my usual baking and decorating, even though my heart wasn't in it. We were looking forward to Judy, Corky and Brandon, and Kim, Dan and Danny, spending Christmas Eve and Christmas Day with us in Clarion.

On Christmas Eve, seven adults and five kids crowded into my mother's new trailer. Her valiant efforts to decorate included a six-foot blue spruce which took up most of the corner in her living room. Christmas music was coming from the stereo. Todd, Nathan, and Brandon, my sister Judy's son, were excited about the arrival of Santa later that night. Everyone else was wearing a false smile. After we had all been seated, a gloomy silence fell over the room. It felt like we were sharing the same thought—*It's not Christmas without Dad.*

Suddenly, the storm door on the trailer blew open and swiftly blew shut with a loud bang. I filled the dreadful silence by saying, "Now we can begin our Christmas celebration. Dad just blew in."

CHAPTER 35

Unraveling

1974-1975

THE BLEAK JANUARY weather matched my melancholic mood. Many mornings, I was barely able to get out of bed to face the day. Instead of looking forward, I could only look back—remembering the turbulent events of the past few months. Sleeping was nearly as bad as waking; my dreams were filled with scenes from the past.

I awoke one morning to a pillow case soaked with sweat. Or was it tears? I had dreamed my father came to me and told me he had cancer. The devastation of the dream quickly faded upon awakening. "Thank God it was only a dream! I'll have to tell Dad about it later."

The irony of this thought made my blood run cold. How can I tell him I dreamed of him dying when he's already dead? The dam holding back my unspent tears finally broke. So did I. Randy found me still in bed, buried under the covers when he came home for lunch. My eyes were puffy from crying and my long, brown hair was matted against my cheeks and neck.

"Holy hell!" he exclaimed upon seeing me. He held me close while I shared my dream with him. "I'm calling a doctor. In all the years, we've been together, I've never seen you this depressed. You need medication or something to help you get through this."

"What I need is time alone today. Would you take Nathan to Mom's before you go back to work? I gave him cereal earlier, and he's been glued to the television all morning."

"Maybe I should stay home, I'm not comfortable leaving you alone today."

"Please trust me. I'm not suicidal like my mother. I just need time by myself to think."

Randy reluctantly agreed to my request. When I heard his truck pull away, I called Pastor Daniels. As usual, he was the angel I needed. Through our long talk and prayers, I found the strength to forge ahead.

My first step in pulling myself out of this deep depression, was to look for a job. I had recently read an ad in the classified section of the *Clarion News*, seeking an advertising sales person. I called and set an appointment to meet with the sales manager. Although I had no prior sales experience, I did my best to sell myself during the interview. An hour after I had left the office, I received a call from Shirley, the sales manager, telling me I was hired. My new job was a blessing. It provided me with an opportunity to learn a skill, pull myself out of my depressed state and make extra income for our family. It gave me a new lease on life.

After Randy's accident, my mother fulfilled her promise by giving us five thousand dollars to start a business. We used part of that money to buy a used truck and some masonry equipment. With some additional assistance from the Small Business Administration at Clarion State College, Randy was able to start his masonry construction business in January, 1974. He quickly found small jobs in the area through the contacts he had made while working for John. He seemed happier than he had been in a while.

Mom and the girls were slowly healing. Linda was very involved with her school activities and friends, and my mom was busy watching Nathan while I worked. I enrolled my little sister, Lisa in the Clarion Easy Steppers where she immediately displayed her talent for baton twirling. She loved it!

The darkest cloud hanging over our heads was Randy's upcoming trial. The next few months were filled with the emotional ups and downs of scheduled preliminary hearings. Each time a date was set for Randy to appear before the district magistrate, we would receive a call about eight that morning informing us the trial had been postponed. Before each hearing, Randy and I mentally prepared ourselves for the outcome. Because we desperately needed to know what charges he'd be facing and how it would affect our lives, these court delays were psychologically draining. The last minute cancelations significantly affected Tom and Sue, too. Every time a hearing was scheduled, Tom took off a day of school to attend the court appearance. On those days, they would leave Jamestown at 6:00 a.m., only to learn upon their arrival at our house, the hearing had been rescheduled. In 1974, there were no cell phones, so we weren't able to contact them once they started for Clarion. The fifth time a court date was set we didn't tell them. We didn't want to put them in this stressful situation again.

The day of the preliminary hearing, our attorney accompanied us. We had prepared ourselves for the worst so we wouldn't be shocked if Randy was charged with vehicular homicide. The District Magistrate's decision didn't surprise us. He ruled that Randy would stand trial for vehicular homicide while driving under the influence of alcohol. A Grand Jury hearing was the next step in our legal journey; a trial we were not permitted to attend.

Randy's fate lay in the hands of our competent attorney. Again we anxiously waited for a court date.

Through all of this emotional upheaval, our marriage started to fall apart. Although Randy didn't stop for drinks every night after work, he still carried a six-pack in his truck. I was appalled the first time I noticed the empty Budweiser cans in the back seat. I stormed into the house, holding a crinkled can in my hand and angrily confronted him.

"Are you out of your mind? How can you possibly drink and drive knowing what you're facing? No, make that what we're facing!" I screamed.

"I don't usually drink while I'm driving. I have one or two on my breaks," he weakly replied.

"And that makes a difference? You don't think there's a chance you could be pulled over by a cop?" I boldly retorted. "You're possibly facing twenty years in jail. If that's not enough of a deterrent, maybe you should think about your sons!' Our argument ended with his weak promise never to do it again. He lied.

Every year, we took Todd to Children's Hospital in Pittsburgh for cleft palate check-ups. During our last appointment, the otolaryngologist scheduled a date to surgically insert plastic tubes into Todd's ears to prevent his frequent ear infections. Although the procedure required general anesthesia, the procedure was relatively simple, with little or no side-effects. The doctor explained most patients awaken within an hour or two and are able to return to normal activities the next day. Randy and I decided to make this trip a mini vacation by booking a room at a downtown hotel and taking the boys to the Pittsburgh Zoo the next day. Todd was very excited.

The night before our appointment, John C, Randy's former boss, showed up at our house to talk to Randy. I was irritated by his unexpected visit. After talking to John awhile on the front porch, Randy opened the door and shouted, "I'm going for a ride with John to his job site. He needs some help fixing a problem."

When I reminded him that we were leaving at eight-thirty in the morning for Pittsburgh, he promised me he wouldn't be gone long. Once again, I watched as the hours on the clock slowly ticked by. Furious and frantic when he still wasn't home at 2:30 a.m., I decided to go in search of him. I awakened my next-door neighbor to let her know where I was going. I asked her to keep an eye on our house. Then I softly shook Todd awake to tell him I was leaving for a few minutes but would be right back. I climbed into the pickup and headed to Rhea's Corners, two miles from our house.

I pulled into the parking lot and immediately spotted John's truck. By this time, I was steaming mad. Peering through the window, I could see John passed out in the driver's seat. Randy was passed out on the passenger's side with his head lolling on the back of the seat, his mouth hanging open and his right hand nestling a beer bottle. I ripped the door open and smacked Randy across the face. The sting of the slap awakened him. He stared at me as if he didn't know who I was.

"You drunk! You are a sonofabitch! What in the hell are you doing?" Shaking his head to awaken himself, he slurred, "Whaddaya mean?"

I completely lost it. My intense rage brought out a strength in me I never knew I possessed. I pummeled him with both fists and physically dragged him from John's truck. He staggered as I pushed him into our pickup. After slamming the passenger door shut and locking him in, I returned to John's truck. By now, John was fully awake.

"What's going on?" he groggily asked.

"I came to get my drunken husband to take him home. Don't you ever, ever come to my house or call my husband again; do you hear me, you bastard?" I slammed the truck door closed and returned to my vehicle. I didn't say another word on the drive home.

When we returned to our house, Randy tried to apologize. I ignored his apology and told him to go to bed because we had a big day ahead.

After catching a couple of hours sleep on the couch, I was awakened by the yellow streaks of light streaming through the living room windows. I immediately woke everyone up and took Nathan into the bathroom for a bath. Randy stood in the doorway, trying to apologize while I was drying Nathan off.

Brushing past him, I said, "Just get ready to go to Pittsburgh. I don't want to talk about it now."

He grabbed my arm. "Well, I do. What the hell happened last night?" I tried to remain calm while recapping the events of the night before, but the further I got into the story, the angrier I became. Exasperated, I exploded.

Disgusted by my outburst, Randy shoved me into the tub full of water.

Dripping wet, I stepped out of the tub and screamed, "I'm done! I can't take anymore. When we get back from Pittsburgh, I want you out of here. I've had a hard enough time dealing with an alcoholic mother, and I will NOT let my sons be raised by an alcoholic father!"

During our stay in Pittsburgh, we slowly worked things out. Randy promised me he would never drink and drive again. He also told me he'd cut back his alcohol consumption. I forgave him.

One afternoon in late October, I received an unexpected call at work from our attorney.

"Diana, this is Barry. I just left the Grand Jury hearing and the vehicular homicide charges against Randy have been dropped!" My heart began thumping as I digested this news.

"Dropped? Are you kidding? How? Why?" I anxiously inquired. "Through investigating the police reports, I discovered the driver of the truck was the person to cross over the center line, not Randy."

After profusely thanking him, I hung up the phone, laid my head on the desk and bawled. The layers of tension I'd felt over the past year began to slowly lift. I offered a prayer of thanks to the good Lord and my guardian angel. I left the office to go to Randy's work site and tell him this unbelievable news. Although I was euphoric for our family, my heart went out to the other family. I continued to keep them in my prayers.

With this news, 1974 ended on a high-note. However, in 1975 our problems continued to escalate and our lives slowly unraveled over the next two years.

The calm lifestyle my mother and sisters had maintained since Dad's death began to erode at the beginning of the New Year. Mom had decided she did not like living in a trailer, and against our advice, she sold it and used the money as a down payment on an unaffordable new home in Marianne Estates. Rather than finance the home through a bank, she signed a rent-to-own agreement with the owner. Even though, the down payment lessened the monthly payments, it was still more than she could afford on her present income, so she got a waitress job at a steak house in Clarion. That meant Linda and Lisa would be home alone most evenings. The girls, at fourteen and twelve were capable of caring for themselves, but Randy and I tried to look after them as much as possible.

Through hard work and dedication, Lisa had moved to the number two position in the Easy Steppers. Her marching unit participated in area parades and events throughout the summer and well into the fall. Linda supported her by attending each event. As Lisa's self-appointed cheerleader, Linda coached her from the sidelines while Lisa marched down the street twirling her baton. Like a mother hen, Linda always carried a bottle of water in case Lisa needed a drink. At the end of every parade, Linda met her with a big smile and a hug. Randy and I attended as many of these parades as possible, but Mom only made it to a few.

Because my mother was fulfilling her financial obligations with her SSI checks and her income as a waitress, she rewarded herself by going out for a drink after work. What started as an occasional stop eventually became a nightly occurrence. That's when my sister, Linda, stepped into the role of a surrogate mother.

In January, 1975, Randy had contracted a large masonry job in Punxsutawney, PA, over thirty miles away from our home. He left early in the morning and arrived home late at night; some nights, later than others. When I questioned him about these late nights, he admitted stopping for something to eat and a few beers at a local tavern in Punxsutawney. Because I didn't have the energy to argue about it, I let it slide.

One sunny day in April while looking through the mail, I noticed a card addressed to Randy Sharp. It had a Punxsutawney, PA postmark with no return address. Assuming it was a payment for a job, I opened it. Instead of a check, I discovered a personal card. A cartoonish character with big, sad eyes and a pouting mouth appeared on the cover. The message inside conveyed feelings of loneliness. Randy's name appeared in cursive writing at the top.

The salutation read 'Debbie' with the word 'Help' sprawled across the inside cover.

At one time, receiving a card of this nature would have devastated me; now, I only felt numbness. Through all of the trials and tribulations over the years, I had slowly lost my feelings of love and respect for Randy. When he came home later that day, I asked him about the card. He acted surprised and told me it was from a crazy bartender in Punxsutawney. I was too tired to argue, so I shrugged it off.

About two weeks later, Randy suggested we ask Linda to babysit so we could go to the local Moose Club for dinner. We were talking over a drink before dinner when Randy reached across the table and took my hand. He was very solemn and his voice slightly quivered as he unloaded his story.

Apparently, he and the bartender, Debbie had become emotionally involved during his after-work stops at the bar. They shared their personal problems and had some physical contact but never consummated their relationship through intercourse. I guess he thought this fact exonerated him.

"We came close, but I just couldn't do it. All I could see, was Nathan's smiling face. I ended the relationship after that. I haven't seen or talked to her since," he confessed."Will you forgive me?"

I weighed my words before casually responding, "You must have needed her emotional support after what you'd been through over the past few years. Let's just forget about it."

At that moment, I realized how much my feelings for him had changed. When I could look directly at him and forgive him for his affair, I knew my marriage was over. During dinner, we decided to make some changes in our lives. Because Randy was losing money with his business, he decided to seek full-time employment that would include benefits. Something we desperately needed. A week later he interviewed for a position with the Community Action Agency in Punxsutawney. He was hired to teach local high school students to restore old houses at a project in Stump Creek. This position enabled him to utilize his education and earn more money. I was grateful. In July, we sold our house in Shippenville and rented a small house in Sykesville. For me, the hardest part of this move was leaving my sisters and my job.

I spent the next three months getting Todd settled into school, enrolling him on a midget league football team and becoming involved with the football boosters club. Although I enjoyed being a stay-at-home mother with Nathan, I realized I'd eventually have to go back to work.

At the end of October, I decided to try to get a job as an advertising sales representative at one of the local newspapers. I scheduled interviews with the advertising managers in Punxsutawney and DuBois. At the beginning of each meeting, I was politely informed there were currently no openings available, but they would call me if that changed. A week later I received an unexpected call.

I grabbed the ringing phone and stuck the receiver under my chin. I continued ironing while I answered, "Hello."

An older man with a raspy voice inquired, "Is this Diana Sharp?" "Yes," I replied.

"This is Bruce McMurray from the McMurray Company in Brookville. Your friend Ann (my former workmate at the *Clarion News*) told me you were looking for a job selling advertising. You're looking for a job and I'm looking for a sales person, when do you want to start?'

Overwhelmed by this abrupt question, I began to ask questions. We set a meeting date for that Friday.

I started my new job selling advertising for *The Brookville American* and *The Jeffersonian Democrat* the next week. The course of my life would drastically change with this new opportunity.

CHAPTER 36

The Separation

1976

AT THE BEGINNING of the year, Randy's recently divorced brother, John, moved in with us. His exuberant personality added some levity to our glum lives and provided us with a diversion from our frequent arguments over financial stress. Between student loan payments and legal bills accrued from the accident, we barely made it. It was my responsibility to pay the bills and balance the budget.

One Sunday afternoon, Randy, John, and the boys were watching a sporting event on television while I sat at the kitchen table toiling over the budget. The longer I worked, the more frustrated I became. I finally snapped. I jumped up from the table, shoved all of the papers on the floor and fled upstairs to my bedroom. Obviously this action caught Randy's attention because he ran upstairs and found me lying on the bed staring into space. He sat beside me and asked, "What was that outburst all about?"

I lifted my head from the pillow. Bewildered by his question, I asked, "You honestly don't know?"

"Not really." His comment allowed me to vent. The first thing I explained was my emotional exhaustion from trying to be the mother figure to everyone. The strain of trying to solve my mother's and sisters' problems, balancing our budget and paying the bills, doing all of the housework and working full time had finally taken its toll. I didn't know how much longer I could carry this weight on my shoulders.

"I feel like I'm handling most of our marital responsibilities and I'm drained." After I listed my burdens, Randy readily agreed to be more helpful around the house. He also promised to cut back on his weekly beer and cigarette purchases, which would significantly lessen our monthly expenses. Our discussion offered me hope.

While things seemed to be improving at our house, the conditions at my mother's house worsened. My mother was dating several men, one of whom she brought home after an evening out. Linda called me early Saturday morning to make me aware that this man had spent the night. After explaining the situation to Randy, I got in the car and drove forty miles to Clarion to confront my mother.

I found her sitting in her usual spot at the kitchen table with a cigarette burning in the ashtray and a beer can beside her as she talked on the phone. The strap of her flimsy nightgown had slid down her left arm and her hair looked like it hadn't been combed in days. I noticed the surprised look in her mascara smudged eyes when she saw me come in the door. "Hey, what are you doing here?"

Ignoring her, I marched into her bedroom and shook the sleeping figure in the bed. A skinny guy with curly black hair and a five o'clock shadow stared back at me.

"Get up, get dressed and get your ass out of my mother's house, right now!" I demanded. Then I stormed out of the bedroom, into the kitchen. A few minutes later, I spotted the strange man in the bedroom buttoning his shirt as he ran out the front door. Meanwhile, Mom tried to justify the situation. I stopped her midstream and declared, "No more excuses. No more lies. You have exactly one month to get your life turned around or I'm calling social services."

I motioned for Linda and Lisa to follow me to my car. I had told Linda when we talked on the phone to pack some things because I was coming to get them. Lisa grabbed their bags and they followed me out the door. During the ride to Sykesville, they shared more of their stories. I promised them things would change soon.

I drove Linda and Lisa back home on Sunday evening. Following a long, serious discussion that ended with me threatening to take custody of my sisters if things didn't improve, my mother agreed to seek counseling.

Work was my escape. My morning drive to Brookville gave me time to sort out my thoughts. I understood I had to make changes in my life before I could help my sisters, I just didn't know what those changes should be.

I had made some good friends at the McMurray Company, Bruce being at the top of my list. I thought of him as a father figure and sometimes confided in him. One afternoon I was working at the layout table when Bruce poked my shoulder and said, "I have someone I want you to meet."

Curious, I turned around and found myself staring at a very handsome, six-foot-three man with sandy brown, curly hair and mischievous brown eyes. I knew instantly it was Jim, the guy I had been hired to replace. I felt threatened by his presence. Instead of my usual warm greeting I pushed my chin outward and announced, "So, you're the great Jim Farley! I'm not sure if I should kiss your feet or your ass!" They both laughed.

My response had been prompted by the stories I had heard over the past five months. Many of the office staff shared humorous tales about him while others praised his writing and photographic skills. These stories had intimidated me. I was greatly relieved when Bruce announced he had lured him back from Florida to work on the editorial staff, not in the sales department. I was a little embarrassed by my outburst.

My daily drives to work suddenly became more pleasurable.

Although some of the problems at home had been temporarily resolved, it wasn't long before they returned. Once again, I found myself caring for two men and two children with little or no help. I didn't expect Todd and Nathan to share my burdens, but I certainly expected Randy to chip in. My second explosion occurred one Saturday morning. The guys were sprawled all over the living room watching cartoons with the boys, while I crawled on my hands and knees in the kitchen scrubbing the floor. Hearing Randy's hearty laughter over some cartoon antic was the last straw. I picked up the bucket full of dirty water and flung it into the living room.

"There! Now it's your turn to clean the floor!" Thankfully the floor was tiled and not carpeted.

I stormed outside to smoke a cigarette. Randy followed. This time we didn't work out any solutions. Our discussion quickly turned into a full-fledged shouting match. I ended it by announcing I needed to get away; I was going to Mom's for the night. Before leaving, I pulled Todd and Nathan into my arms and apologized for yet another fight. Todd whispered into my ear, "Mom, it seems like every time you and Dad take two steps forward, you get kicked back about three more." I thought it was a profound statement for a ten-year-old boy to make. Todd's words reverberated through my head on my drive to Clarion.

On the way to my mother's, I thought about the many recent arguments Randy and I had been having in front of the boys. What's happening to us? What can we do to change it? Our family life is starting to feel like Mom's and Dad's. God help us.

My overnight stay at Mom's helped. She was trying very hard to quit drinking. Consequently, she was deeply depressed. She had not taken my advice to seek counseling, but I didn't think this was the time to tell her I had contacted social services. They were aware of the situation and waiting for more information from me before they investigated it further. I feared it would push her over the deep end.

Instead, I changed the subject by engaging her in my problems. For once, she listened attentively and offered me her motherly advice. It was nice to be on the receiving end of her compassion. I returned home the next day more relaxed.

A week later, Linda called me at work and told me she had just called an ambulance because my mother had slashed her wrist. I sped along I-80 and arrived at the Clarion Hospital twenty minutes later. Mom's doctor suggested sending her to a psychiatric center at the Oil City hospital. When I offered to stay in Clarion with Linda and Lisa, my mother agreed to go. For the next ten days, Randy and John cared for the boys while I took care of my sisters. Every morning after getting the girls off to school, I drove to work in Brookville.

Most days I couldn't wait to get there.

The Road Back to Hell

Over the previous weeks, Jim and I had developed a very close friendship. We discovered we both possessed a quick-witted sense of humor and we tried to out-do one another with our barbs. Through lightly sharing some of our life experiences and goals, we discovered we had a lot in common. When he learned about my mother's situation, he offered to drive me to the Oil City Hospital for a visit. Coincidentally, his grandmother had pneumonia and was also a patient there. He told me he planned to visit her and would be driving through Clarion. It would be easy to pick me up on his way to Oil City.

That evening, when he stopped at my mother's house to get me, I told my sisters a friend from work was giving me a ride to the hospital. At that time, I believed this was the truth, he was just a friend. It was during our long conversation on the way home, I realized my feelings for him were more than friendship. His kind words of advice and unique sense of humor in the face of trauma drew me in. When I was with him, I felt safe and happy. We laughed a lot.

I spent that night tossing and turning, imagining my life with someone like him—strong, intelligent, witty and caring. The fact that he was extremely good-looking didn't hurt. By morning, I convinced myself to forget these frivolous thoughts and get back to the reality of my life.

During her stay in the hospital, my mother had decided to move back to Jamestown at the end of the school year. This news was devastating, but I didn't possess the emotional strength to oppose her decision. Instead, I prayed she would change her mind.

I missed Todd and Nathan while I was staying at Mom's, so Randy brought them to Clarion for the weekend. I was refreshed by their visit and anxious to return home as soon as possible. My mother had been in the hospital for ten days when she was released. A few days later, I returned to my home in Sykesville and happily resumed my motherly duties.

At night, I found it difficult to lie beside Randy. Over time, I had slowly turned away from his sexual advances because his breath reeked of beer and the dead weight of his body lying on me became unbearable. One night while lying in bed, he reached out to me. I dutifully complied, silently crying throughout the whole experience. When I heard him snoring, I quietly slipped out of bed and went downstairs for a cup of coffee.

John slept on the couch in the living room and was awakened by the sound of my feet pacing up and down the kitchen floor.

"Having trouble sleeping?" he asked while pouring himself a cup of coffee. "A little," I murmured.

"Want to talk about it?" Those five words were all I needed to pour my heart out to my brother-in-law. I confessed that I had met someone and although I hadn't been unfaithful physically, I definitely had adulterous feelings for him. My pent-up feelings flowed out of me like an unleashed river. John listened to every word.

"John, I love your brother but I'm no longer in love with him. I feel like I'm raising three kids instead of two. The traumas we've been through with his drinking and my family have finally taken their toll. I don't know what to do. Sometimes I think maybe we should separate for a while."

Expecting a lecture, I was shocked when John said, "Separating may a be good idea. It might give you each time to figure things out."

A few days later, Randy and I talked at length about our problems and agreed to seek marital counseling. I made an appointment with a recommended psychologist, Ann G, in DuBois. During our first session, we shared our story and the problems we encountered as a couple. After that, we met with Ann individually one week and the next week as a couple. These meetings continued for two months.

During my individual sessions with Ann, I was extremely comfortable and able to express my inner-most feelings, doubts, and fears while Randy experienced some difficulty sharing with her one-on-one. It was much easier for him to open up when we met as a couple. At my last personal meeting with Ann, I vocalized my deepest concern.

"My concern is how the separation will affect Todd and Nathan. I've discussed the possibility of a separation with Todd and let him know I would totally understand if he chose to live with Randy. At his age, he and his father share a special bond, especially when it comes to sports. I feel differently about Nathan; he's only four and looks to me for everything. He needs me now, at this time in his life, more than he does his father."

Ann pondered this for a moment. "How did Todd react to your suggestion?"

Trying to hold back my tears, I covered my eyes with tented fingers. When I removed my hands from my face, the scalding tears trickled freely. I exhaled the deep breath I'd been holding and replied, "He asked who would take care of me if he lived with his dad. Do you believe it?"

I went on to say, "I told Todd how deeply touched I was by his concern for me, but he shouldn't worry about me. At his age, his most important job is to be happy. If living with his dad would be better for him, I could accept it. I encouraged him by saying I'd attend all of his games and that he could stay with me whenever he wanted. I exuded confidence that I really didn't feel."

I stressed this was the most difficult conversation I had ever had.

Todd's well-being was extremely important to me and, as his mother, I would sacrifice my happiness for his. I explained that after spending countless hours analyzing the problems in our marriage, and considering possible solutions, I had concluded sacrificing my happiness for his made me a better mother.

Ann's response will forever live in my memory. "Diana, you're an excellent mother and caregiver, that's why you're willing to do this. Don't ever question your motherhood."

The last week of May, Randy and I met with Ann. We sat together on the sofa facing her desk. When she finished reviewing her notes, she slowly lifted her elfin-like face, pushed her soft brown hair behind her ears and gently expressed her opinion.

"I've spent the past eight weeks talking to you together as a couple, and separately as individuals. After carefully listening to what each of you shared with me, I'm recommending a separation. Because you were married so young, you were never able to truly grow up and develop your individual potentials. You've also dealt with enormous problems in your short marriage that many people don't encounter in a lifetime. A separation will allow both of you the opportunity to find yourselves. After a while, you may decide to try to make your marriage work. In the meantime, I believe a separation is beneficial for everyone, including your children. You may find you're stronger parents apart."

I took Todd and Nathan with me while I stayed with my mother the first two weeks in June to help her get ready for the move to Jamestown. This short separation afforded Randy and me the time we needed to digest everything we'd learned during our counseling sessions. We definitely needed space to make sensible decisions about our future.

Linda and Lisa were devastated about the upcoming move. The four kids played ball together in the park across from my mother's house, swam in the Clarion pool and watched their favorite television shows while Mom and I handled the daunting task of packing. My mother planned to move the day after Brookville's Laurel Festival parade so Lisa could participate in one more event with the Easy-Steppers. Linda spent Friday night at a friend's house. She was surprised when she discovered the slumber party was actually a going-away party in her honor. The happy memories of that night and her three glorious years at Clarion Junior High School stayed with Linda for years.

During my stay, Mom and I talked non-stop about her future and mine. When she came home from the hospital, she acted more like the mother she had been after Dad's death. While I was skeptical about her uprooting Linda and Lisa again, I became more confident during my stay with her, about her ability to raise the girls. I had hope.

My mother adored Randy and our upcoming separation upset her. Our long discussions allowed her to better understand the reasons for it. During one of our late-night conversations, I revealed my innermost fears.

"Mom, I'm completely worn-out and depressed. I don't have the strength to carry everyone's burdens any longer. Spending time with you and watching the changes you've made has convinced me you're very capable of caring for the girls on your own. Right now, my number one concern is for my sons."

Mom sipped her coffee, took a long drag off her cigarette and responded, "You've always carried everyone's burdens; I'm sorry about that. It was wrong. I shouldn't have leaned on you so much over the years. I'm sad your marriage isn't working, but I know you'll do what's best in the end. I have the utmost confidence in you." She reached over, wrapped her arms around me and held me close as I sobbed into her neck.

When my crying subsided, she pulled away, looked directly into my eyes and in her smoky voice asked, "What was the final factor in your decision to separate?"

I paused before answering. "Honestly? I was afraid of becoming like you. Lately, I've been drinking a couple of beers whenever I'm upset. I'm also on the verge of having an affair to escape my problems. I can't do that to my sons or Randy. I feel like I'm falling into a cesspool and swimming like hell to stay afloat. The same cesspool I've been trying to escape from all of my life."

"Don't worry, you'll never be like me, you're too strong. Take this opportunity to find yourself and fulfill your dreams. You deserve it. It'll be best for everyone in the end." At that moment, my mother was the woman I remembered when I was four, offering me her heartfelt advice and love. I needed her and she was there.

Randy came to Clarion the weekend of my mother's move because we needed to talk and he wanted to say good-bye to Mom, Linda, and Lisa. The two of us went out to eat on Friday night. After dinner, we drove to the college stadium and sat in the parking lot talking into the wee hours of the morning. We mutually agreed that the separation was necessary. Whether it would be temporary or permanent remained to be seen. He'd found an affordable, one-room apartment in Sykesville and planned to move the beginning of the next week. The proximity to our house enabled him to see the boys whenever he wanted. He also planned to take a two-week leave of absence from his job to admit himself into an alcohol rehabilitation program in the DuBois Hospital. I was proud of his decisions.

"These past few weeks made me realize how many problems my drinking has caused. I need to stop drinking," he confessed. "My other problem is loneliness. I've called a few girls we know and asked them for a date, but they refused because of their friendship with you."

"Have you called Debbie?' I asked. "I'm surprised you'd mention her."

"Why? She seems like the perfect choice. You had feelings for her before and she apparently cares about you or she wouldn't have sent that card. I think you should try."

"Shit! You sound more like my sister than my wife," he chuckled. Smiling like a Cheshire cat, I responded, "Maybe that's because lately I feel more like your sister than your wife."

Our entire family attended the Laurel Festival Parade in Brookville to watch Lisa. When her unit marched by, we hooted and hollered as she proudly threw her baton high into the air, gracefully catching it. Her confident smile and twinkling eyes filled me with pride. Linda strode beside her, encouraging Lisa every step of the way. When I noticed the tiny tear trickling down Mom's beaming face, I offered a silent prayer. "Thank you, God. Please watch over them on their new journey."

In the middle of the night, I was awakened by the sound of someone sobbing. It was coming from Linda's bedroom. I slipped out of Mom's bed and walked into her room. I lay down beside her and listened as she shared her deep sadness and fears about leaving Clarion. I desperately wanted to tell her she could live with me, but I couldn't. Instead, I gently rubbed her eyebrows and held her close as my mother used to do to me.

Early the next morning, Uncle Kenny and his buddy, Jerry pulled into Mom's driveway in a large, rented U-haul. After coffee and donuts, everyone started filling the truck. By noon, it was packed full of furniture and Mom's car overflowed with clothing and personal items. Randy, Todd, Nathan and I stood there waving to them, long after they pulled away. My heart was breaking.

As planned, Randy moved into his new apartment and spent two weeks in a psychiatric unit for rehabilitation. When he got out, he contacted Debbie. I started dating Jim. I decided to move from Sykesville to Brookville the first weekend in August. The boys were adjusting fairly well to the changes. In fact, they seemed calmer now that the fighting had stopped.

Randy agreed to help me move into my new house on August 6, 1976. This was the only date that worked for both of us. It was also our tenth wedding anniversary. A friend from work offered to stay at my new house and care for the boys while Randy and I made several trips to Sykesville for the rest of my belongings. During our final drive to Brookville, Randy laid a bombshell.

"I'm not sure how to tell you this but I have a real problem." So far, everything seemed to be going well. I couldn't imagine what it was. "I can't afford to keep the apartment anymore. I need to move in with you and the boys for a few weeks until I get back on my feet financially."

Oh my God. Here we go again.

I remained speechless for a while. Unable to see any solution to this problem I reluctantly agreed. The Sharps would remain a family for a while longer.

CHAPTER 37

The Funeral

1976

RANDY AND I had agreed to try to platonically live together for an undetermined length of time. I slept in one bedroom and he slept in another. We shared our meals together, spent time with the boys and briefly communicated. Randy continued to date Debbie while I tried to maintain a relationship with Jim. Neither Jim nor Debbie ever came to our house. This had worked for about three weeks before the arguments began anew. When I realized how much the tension affected Todd and Nathan, I knew something had to change. Obviously, the current situation was not working.

I decided to go to Jamestown to inform Randy's family why we were officially separating. After that, I would need to find another place to live. I also wanted to see how Mom and the girls were faring. On a sunny Friday afternoon in August, the boys and I went to Jamestown.

Mom wasn't expecting us until Saturday and she wasn't home when we arrived about 5:00 pm. When we walked in the door, Linda and Lisa were overjoyed. When I asked where Mom had gone, Lisa gazed down at her feet while Linda tried to explain my mother's absence. "Um, she had to go to the store but she should be back soon." I knew by the sound of her voice and the look in her eyes she was covering something up.

"Linda, tell me the truth."

She couldn't. Lisa blurted out, "She's at Smokey's."

My stomach churned. This is not what I was expecting to hear.

"Let's get supper started and we'll talk later," I replied while seething inside.

Linda spoke up. "There's not much here to cook, Diana, that's why she was going to the store."

I ordered two pizzas. I tried to brighten the atmosphere by sharing crazy stories about Todd and Nathan's recent escapades. This opened the door for laughter and jokes, my remedy for everything. Meanwhile, a tornado was brewing in my mind.

When my mother finally walked in at midnight, I barely spoke to her.

The next morning, Todd, Nathan and I left to visit the Sharps. Our first stop was Tom and Sue's house. I had called the day before to tell them we were coming up, so I wasn't surprised to smell the aroma of Sue's freshly baked coffee cake when we walked in the door. Billy Joe and Matthew dragged their cousins into the toy room. Stephanie and Lorrie weren't home, they'd spent the night with friends. Without the kids around, I found it much easier to talk to Tom and Sue.

Tom silently nodded his head while I explained my reasons for leaving Randy. When I finished, Sue spoke up, "This doesn't come as a surprise. I've seen it coming for a long time." Sue had witnessed many problematic situations throughout our marriage.

Over the years, Randy and Sue had clashed on several occasions which is why she wasn't surprised by my decision. Whatever Tom felt about it, he kept to himself. We left their house and went to see Randy's sister, Janet and her husband, Dan. Although Janet was saddened by my news, she seemed to understand. She made me promise to stay connected with their family even if we divorced. I promised. My last stop was at my mother-in-law's apartment. When I first met Marion, she seemed very standoffish but I soon learned that was 'her way'. As the years passed, we became much closer. The problems Randy and I had experienced over the years had strengthened the bond between Marion and me. Being a divorced woman herself made it easier for her to accept the news of our separation. As I was leaving, she hugged me and asked me to stay in touch.

After we had left Marion's, we returned to my mother's apartment. Realizing there was nothing I could say or do to make Mom change anything about her life, I didn't talk about it. Just before this visit, I had received a call from the Social Service office in Clarion asking me about my sisters, and if I was still interested in having them placed in my care. I was taken aback by this call, because with all of the issues in my own family, I no longer had the strength to help Linda and Lisa at that time. When I explained that they had moved back to New York State with my mother, the caseworker politely informed me she would remove their names from her list. Rather than get into a deep conversation about problems I wasn't capable of coping with at this point, I made idle chatter with my mother for the rest of the evening.

Before leaving on Sunday, the boys and I had two more stops to make.

Sue had invited us for breakfast, so that was our first stop. As we were preparing to leave, Nathan asked if Matthew could come with us while we visited my great-grandmother. Knowing he wanted to spend more time with Matthew, I agreed. Gussie was delighted to see us. The boys sat in front of the television while we sat at the dining room table pouring over an old photo album. While flicking through the pages, I found a picture of a woman I'd never met. She was wearing a long-skirted dress, her hair was pulled into a bun on top of her head and she smiled just like Gussie. "Who is this?' I asked.

"That's my sister, Amelia," Gussie replied.

Goose bumps covered the flesh on my arms. "She's the lady in my dreams!" I exclaimed. "Remember? I used to tell you about my dreams of running into the arms of a beautiful woman and burying my face in her long skirt? She was protecting me from the man in a black cape who was getting down from a dark carriage and starting towards our house."

Gussie's eyes lit up. She smiled and said, "Amelia must be your guardian angel." I was relieved by those words because I needed a guardian angel now more than ever before.

Gussie went on to say, "You've had a lot to deal with over the years. You've had more than your share of problems with your mother and father. And now you're dealing with problems in your own marriage. If you get divorced, maybe you'll find someone who will make you happy." My great-grandmother knew and understood me better than anyone in my life.

Encouraged by her words, I reached over and gently hugged her.

About that time, Matthew came into the dining room to tell me he had a bad headache. I instructed the boys to go to the car while I stood in the foyer with my arms around my tiny, five-foot, great-grandmother. I kissed her cheek and thanked her for her love and support. The twinkle in her eyes, when she looked into mine, made me feel more confident about my future.

As soon as we got to Sue's house, I made her aware of Matthew's headache. After saying our farewells, we started back to Brookville. That evening, Sue called to tell me they'd taken Matthew to the WCA Hospital because he began to look jaundiced and had a fever. He was diagnosed with Hepatitis C. Since it was contagious, the doctors recommended anyone who had contact with him over the past twenty-four hours, get inoculated. I took Todd and Nathan to our family physician the next day.

I was very concerned about Matthew and called Marian every day to check on his progress. His condition worsened and on Friday he went into a coma and was taken to Children's Hospital in Buffalo. The seriousness of this situation took precedence over any problems Randy and I had been having. Every night, I prayed for Matthew and his family. Throughout that week, he was never far from my thoughts. A week later, I received a call from Marian at work telling me Matthew had passed away.

All I could think about was how devastating Matthew's death would be for his family. How would I feel if I lost one of my sons? The amount of heartache and pain Tom and Sue were going through was unimaginable. By comparison, what I had personally been dealing with seemed inconsequential. I needed to push away my own problems and get to Tom and Sue's as soon as possible to offer my love and support.

Overwhelmed with grief, I could barely function. Jim noticed the expression on my face from the other side of the office. He quickly walked over to my desk and gently asked me what was wrong. He held me in his arms while I cried into his chest. I didn't want to leave the safety of his arms. I finally pulled away and said, "I'm calling Randy at work to tell him. We need to get the boys and go to Jamestown."

He hugged me and left the office so I could talk privately with Randy. I started crying again when I shared this devastating news with Randy. Instead of saying that he would come to Brookville to get me and the boys, he told me to go Jamestown without him because he had things to finish in the office. He said he'd drive to Tom's later that night. His reaction shocked me. What could possibly be more important than getting to your brother when he needs you?

Before hanging up, I said, "Randy, this is not the time for us to tell anyone about our problems. I think it's best to act like a normal couple while we're there. Tom and Sue are going through the most difficult time of their lives. We don't need to draw any attention to us. Do you agree?" I don't believe he answered me before hanging up. I left the office, picked up the boys from school and daycare and went home to pack.

On the way to Jamestown, I did my best to prepare my sons for what lay ahead. Two hours later I parked on the street in front of Tom and Sue's house. Their driveway was full of cars. I sat there for several minutes gathering the strength to walk through that door. Tom saw me the moment I opened the door. He crossed the room and tightly embraced me. I held his trembling body close to mine and tried to soothe his aching sobs. Sue appeared to be in a trance when she approached me. "Can you believe it?' she asked.

"No Sue, I can't. It all seems like a nightmare," I rubbed my hands across her slouching shoulders and drew her near.

I busied myself refilling trays with the enormous supply of food friends and neighbors had brought. I offered my heartfelt condolences to other family members and friends as I filled their empty coffee cups. I couldn't fathom the pain Tom, Sue, Stephanie, Laurie and Billy Joe were enduring.

Todd approached me several times, asking when his dad would arrive.

Nathan sat in a corner playing with another five-year-old boy, occasionally glancing around the room as if he expected Matthew to appear any moment.

Where are you, Randy? The boys and your brother need you.

He finally arrived about nine that night. After expressing his sympathies to Tom and Sue, he went in search of Todd and Nathan, completely ignoring me. As people started to leave, I approached him and asked what his plans were for the night.

"I'm sleeping here with Todd. You and Nathan can spend the night at your mother's," he curtly replied. Nathan and Matthew were close in age and I assumed Randy thought it would be better for Tom and Sue if Nathan weren't there when they woke up the next day. I retrieved Nathan from the living room and said goodbye to Tom and Sue.

The next morning, I went to the funeral home alone. The Sharp family gathered outside, waiting to enter together at 10:00 am. I silently stood beside Randy. When the doors to the funeral home opened, he brushed past me and went inside. I followed at the end of the line. Throughout the day, Randy ignored me and sat off by himself. Several relatives asked if everything was okay. I assured them everything was fine; Randy was just overwhelmed with the loss of Matthew. I wasn't bothered that Randy ignored me, I was upset because his actions were drawing everyone's attention.

All family members were invited to the Sharps between the afternoon and evening viewings. Several of the neighbors were providing a buffet dinner. As everyone was leaving, Sue walked over to me, took my hands and asked, "You're coming to the house, right?"

I looked into her pain filled eyes and said, "Sue, as much as I want to be with you, I think it's best if I leave. Randy hasn't said a word to me all day and every time I have tried to talk to him he storms off in the opposite direction. Rather than draw any more attention to us, I'm going to go my mother's house. I'll be back for the funeral on Monday. If anyone asks where I am, just tell them I'm sick. I'm very sorry."

"I understand." Here stood a woman who had just lost her son. The last thing she needed was more drama. My absence would prevent that. We hugged each other tightly and I started for the door.

"Why don't you bring Nathan to my house before you go to your mothers? I think it would be good for the kids to all be together tonight." I nodded my head in approval.

On the way to my mother's, I realized I couldn't stay there. I knew I couldn't deal with any more emotional problems. Thankfully she was home with the girls, peacefully watching television. When I explained my feelings to her, she supported my decision to leave and come back for the funeral on Monday. I called Randy at the Sharps and told him my plans. He didn't try to dissuade me. I said I'd be over in five minutes and asked him to come to the car to get Nathan. I sat in the car watching as Nathan reached up for his father's hand and they slowly walked into the house together.

Although I didn't really have a plan, I knew I had to get away. The searing pain in my heart had deepened over the past two days. As I drove aimlessly south on Rt. 62, I tried to shut down my mind and my emotions. When I arrived in Warren, I realized exactly where my car was heading. I pulled into my Grandmother Conklin's driveway and was relieved to see the light streaming through her windows. Just like Gussie, Granny C welcomed me with open arms and a loving heart. We talked until midnight. Just as I was about to turn off the light beside my bed, she came into the room, kissed me good-night and whispered, "You'll always be my girl, remember that. I'll keep praying for you."

The next morning I drove home.

CHAPTER 38

Gotta' Get Off of This Ride

August, 1976

WHEN I DROVE down the hill into Brookville, the heaviness in my heart began to lift. Seeing the tree-lined streets of this quaint Victorian town brought me some peace. I had started to embrace this small community; it felt like home. My mood was a little lighter when I got out of the car and walked up the steps to my front door.

As soon as I opened the door and dropped my bags on the worn carpet, the memories of the past twenty years descended upon me like lava flowing from a volcano. I was buried. I sank to the floor, laid my head in my hands and sobbed. I sat there for a long time with my eyes tightly shut.

I could see my mother's once beautiful face as it turned puffy and worn, like a whore's. My father is holding his large hand out to me, but when I reach for him, he vanishes. One minute, I hear the soft words of his voice as he sings to my mother from his seat at the piano. The next moment, the voice is my mother's as she shouts vulgar, harsh accusations. She stands there, taunting him with her seductive smile. The Ice Cream Man is hovering in the background as his gleaming eyes observe the destruction in his wake.

Afraid, I closed my eyes tighter. My face is glowing as I hold each one of my newborn sisters in my arms. I watch as the high winds of despair extinguish the innocence in their eyes. They raise their arms, begging me to deliver them from the storms in their lives. But I no longer possess the strength to respond, and Judy and Kim begin to walk away, down a seedy road taking them nowhere. Linda and Lisa are wandering around lost, looking for someone to guide them.

Now I'm an effervescent girl of fifteen reaching for the stars, until they become unreachable. I see myself struggling to build a mountain out of a little hope. But then, I peer over the edge of a precipice and see myself spiraling downward.

For the first time, I clearly understood I did not have the strength or the necessary skills to help my mother overcome her demons. When I accepted the fact I did not possess the saintly powers needed to save my beloved sisters, I let out a long sigh. Relief flooded through me.

I walked into the kitchen, brewed some fresh coffee, carried the steaming cup into the living room and sat in the recliner. As I glanced around the room, my eyes were drawn to a photo of my two sons, Todd and Nathan, that hung on the wall. I carried it back to my seat and stared at it for quite some time.

In this photo, Todd is seven and Nathan is two. Todd's tilted head is leaning towards the left and his right arm is wrapped around his two-year-old brother's waist as if he's protecting him from falling. Dark-brown, Beatle-length bangs cover his forehead. His big brown eyes are focused on the photographer, to whom he offers a confident smile. Nathan is seated beside Todd and his resemblance to his older brother is striking. He also has brown hair, although it's a shade lighter and much finer than Todd's. His chubby little chin is covered with a slight rash caused by drooling. He, too, is focused on the photographer with his lips pursed, creating a determined grin.

While lingering over this photo, I'm reminded of the joy these two boys have given me. I shudder when I think I almost gave Todd up for adoption. What would his life have been like if he had grown up in a different home? I know my life would have been empty without him. I would have missed his first words, his first steps and all of the days that followed as he grew into a loving young boy.

When I studied Nathan's adorable face, I remember the joy I felt the day I found out I was pregnant. Holding him close to my chest after the nurse first laid him in my arms, I was overwhelmed with maternal love and pride. I vowed to protect him forever.

While my sons resemble each other physically, their personalities are quite different. Todd is much more reserved than his younger brother and easily entertains himself. Nathan is vivacious and basks in the attention he receives from his mother.

I got up from the chair and put one of my favorite eight track tapes in the player. Pulling the soft comforter over my body and holding the photo of my sons close to my chest, I drifted to sleep listening to Dionne Warwick singing one of my favorite songs, the theme song from "Valley of the Dolls". I awoke several hours later with the lyrics of that song floating through my mind.

Gonna' get off, gotta' get off, have to get off from this ride. How was I caught in this game? When did I stop feeling sure, feeling safe, and start wondering why? What's in back of the sky? Gonna' get off of this merry-go-round. Need to get on where I'm bound.

It was then that I understood precisely what I had to do. My two sons had to become my top priority. In order to provide them with the security and love they needed, I had to create a stable environment for them and a calmer life for myself. At that moment, it was obvious— I was 'gonna' get-off -of -this- ride'.

I did. I walked away from the burdens of the past and into a new life.

CHAPTER 39

My Journey to North Carolina

December 5, 2005

THE EVERGREENS LINING my driveway were laden with thick white blankets of snow forcing their limbs to sag downward as I started on my journey to North Carolina. Instead of going to Chapel Hill to support my younger sister, Kim, as she struggled for her life, I was driving to her funeral.

Early Sunday morning, my niece, Amy had called to tell me Kim was undergoing emergency surgery to stop the bleed in her brain. The operation would take four to five hours and Kim had a fifty/fifty chance of survival. She encouraged me to stay home until the surgery had been completed. She didn't want me traveling by myself if the news was grave. Kim made it through the surgery, but not the night.

On Monday, the weather had improved and I decided to drive the five hundred miles to Kenly, North Carolina, rather than fly. The long drive would provide me with the time I needed to sort through my thoughts and fears.

Although I had walked away in 1976, I had continued to worry about Judy, Kim, Linda, and Lisa. I had never completely abandoned them. My fear of this trip was based on the unknown. I realized the moment I saw my family, my resolve to remain uninvolved in their lives would vanish. Was I dreading becoming involved in their lives again or was I anxious to embrace them and re-open my heart to their needs?

For the remainder of the trip, I focused on what had transpired in their lives over the past twenty-nine years.

On the day my mother was diagnosed with pancreatic cancer, I was sitting by her side. For the next two months, I made weekly treks to

The Road Back to Hell

Jamestown to visit her in the hospital. My final summons came early on Sunday morning, August 4, 1982. My sister Kim called because the doctors had instructed her to alert everyone in the family they should come to the hospital. They believed my mother was dying. When I arrived two hours later, my sisters and their husbands were surrounding her bed. My mom was in a semiconscious state when I took her hand in mine to let her know I was there. Pastor Daniels stopped in after church and prayed with us. Our watchful vigil continued throughout the day and into early evening.

About seven-thirty that night, Mom sat up, looked around the room and said, "What's going on? Is this a party?" We looked at one another as if to say, "What the hell *is* going on?" That collective, unspoken thought brought some comic relief to a long, stressful day.

I spoke up and said, "Actually Mom, it is a party. Today is Judy's birthday, now she can go home and celebrate with her family."

That night, my 'resurrected' mother and I talked until dawn, openly expressing our feelings about the problems and the joys we had shared over the years. She told me she had always loved my father but had been unable to remain faithful to him. Frank had stolen a part of her heart that bound her to him until her dying days. My mother had called Frank from the hospital and asked him to come to see her. I never knew if he made that visit or not. When Grandma Conklin paid a final visit to Mom, she told her she had been aware of Mom's affair with Frank. And while my grandmother had struggled with it for years, she wanted Mom to know she had finally forgiven her.

Unfortunately, I could not say those words to my mother.

When my mother conveyed her sorrow for all of the pain she had caused and expressed remorse for abandoning my sisters, again I could not tell her I forgave her. Instead, I said I had loved her through the years, even when that love was tested. I thanked her for all the love she bestowed on me when I was a small child. Then I thanked her for her biggest gift, bringing Stew into our lives. I believe those words were enough to bring my mother peace. She went into a coma the next day and remained that way until her death on August 17, 1982.

Diana Lynn

My beloved great-grandmother, Annie Augusta Foote had passed away the year before at the age of 96. Understanding that she had lived a full and happy life brought me comfort. Every night, I include her in my prayers, thanking her for the love and support she so willing gave to me and the values she instilled in me. I feel as if she still watches over me like a guardian angel.

Over the years, the lives of Judy, Kim, Linda and Lisa had continued to be filled with chaos, pain, and heartache.

Judy and Corky started living together in January, 1972. Judy gave birth to her son, Brandon, in July of that year. Although Corky wasn't his biological father, he raised him as a son. Together they had a son, Jonathon, on March 31, 1975. They married on Dad's birthday, November 9, 1988. They spent their early years living like hippies while raising their sons in this freestyle environment. Judy and Corky spent many nights and most of the weekends drinking beer and smoking pot. With little supervision and guidance, both of their sons continually got into trouble with the law, often spending time in jail. The opportunity for change for Judy and her husband came about the day they took John's daughter, Anastasia, into their home and into their hearts. Because John and Anastasia's mother were separated, she spent many weekends with her grandparents. One day, Anastasia arrived at Judy's looking very disheveled and covered in cigarette burns. Judy and Corky immediately took her to the emergency room at WCA Hospital.

The next trip was to court to fight for custody of their grandchild.

Anastasia was three years old when the courts awarded Judy, Corky and John, joint custody. From that moment on, my sister and her husband have devoted their lives to giving their granddaughter all of the love, attention, support and guidance she would need to succeed in life. Today, Anastasia is a lovely seventeen-year-old girl, who has excelled in dance, sports, and academics. She is graduating in June, 2016 as an honors student with an advanced academic diploma from Jamestown High School and a cosmetology certificate from Erie 2 Chautauqua-Cattaragus BOCES. Anastasia is a survivor with a bright future ahead.

The Road Back to Hell

Kim's marriage to Dan was much like my parent's marriage, with lots of fighting and separations. Their only son, Danny was born in 1972, followed by two sisters, Amy and Christine. After fifteen years of marriage, they divorced. Through the years, Kim remained closer to our mother than any of us. Unfortunately, she followed in Mom's footsteps by becoming a heavy drinker who spent a lot of time in bars, neglecting her three small children.

Recognizing my niece, Amy's need for attention, I invited her to spend a week or so with me in Brookville each summer. During her last visit, I noticed how difficult it was for her to interact with the other children who were playing in the park. Her lack of self-confidence was evident. I desperately wanted her to live with my family in Brookville. That wasn't possible for two reasons —Kim would never allow it and Jim didn't deserve the extra stress.

On the drive to Warren where we were to meet Kim, Amy and I were both broken hearted. When we arrived at Granny C's house, Kim wasn't there to get her. She was in a bar in Jamestown, partying with her friends. Amy spent the night at my grandmother's house and I went home and wrote Kim a letter, berating her for the way she was raising her children. I begged her to get some help. She responded with a letter stating I should mind my own business and stay out of her life. I did for almost twenty years.

While living in Jamestown, Kim became involved in a very abusive relationship which lasted for over seven years. After finally finding the courage to leave him, she met Gary, the man who would help change her life. In the early 1990's, they packed everything they owned and moved to North Carolina, hoping to start a new life together. It worked. Kim quit drinking, began working at a Caterpillar plant where she soon became a floor manager and bought her first home. She devoted her time to her older children and her beloved grandchildren. I'll always remember our last conversation, when Kim proudly extolled the scholastic and musical accomplishments of her fifteen- year-old granddaughter, Ashlyn. It was comforting to know the final years of Kim's life were filled with joy because of her husband, children, and grandchildren.

Kim would be extremely proud today, knowing that Ashlyn graduated from the University of North Carolina; her daughter, Amy will be graduating from that same school in May, 2016 and her granddaughter, Miranda is planning to attend there when she graduates from high school.

Linda and Lisa suffered the most from my mother's negligence. While in high school, Linda continued to 'mother' Lisa and their bond grew stronger. There were many nights Mom never came home. The cupboards were often bare as they struggled to survive. In 1979, Linda was a senior in high school and capable of caring for herself. However, Lisa was only sixteen and needed a mother's supervision. When I learned of these conditions, I brought Lisa to Brookville to live with us.

During her stay, she told me stories about my mother that made me ill. Many times she and Linda felt motherless. Lisa was angry because our mother had given birth to four daughters she was not capable of rearing. She told me about the nights she woke up, alone and frightened because Mom wasn't home. On those nights, she crawled into bed with Linda, who would hold her in her arms until she fell asleep. She described Mom's narcissistic behavior as she squandered most of the income from the social security checks on herself, rather than providing food and clothing for the girls.

When Lisa was twelve, my mother gave her just enough money to take the bus to the Chautauqua Mall to buy Mom a new bra. She was terrified of making the trip alone. After paying the bus fare and buying Mom's bra, there wasn't enough left for Lisa to buy herself anything to eat. This experience, embedded in Lisa's memory, and other stories like this made me almost hate my mother.

Before coming to live with us, Lisa had met and fallen in love with Sam, a guy she had met in school. She missed him during her stay with us and decided to return to Jamestown and Sam, when the school year in Brookville ended. With Sam's support and guidance, she was able to survive under my mother's roof. In January of 1981, Mom announced she was moving to Arizona in the summer. She gave Lisa two choices— marry Sam or go to Arizona with her. Lisa married Sam on June 27th, two weeks after graduation. My mother never fulfilled her threat to move to Arizona, and Lisa believes it was a way for Mom to relinquish her maternal obligations. Although Sam and Lisa loved each other deeply, they found they couldn't live together. To avoid raising her two children, Sammy and Andrea, in a dysfunctional home, they divorced. After that, Lisa began dating a man who became very abusive. Soon after she found the strength to kick him out of her apartment, she met Joe. He whisked her off her feet—all the way to North Carolina. North Carolina seemed to be the place where my sisters could get a fresh start. Lisa now devotes her life to Joe, her daughter, Andrea, her son, Sam and her four beautiful grandchildren.

Of my four sisters, Linda was the one with the most drive. She was the first to graduate from high school and the only one to attend two years of college. After graduating, she met a guy who had just moved to Jamestown from Tennessee. She married him and they had three children. Over time, he became abusive to Linda, both mentally and physically. When she could no longer take the abuse, she reached out to me. I encouraged her to move with her children to Clarion, only fifteen miles from my home. After she had agreed, I rented a trailer in Clarion and drove her to an interview with Headstart. When she was hired, I helped her buy a car. We were both hopeful this would be the beginning of a new life for her and her children. Everything was going well until her husband began visiting her and the kids in Clarion almost every weekend. After weeks of begging Linda to return to Jamestown, she reluctantly agreed to go back. She wanted her children to have the benefit of living with both parents. When she and the children moved back, she found the living conditions were not as he had promised, nor was his promise to never to hit her again.

On New Year's Eve, 1993, they went out for the night with some members of her husband's family. During the course of the evening, he became heavily intoxicated and beat Linda to the point she needed hospitalization. From there, it was all down-hill.

The next twenty years of her life were filled with upheaval and heartache. Even when Linda was at her lowest point, she put her children's welfare first, unlike our mother. Consequently, her son Joshua is married with two lovely children and has a successful position as a computer technician at a local hospital. Her daughter, Sara, has worked her way through college and is teaching in Utah. Of all of the Smith girls, Linda has suffered the most. Despite their unstable lives, she takes great pride in knowing that she has given her children what they needed most, her love and support. Something she never had. I hope someday she will write her story.

After recalling all of the stories and problems from the past, I wasn't certain if I had the strength to offer my family the support they needed now. If I opened that door, would their struggles overtake me? The closer I came to Kenly, North Carolina, the stronger this fear became.

"Please God, give me the strength to deal with whatever lies ahead," I prayed as I pulled onto the road heading into Kenly. The moment I parked my car outside of Amy's rundown rental and saw the need in all of their eyes, I dropped my defensive shield and welcomed them into my arms and my heart.

The night before Kim's funeral, I rented a motel room for Judy, Linda, Lisa and me. We spent that evening drinking, smoking, laughing, and crying as we shared the memories of our past. We took turns supporting one another through these dark hours. Judy and Lisa had never been particularly close, but on this night, Judy provided the love and guidance Lisa so desperately needed. When Kim died, Lisa had lost her closest friend, confidante and surrogate mother. Judy listened while Lisa talked and held her in her arms while she cried.

While holding Linda, I attentively listened as she repeatedly stated she wished she had died rather than Kim. She didn't feel worthy of living. I felt her pain. I understood Linda better than anyone in her life. Kim, Lisa and I had been Mom's favorites. Judy had support from me and Dad. Although my dad had loved Linda as he did all of us, she still lacked my mother's attention and support. I filled the motherly role she needed that night, and our relationship has flourished over the years. I'm looking forward to the day Linda finds the peace and happiness she deserves.

The Road Back to Hell

The day of the funeral, my sisters and I joined hands as we walked up to the casket to say our final goodbyes to Kim. While sitting in the pew listening to the many accolades being offered by the minister, family members, friends and co-workers about Kim's life, I found peace. I finally realized that as sad as our growing-up years had been, we had all emerged as survivors and were doing the best we could to live happy and productive lives.

I had believed that when I left for North Carolina, I was driving the road back to hell. When I left Kenly that day in December, 2005, I knew I was driving toward everlasting hope.

Epilogue

In 1976, when I walked away from the chaos, my life significantly improved. After reaching the lowest point in my life, I realized I could no longer offer emotional support to anyone in my family. At that time, I was the one desperately needing someone to offer me emotional support. Jim filled that role and has continued to do so for almost forty years. We married on July 26, 1980. Through his unconditional love, support and guidance I regained my self-confidence and drive. We worked together remodeling our home on Pickering Street, created a family environment for Todd and Nathan, and set mutual goals for our future. In 1984, we purchased a local radio station which enabled me to become a community leader in Brookville, the town I call home. Jim helped make my dreams come true and I thank God for him every day.

We worked together to provide Todd and Nathan with a stable home environment while encouraging them to excel in school and sports. Soon after our divorce, Randy married Debbie, and the boys spent a considerable amount of time with them in Punxsutawney on weekends and during the summer. Even though Randy and I were divorced, we took great pride in the accomplishments of our sons, Todd and Nathan.

My oldest son, Todd, lives in southern Maryland with his wife, Shawna. Todd excelled academically and athletically in high school. He graduated with a teaching degree from Indiana University of Pennsylvania in 1988 and is currently teaching and coaching at La Plata High School. His wife, Shawna, works for the United States Census Bureau in Washington, DC. Their oldest son, Matthew, graduated from the US Naval Academy in 2011. Upon graduation he enlisted in the Marines where he is currently serving as a Captain in San Diego, California. Their younger son, Dane, graduated with a degree in Civil Engineering. He's currently employed by an engineering firm in Arlington, Virginia where he and his wife, Rebecca, reside. Some of my most memorable times have been the nights I spent with Todd and his family, sitting around the campfire in their backyard, sharing love and laughter into the wee hours of the morning.

Nathan was an honor student who also excelled in sports while attending Brookville Area High School. Upon graduation in 1989, he attended Indiana University of Pennsylvania where he majored in finance and minored in communications. While in college, he also served as President of the Sigma Nu fraternity for two terms. He is currently the General Manager of our family business, Mega Rock, WMKX-WJNG-FM.

Nathan and his wife, Jody are the proud parents of three children- Elliot, Sophie and Truman. Elliot is a junior at Brookville Area High School and is considering a career in psychology. As a freshman, Sophie excels in academics, girls' basketball and golf. Truman is an active fifth grader who is interested in science. I'm grateful to have them living in Brookville, where I'm able to watch them grow and to take part in their lives. My experiences as their grandmother have provided me with hours of joy and lots of happy memories.

The accomplishments of my sons, my daughters-in-law and my grandchildren have been a great source of pride for me. I often think about how different my life might have turned out if I had not decided to keep Todd on October 22, 1965. Without Todd, there might have never been a Nathan. I was fortunate to have the support of my family and friends while making this decision.

When my sisters, Judy, Linda, Lisa, and I reunited at Kim's funeral in 2005, I vowed to do anything I could to offer them what they had lacked most in life— a sense of security. In 2006, I helped Judy and Corky purchase a home, so they would be able to offer their granddaughter a stable environment in which to grow. I helped Lisa purchase a house in Metter, Georgia in 2012 for the same reasons. Although I haven't assisted Linda with the purchase of a home, I have helped with her travel expenses and other areas where's she needed some support. Being able to share with my siblings has brought me great joy.

Over the years, my sisters, Judy, Kim, Linda and Lisa were able to turn their lives around. The maternal abandonment of our mother during adolescent years, left all four of my sisters unprepared to deal with motherhood. Although they tried their best, sometimes they failed. With the birth of their grandchildren, they were each given a second chance. By actively participating in their grandchildren's lives and providing them with them with the nurturing love and attention they needed, they each gained the self-confidence they had lacked in their earlier years.

During my frequent conversations with Judy, Linda and Lisa, I'm always delighted when they share the latest accomplishments of their sons, daughters and grandchildren. Life is much better when you can talk about the happy times rather than the sad.

Although Kim is no longer with us, I know she would be very proud when her daughter, Amy, graduates in May, 2016 with an accounting degree from the University of North Carolina. It will be an honor for me to be there to congratulate my forty-year-old niece for her accomplishments.

It is with great pride that I honor all of the survivors in my family and look forward to congratulating all who succeed in the future.

The next step on my journey is to participate in some type of local mentoring program for at-risk teenage girls. If my story can persuade someone to change her or his mind-set from, "No, I Can't" to "Yes, I Can," my mission will be accomplished.

Thank you for joining me on my journey!

The Next Road on My Journey

While writing this memoir, I tried to analyze what characteristics I possessed that had enabled me to become a survivor. While I was doing some research for my book, I read an article that helped to answer my question. The article compared raising a child to growing a plant. In order for a plant to become strong and tall, it has to be carefully nurtured in the early stages of growth. The same is true in raising a child. If you want your child to grow into a happy, confident adult, it's critical they receive the undivided attention and devotion of their parents during the first few years of their life. As the oldest of five girls, I was the child who benefitted the most from the stability my parents provided during the early years of their marriage. The undivided attention and love they lavished on me, instilled in me the self-confidence, drive and ambition I would need to overcome many great obstacles in my life.

As my parents' marriage disintegrated, so did the life of the Smith family. With the birth of each new daughter, our family life worsened.

Consequently, my four younger sisters, Judy, Kim, Linda, and Lisa didn't receive the nurturing care they desperately needed during the early stages of their lives. For years, I struggled with guilt because I had received what they had not—an abundance of my parents' love and attention. Assuming the mother role at twelve allowed me to try to give them what they had missed. By then it was too late.

The special bond I had with my father is proof that a child's environment plays a vital role in molding a child's life. As my adoptive father, his blood did not flow through my veins. Yet the love, wisdom and continuous guidance he shared with me impacted my life very deeply. His belief in me offered me hope, enabling me to remain optimistic throughout most of my life. Even though Judy and Kim were his only biological daughters, all five of his daughters were the recipients of his unconditional love. He was our rock.

Although I've painted my father as a saint, he wasn't. He had many faults. His biggest being his inexplicable love and devotion to my mother. She had the power to control him. It was difficult to silently watch as he slowly fell from the pedestal I'd placed him on. I became angry with my mother because she drew him in and kicked him out so often, causing many of the traumas in our lives. I became angry with Dad because he couldn't stand up to her. My anger turned to fury as I watched my sisters suffer because of Mom's alcoholism, her melodramatic behavior and the unstable home environment she created. The day she chose Frank over her husband and children, I began to hate her.

As a young girl, I had adored my mother. Over the years, it became more difficult for me to accept the changes in her. When I studied photos of her as a child, and later a teen, I began to see a very troubled young woman. While remembering passing comments several family members had made about Mom's life growing up, I started to believe she may have been sexually assaulted as a child. I thought her narcissistic behavior and obsession with her appearance stemmed from her lack of self-esteem. By making herself attractive, she easily attracted men, which seemed to fulfill her desire for self- worth. Often times, when she was on a personal high, she'd instigate a fight with my father and send him packing, only to reel him back in when she hit rock bottom. While Dad was never able to resist her, Frank often treated her like a slut, yet she clung to him like a life raft. Her promiscuity, suicide attempts and alcohol abuse were also signs she may have been suffering from undiagnosed mental issues. Sometimes she would be a wonderful, attentive mother, while other times, she simply abandoned her maternal obligations.

Unfortunately, there were few mental health services available to help my mother in the 1960's and 1970's. Consequently, she never received the treatment she desperately needed. I still question what my mother may have endured while growing up that could have played a significant part in her emotional problems. Was she sexually abused as a young girl? Why did she feel the need to attract new men into her life? Why couldn't she be happy with Stew? What made her resent Judy and Linda?

I also have unanswered questions about my father. As a young man with a solid home life, a nurturing mother and so much talent, why wasn't he more successful? Why was he constantly changing jobs, rather than sticking with one and working his way up the ladder? What was it that drew him to Bonnie again and again?

The Road Back to Hell

Desperately needing some answers, I have been actively researching mental health issues, contacting family members and talking with experts in the mental health field. I sent a copy of my book to my former counselor, Gina Knight, M.S., asking her to read my book and offer me a general assessment of my mother's psychological problems. I explained to her I had recently learned some things that strongly indicated my mother could have been sexually abused as teen by either her father or her brother, Kenny. Unable to personally evaluate my mother, Gina hypothesized from the descriptions in my book and by reading my mother's diary that Mom's problems very well may have stemmed from early sexual abuse. This led to the strong possibility that my mother may have had suffered from BDP- Borderline Personality Disorder. Research shows there is a high occurrence of alcoholism with BPD sufferers. Two other professionals whom I consulted also confirmed this possibility.

After reading my book, each of my sisters— Judy, Linda and Lisa, have had flashbacks into their past, which have provided even more insight into their chaotic lives.

They're recording their untold stories which occurred after I left home in 1967 up until the time our mother passed away in 1982.

All of these factors contributed to my decision to write another book about the dysfunctional life of the Smith Family. By writing my sister's stories, using the facts I obtain through my research, contacting other family members and including my personal perceptions, I plan to write a book which will shed more light on the reasons behind all of the insanity. I'll also be inserting some stories I omitted in this book, as well as adding more photos.

I pray that when I've finished my quest, I will finally be able to forgive my mother. The last night we ever spent together, in her hospital room, I was able to tell her I loved her.

Now I need to let her know I've forgiven her. I hope I can.

Please visit me at
www.dianalynnauthor.com
facebook- Diana Lynn

Acknowledgments

My life-long dream of writing this story would never have been fulfilled without the love and support of my family and my closest friends. Special thanks to my husband, Jim, for his encouragement, understanding and his belief in me. By sharing their heartfelt stories about our past, my sisters— Judy, Linda, and Lisa enabled me to complete my memoir. We formed a very special bond as we walked the 'road back to hell' together. I am eternally grateful to my two sons, Todd and Nathan, for their love and encouragement. Thanks to my grandson, Elliot, for listening to many of my stories while riding with me in the car. My niece, Amy, provided insightful information about the life of her mother, my sister Kim. While visiting my aunt, Jean Woodard, I learned some interesting stories about my early years. One of the funniest stories she shared was telling me I could talk in complete sentences before my first birthday. Anyone who knows me will find this believable.

The first seeds of my story were nurtured through the encouragement of my Chautauqua mentor, Diana Hume George, and my friend, Judy Feldman. Eileen Arthurs, a personal friend and author, offered suggestions and editorial support in the early stages of my writing. Linda Joy Myers and Brooke Warner, mentors of the writing course, 'Writing Your Memoir in Six Months,' enabled me to focus on my writing and provided the weekly accountability I needed to complete this book. Deb Trotter, my writing partner during this course, became a good friend and supporter of my work.

I've been fortunate for the many friends who have traveled with me on my journey. I offer special thanks to Mary Kay Slimak, Camille Reitz, and Judith Anderson for listening to me, encouraging me and sharing some tears while I worked on this book. Sue Sharp has walked beside me through many of my trials and tribulations. Her love and support are priceless. JoAnne Ottoson Johnson, Sue Young Schifano, Barbara Kling Anderson, Mary Anderson Radack, Lorrie Marker Bush and Cherrie Swanson, are my Jamestown friends, who provided some of the happiest memories of my junior and high school years. I would also like to thank Cathy Dinger, Cara Stockdale and Joan Hillard for their encouragement and spiritual support. The members of my 'No Sub, Card Club'-- Camille Reitz, Mary Kay Slimak, Beth Gerg, Shelly Wilson, Judith Anderson, Heidi Hoak and Sue Erlandson are more like sisters than friends, and have been my cheerleaders throughout this writing endeavor.

Many thanks to Kristine Gasbarre, author of "How to Love an American Man: A True Story", and co-writer with Regina Calcaterra of the best-selling memoir, "Etched in Sand", for her encouragement while I was completing my book. I am grateful to my former counselor, Gina Knight, M.S., for offering her professional opinions about my mother's mental health issues and my friend, Diana Smail, for proof reading this book.

I would like to express my gratitude to Cara Stockdale and Rebekah Frampton for preparing this memoir for publication. Thanks to Robert Braun for granting permission to use the quote at the beginning of Chapter 2. My apologies to anyone I have been remiss in acknowledging.

I wish to honor my deceased parents, Bonnie Jean and Stewart Edwin Smith, for showering me with love and stability during the formative years of my life. Their love and guidance provided me with the self-confidence, strength and drive I needed to succeed.

My life has been blessed with family members and friends who significantly influenced my life—my great-grandmother, Annie Augusta Foote Wilson; my paternal grandmother, Jennette Conklin; and my paternal grandfather, Elmer Woodard. My former pastor, Reverend Gerald Daniels and my fifth-grade teacher, Miss Loretta Funk are two people who greatly inspired and supported me while I was growing up. I am eternally grateful to all of my angels on earth and in heaven.

I extend my thanks to you, the reader, for joining me on my 'road back to hell'.

This is the photo I had taken for my parents for Christmas in 1964. I'm seated in the middle holding Lisa on my lap. Judy is standing on my left, and Kim and Linda are on my right.

This photo of Stew and Jennette, his mother, was taken in 1939.

Adeline Powell Woodard at 15 – 1927

Woodard outing 1942. Bonnie is sitting on the hood of a '37 Studebaker. Kenny on the left; Jerry on the right. Elmer and Adeline in back.

The Road Back to Hell

Picnic at Allen Park – 1942. Front to back: left side- Gussie, Bonnie, Sharon, Carol; right side- Kenny, Elmer Virgil, Grandma Goodwill

Dad in top row, 3rd from right, peering down at girl in 2nd row 2nd from left.

Dad playing the piano at Granny C's

Bonnie and Stew's wedding on May 26, 1951 in the Frewsburg Methodist Church.

Mom's bridal shower held at Grandma Conklin's house. Left to right-
Mom's mother, Adeline, Mom and her grandmother, Gussie.

I'm two in this photo. I'm trying to sneak around
the table to surprise Mom and Dad.

Diana Lynn

My mother and me in February, 1951.

A professional photo of me, Kim, and Judy in 1957.

Bad day at Granny C's. From bottom (left) Mom, me, GrannyC holding Judy, Grandpa Conklin, Gene and Dad

Our family in Modesto, California in 1957.

The photo of me as Stephen Foster that appeared on the front page of the *Jamestown Post-Journal*.

Kim and Judy in their new Christmas dresses in 1960.

The Road Back to Hell

This photo was taken at my parents' home on Broadhead Avenue in 1966. Left to right- Lisa, age 3; Linda, age 5 and Todd age 1.

This picture was taken in 1972. Nathan had just turned 1 and Todd is 6. It's one of my of my favorites.

The Smith Sisters in 1981.
Left to right- Judy, Kim, Linda, Lisa and me.

The Smith Sisters with Granny C in 1985. Left to right-
Lisa, Granny C, Judy, Kim, Linda and me.

This professional photo was presented to me as a Christmas gift in 1993.

This photo was taken on South Pickering Street in Brookville in 1977. Left to right- Todd, me and Nathan.

Diana Lynn

This is the photograph of my mother, father, and me as we gaily walked down Main Street on Easter Day, April 19, 1953. It appeared on the front page of the *Jamestown Post-Journal*. (The two people on each side of us were cropped into the photo)

Made in the USA
Columbia, SC
04 August 2017